Grave Undertakings

Grave Undertakings

Mortician by Day, Model by Night— One Woman's True-Life Adventures

Alexandra Kathryn Mosca

New Horizon Press
Far Hills, New Jersey

New Horizon Press
P.O. Box 669
Far Hills, NJ 07931

Alexandra K. Mosca
     Grave Undertakings: Mortician by Day, Model by Night—
     One Woman's True-Life Adventures

Cover Design: Robert Aulicino
Front Cover Photo: Peter Provenzano
Interior Design: Susan M. Sanderson

Library of Congress Control Number: 2002101396
ISBN: 0-88282-223-3
New Horizon Press

Manufactured in the U.S.A.

2007   2006   2005   2004   2003   /   5   4   3   2   1

For Peter, the dearest friend anyone could ever have.
You always said I should write a book.

Author's Note

This book is based on my actual experiences and reflects my perception of the past, present and future. The personalities, events, actions and conversations portrayed within the story have been reconstructed from my memory and the memories of participants. In an effort to safeguard individual privacy, I have changed the names of certain people and, in some cases, altered otherwise identifying characteristics. Events involving the characters happened as described; only minor details have been changed.

Table of Contents

Acknowledgements

My sincere thanks to:

Edward J. Defort, who gave me my first important writing opportunity and allowed me to work on projects dear to me;

Anthony M. DeStefano, for his guidance, insight and input on this project and his tireless reading of my chapters;

Dr. Philip A. Pecorino, for his help with my original book proposal and his continued encouragement and belief in my ability;

My publisher, for being imaginative and forward-thinking in taking a chance with this book.

Prologue

The first funeral that I remember attending was my grandmother's. Strangely enough, it was not an altogether unpleasant experience for a nine-year-old. In fact, with all due respect, it bordered on fun. She had died from a heart attack at the age of seventy-two, which I considered at the time very old.

After my mother told me what had happened, the first order of the day was to go shopping at the local mall for appropriate funeral clothing. My mother said we needed something new for each day of the wake and something extra special for the day of the funeral. Not to be appropriately dressed, according to my mother, was unthinkable. I received some beautiful new dresses. Not all were black, because my mother said it was okay for a child to wear colors like blue or purple. Besides the new clothes, my mother told me that we would be eating dinner out for the next few days. It began to seem more like a holiday to me.

"After all," she told me, "people who are in mourning cannot be expected to cook." So each day at five o'clock, when the afternoon visiting hours ended, we went to a restaurant for dinner...a really nice restaurant. Usually Italian, sometimes seafood. There was a rhythm to the days preceding the funeral, which was somewhat comforting even in its peculiarity. The mundane regularity of life ceased for the time being, halted by death. And for some reason, I liked that.

The funeral home was located in the Bronx, where my grandparents had lived and where I spent the first few years of my life. It was a stately, stone building. Not at all scary or spooky like what you might see on a television show, it looked more like a small catering house than a transient resting place for dead bodies before burial.

Inside, a large lobby had all varieties of religious paraphernalia encased in cabinets and lining the walls. Crucifixes, crosses, vestments, chalices; things regularly seen in church were decorations here and all were for sale.

I looked around and saw many people—some relatives, some friends of my parents and grandparents—whom I did not see regularly. They all made a fuss over me, saying how pretty I was, how I'd grown and what a lovely dress I was wearing.

"You are the prettiest of all your cousins," one aunt whispered to me.

"And how is school? Do you realize what a lucky girl you are, that your parents can afford to send you to that kind of school?" another asked.

"That kind of school" was a reference to the expensive private school I attended, which was housed in a mansion overlooking the Long Island Sound. People were always reminding me how lucky I was to have parents who "had money"—or what passed for having money in those days. We wintered in Miami Beach and my days were filled with ballet, French and horseback riding lessons, as well as shopping for clothes, books (I had every volume of the Nancy Drew mystery series!) and each new Barbie Doll and Barbie accessory which came on the market. I thought we must be as rich as everyone said we were, but later realized my family was, in reality, no more than "upper middle class."

"Gee, funerals are kind of neat," I murmured to an uncle sitting next to me. "You get new clothes, eat in restaurants every night, get lots of compliments and even get to drink some wine at dinner—and I'm only nine."

My uncle smiled down at me. He, of course, realized I was very young and light years away from any awareness of my own mortality. Death, for me, was something that happened to other people. Mostly old people, unless you were unfortunate enough to have an accident or get very sick, but that was rare, my aunt had reassured me.

My grandmother lay in her casket at the head of the softly lit room, a living room of sorts, except for the rows of metal folding chairs. In front of a backdrop of rich, red drapery, flanked by an outsized ebony cross, the shiny metal casket encasing her body gleamed. I boldly strode up to the casket, curiously inspecting the scene and her body.

My grandmother was dressed in her favorite blue dress, which was trimmed in white lace. Her long, gray hair was braided atop her head, just as she had worn it every day of her life. A touch of cosmetics accentuated her strong features. People kept saying that "she looked just like she was sleeping." An analogy that both comforted and caused a flicker of unease, for I knew this was not a sleep from which she would wake.

A lot of people were crying and one of my elderly aunts shrieked at regular intervals. But I didn't cry. I don't know why, but the tears just didn't come. My parents, aunts and uncles were troubled that I never shed a tear. It wasn't that I didn't love my grandmother, because I truly did. I was her favorite grandchild (or so she told me, though now I suspect she said that to all of her grandchildren). However, the fact that I'd never see her again had not truly sunk in. Still, even as a nine-year old, I was pragmatic enough to accept that death was a natural part of life. I was proud that I didn't carry on like my sissy cousins who stayed in the lobby or the back of the room, afraid to come up to the casket. They were afraid of dead bodies, like the dead could do something to hurt you. Howling and weeping from their safe distances, it didn't sound like they were grieving—it sounded more like they were being tortured.

"Tsk, tsk, such an unemotional child," came a disapproving comment directed at me.

Somehow, even in my childhood innocence, I sensed the theatrics in the room. This funeral stuff was more about drama and tradition and how you dressed and acted, than it was about how you really felt. After all, that wasn't really my grandmother in the casket; she was in heaven. That was merely her body, her spirit was more important. I'd learned my lessons well in Sunday school.

The day of the funeral, I felt special riding in the long, black limousine. First, we went to the funeral home, where we took a last look, then to church for a lengthy service. I watched my parents as they carefully glanced at others for cues on how to act in church, when to sit and stand and pray. That they were not regular churchgoers was readily apparent. Then it was on to the cemetery, where, bored by now, I read the inscriptions on the surrounding stones, as the priest droned on with the graveside prayers. At last he finished and we went to yet another restaurant for the funeral luncheon.

My head spinning from the half glass of wine I was allowed, I slipped from the present into days past and turned over in my mind all of the things my grandmother and I had done together and would never do again. Picking fruit off the abundant, fragrant trees in her carefully tended backyard: cherries, apples and figs. Planting marigolds and geraniums in the spring. Watching "her story," as she called her favorite soap opera, on television. And cultivating yogurt on the windowsill, a practice that came from her Greek heritage.

As images revolved in my mind, I began to feel sad. Well, sure I did, that was natural, I told myself. All the kids at school whose grandparents had died had felt sad. Surely it wasn't surprising that I would feel the same when my grandmother died, except for one thing: the woman who had died wasn't my grandmother by heritage. Nor were the people I called mother and father my natural parents.

We were not related by blood—they were my adoptive parents. Believing they were unable to have children of their own, they had adopted me in Europe when I was just a few months old. The particulars of my adoption were always shrouded in secrecy. Even the country I was born in remained unclear. I had no original birth certificate and without this tangible proof of my birth, I sometimes felt as if I had no date or place of origin. A feeling of unreality permeated my young life. I felt different from other children. I was still a young child when I learned that adoption was a secretive, shadowy entity, something spoken about in whispers. "She's adopted," I'd hear adults murmur quietly when they thought I was out of earshot.

It wasn't merely feelings of disconnection I felt. My adoptive parents were frequently cruel and not supportive: physically, emotionally and mentally. To escape, many times I sought solace through my extensive collection of books and Barbies.

My early life seemed to be a picture of privilege; from the upscale neighborhood we lived in to the exclusive private school I attended, everything seemed perfect. Just like in the funeral industry, image was paramount, and we presented the "right" image.

My mother was preoccupied with the word "right." Having the *right* friends; living in the *right* neighborhood; wearing the *right* clothes; driving the *right* car; going to the *right* schools. Yet, however much she struggled to make things "right," they never seemed "right enough" for my mother.

"They're not our kind of people," she'd say with a subtle sneer of those who didn't measure up to her standards.

As a consequence, my childhood was lonely—few playmates seemed to pass muster. Still, my days were full of lessons—music, language, riding, dance—all designed to make me as "right" as could be.

"Look at what we do for our adopted child," my parents would tell others, patting themselves on their backs for their good deeds. The implied message was clear: I was lucky to have been adopted by them.

Privately, it was another story. I lived in constant fear of being returned to the orphanage. My adoptive mother's warped idea of discipline was to drive me to an upstate orphanage and threaten to leave me "with the other orphans." My adoptive father's idea of keeping a child in line was far worse.

A violent, abusive, crude man given to loud tirades, violence seemed to be second nature to him. Conversation was out of the question and a waste of time when a beating would suffice. My adoptive mother turned a blind eye to the beatings he gave me, never once trying to stop him. Not even the time when, after playing baseball with some boy cousins, he punched me in the face—hard enough to break my nose.

"Well-brought-up young ladies do not play boys' games!" he bellowed.

Blood pouring from my nose, I went to my mother, who said, "Look what you did to the beautiful dress we bought you. Do you know how much it cost?"

Another time, as my mother stirred a big pot of spaghetti sauce on the stove, my father picked it up and hurled it at me in a rage. I got out of the way just in time. The pot crashed through the kitchen window into the backyard, splattering bright red liquid everywhere.

"Look what you made me do! Now clean it up!" he screamed.

I rarely invited schoolmates to the house as I never knew what kind of mood he would be in. I desperately did not want to be embarrassed by his outbursts in front of my friends. Instead, I went to their homes, where I was amazed to discover that other children did not live in fear of their fathers. Those fathers did not come home from work and beat them. Instead, those fathers greeted their children with a hug or kiss and asked questions about school or their activities.

Holidays were hellish. The many gifts I was given were later either destroyed or taken from me to give to "poor" children. One year, I came home from school to find the long hair from my Patty Playpal doll had been hacked off.

"And your hair is next," my mother said menacingly.

Growing up with this lack of stability and security, I was certain that if I misbehaved or displeased them (as I seemed to do daily), I would be given away. Because I was not their real child, the threat of being sent away by my parents was very real and hung grimly over my head throughout my childhood.

There was never a time when I was comforted for daily mishaps, hurt feelings or imagined fears as any child would be. I wished, as a small girl, that someone would just take me in his or her lap and tell me everything was going to be all right. No one ever did. Words of comfort or reassurance were never forthcoming. There's a certain irony in the fact that I chose a profession in which I must comfort others on a daily basis.

Every day of my young life, I longed for my real parents to come and take me home. Sitting by my bedroom window, I watched wistfully, if not expectantly, out the window as cars came and went. Praying to God, I was sure that *He* could see me and would answer my prayer. The next car that drove up and parked in front of the house would be them, here to save me from these awful people and my unhappy existence.But that never happened and I never found sustenance. Instead, I left my adoptive parents' home, in which I felt affection and love were absent, at the age of sixteen, setting out to find or create the identity and the grounding I was sorely missing. And I found it... in a most unlikely way.

One day several months after I left home, my destiny literally walked in the door of the Northern Cross, a local diner where I often ate breakfast. As I sat by the window sipping coffee on that cold, wintry morning, a long, gleaming black limousine parked outside, catching my attention. Impressed, as only a sixteen-year-old can be, I watched as a chauffeur opened the door of the automobile and out stepped a trimly built, sprightly man of about thirty-five, attired impeccably in a single-breasted, black suit. With not a hair out of place, he strode imperiously into the modest diner. Six men followed in his wake, appearing massive in relation to the dapper man on whom they lavished deferential treatment.

On the mornings which followed, the black limousine pulled up outside the diner and its distinguished-looking passenger and men in black suits repeated their entrance until it became a daily ritual. Sitting in a comfortably upholstered booth by the front window, I'd watch them arrive. They made a curious picture, the smaller man so meticulous in his mannerisms and dress, flanked by the six burly types. As time went on, my curiosity about this impressive stranger became greater and greater. Intrigued by him, I made him and his companions the subject of several assignments in my creative writing class. I spun elaborate yarns about who Fred Passarella (I had learned his name) might be: politician, foreign dignitary, dangerous gangster or maybe heir to a fortune.

At last I learned he was the local undertaker. He owned a large funeral home on the boulevard, which could easily be mistaken for a lavish restaurant or catering establishment. I had been right about one thing, he was indeed heir to a large fortune, owing his considerable success to a father who had the foresight to heavily invest in real estate.

Early one morning a few weeks later, he invited me to his table. As we drank our coffee together, he seemed very polite and sincere. He told me what a pretty girl I was; he seemed interested in me, asking me about school and what I wanted to do in the future.

On a number of mornings throughout that year he invited me to join him for coffee. Fred was always a perfect gentleman and over time began to tell me about his funeral business. But then June arrived, high school ended and so did our morning chats. Nevertheless, our fleeting association had piqued my interest in the profession of funeral directing and I began to think of it as a possible career path. A road made increasingly compelling, because from an early age I'd heard it whispered that my own mother had died in childbirth. When I was older, I discovered this was true.

She had died giving birth to me. That is all I ever found out and questions about her and what in particular had killed her haunted me. I began to read medical literature and was mesmerized by the countless mortal illnesses lurking in wait. For comfort, I withdrew into my own private world where I made up stories about my real mother. However, the revelation about my natural mother's death had, I believe, a profound influence on my future career decision, as thoughts about death were ever present in my mind.

CHAPTER 1

Grim Ambitions

As fate would have it, shortly after I graduated from high school, I met my second funeral director, Jimmy Abramo, at a "Las Vegas" night at our local church. Dark haired and in his early thirties, Jimmy spoke with a thick Brooklyn accent which had not left him even years after moving from the borough. As I chatted with him at the dice table, he offered me a summer job as a receptionist. Two months before my eighteenth birthday, I went to work in his funeral business. The job was my entree into the mysterious.

Like many young people, I was inquisitive, idealistic and anxious to tackle interesting endeavors and latch on to new opportunities. Even though funeral directing was not yet my career choice, I thought my job at the funeral home would be a special learning experience and the other employees would have some sort of secret knowledge. By working in a funeral home and associating with funeral directors, I hoped some great answers about the mysteries of death were going to be revealed to me. Of course, they never were. There are no final answers—at least so long as we're alive.

At the time, though, I really did believe that I was becoming part of a compassionate, sensitive, respected group of people:

veritable "pillars of the community," as they are often called. And so I welcomed the chance to meet them, learn more about them and find out what they knew about death's secrets.

Dressed in my Sunday best and more than a little anxious, I went to work that first morning. One of my earliest experiences was being brought along to our "trade embalmer." This is the term that describes the independent contractor who does the embalming for a funeral home in an outside facility—a very common practice.

More often than not, it is the trade embalmers who will deal with such matters as removing the body from the place of death, embalming, dressing, casketing and performing cosmetic procedures. The trade embalmer's job is about the hardest in the industry. They are on call around the clock, on any day or holiday. Being roused from a sound sleep at four in the morning, a blizzard raging outdoors, to remove human remains from a sixth floor walk-up takes an enormous amount of fortitude. Such deeds are also thankless jobs, seldom appreciated by the funeral directors the trade embalmers serve. The funeral directors merely need to make a phone call to the trade embalmers, while snug in their own warm beds. Later, to add insult to injury, the funeral directors usually take the credit and receive praise from the families for the lifelike way their loved ones have been transformed. The embalmers are almost never given thanks and most times do not even meet the families.

On that first visit to the trade embalmer's facility, I saw firsthand the gore behind the sanitized funeral business.

On what seemed an endless row of old, cracked, discolored porcelain tables lay dead bodies in varying degrees of preparation. Embalming machines whirred around me. I would have thought the gray-haired woman on the table nearest to me was sleeping, if it weren't for the inch-long incision I saw in her neck.

Lying on the table next to her was a dark-haired man who had been autopsied. His chest cavity was completely open and an embalmer was reaching in with his hands and removing the deceased's internal organs one by one, tossing them in a nearby bucket filled with formalin. The cadaver's skull plate had been removed as well and was now resting on the sink. With his scalp pulled over his face, the dead man looked as though he was wearing a ghoulish Halloween mask.

An even more gruesome sight caught my attention at another table. The embalmer plunged into a corpse's stomach cavity a long, thin, pointed instrument, which I was informed was called a trocar, and aspirated the gases and liquid contents of the stomach by suction. As he worked, he drank from a cup of coffee which he occasionally perched precariously on the chest of the dead person. I watched the embalmer transfixed, marveling that such an ordinary gesture as drinking coffee could be so repulsive.

Jimmy, my funeral director boss, beckoned me closer to the table where the autopsied body lay. "You gotta watch closely. You'll learn a lot today. This is how we embalm a post," he explained. When I looked at him questioningly, he added, "We call it a 'post,' from post-mortem exam, which is just another word for autopsy."

I nodded and stood as close as I could, staring at the bizarre sight. I hoped I didn't appear frightened. I suspected they were expecting me to faint or act queasy. They were probably looking forward to it. Well, they were going to be disappointed; I stood fixed to the spot. *I can handle this*, I told myself again and again as I looked on.

"Are you watching closely? We're gonna ask questions later," Jimmy said, nudging me closer to the table.

I wanted to tell him that if I got any closer, I'd be on the table with the dead body, but I kept quiet.

The embalmer continued to toss organ after organ into the metal pail. A staccato, clanking noise rang out every time an organ hit the bottom. Blood splashed over the sides of the pail and onto the floor with each toss. Involuntarily, I took a step backward, hoping to avoid getting blood on my clothes.

Jimmy quickly asked, "Whatsa' matter? You scared?"

I realized my insight was correct. The men were testing my fortitude and tolerance to the sights and smells I would have to encounter if I chose a permanent career in this field.

"No, I'm not scared," I said quietly, hoping there was no quiver in my voice.

I found the sights I was seeing in the embalming room were manageable, but the smells were another matter. Human organs after death have a distinct, putrid odor due to the presence of partially digested food interacting with various enzymes. The odors were putrid enough to make anyone nauseous.

At one point in the organ removal process, the embalmer playfully held up the man's liver and asked, "Anybody hungry?"

Just as Jimmy and his companion had glanced in my direction during each step of the embalming procedure to note my reaction, they did so once again after this sophomoric joke. I silently vowed to keep my expression impassive. It would take a lot more than this to rattle me, I promised myself.

At last Jimmy thought I'd seen enough. He announced it was lunchtime. *Lunch!?* At that moment I didn't have much of an appetite and there wasn't much that ever made me lose my appetite.

As we were walking out the door of the embalming room, one of the men suggested a local Italian restaurant.

I swallowed hard and said, "That sounds good."

At lunch, the men eagerly asked me to describe my impressions of the embalming to them as they scanned the menu and ordered a big pasta meal. I usually love Italian food, but when my plate was placed in front of me, for the first time in my life spaghetti sauce did not look appetizing. In fact, it instead resembled the substance coating the organs in that embalming room bucket. I drew in a big breath, however, and forced down the food. I refused to appear squeamish.

Such was my first indoctrination. I knew I'd succeeded in earning my bosses respect when Jimmy slapped me on the back and said, "You did good, kid! Most broads would have puked!"

During the months that followed, I helped Jimmy as much as I could around the funeral home. My duties grew to encompass not only answering the telephones, filing paperwork and greeting bereaved families, but also helping dress bodies, assisting with the make-up and transporting the corpses back and forth to the neighboring counties where our trade embalmers were located.

I was set to enter college that fall and I was determined to finance my education myself. Jimmy kept suggesting I had a real feel and empathy for the funeral business. He said I had a nice, pleasant, sincere way with the families and no fears in dealing with the dead.

Although I was majoring in journalism, by mid-winter I began to seriously consider enrolling in embalming school after college, because of the irresistible lure I was beginning to feel for the funeral business. I continued to work full-time at the funeral home while attending college classes. I felt very grown up dealing daily with adults and such important responsibilities while still in my teens.

What I did not realize at the time, in my youthful exuberance, was the self-imposed exile I was creating for myself. I had no friends my own age, as I worked seven days a week and had moved into the apartment above the funeral home. By late September my workaholic schedule was in place and when I wasn't at work, I was attending classes. There was never any time after school to meet new college friends as I had to rush back to work at the funeral home for afternoon visitation. I looked forward to these hours, but I was always tired and there were times I felt cooped-up. Nevertheless, I believed that I had found my calling. I made some attempts to keep in touch with old high school friends, but they weren't anxious to visit me at the funeral home, except for a few obvious deviants who implored me to call if we ever had a good-looking young woman naked on the embalming table. And I had no time to do the things college freshmen did. So impressed with my new "friends" and life, I never stopped to realize or care about what else I was missing.

I was expected to be mature beyond my years, whether I liked it or not. Wanting to laugh, clown around or even play a radio in the apartment upstairs was impossible. Jimmy always admonished me with the words "Shhh! There are mourners downstairs."

"I hate silence!" I told him one day.

"Get used to it!" he shot back.

I soon found out that the customary job for women working in the funeral field was that of "lady attendant"—cosmetics and hairdressing of the female deceased. In this most feminine end of the business there was a rigid hierarchy; an "old guard," so to speak.

The first woman attendant I met was Tilly Fox. Jimmy opened the door and in strode a red-headed woman of about fifty with a drooping chin and sagging bloodhound jowls. Dressed gaudily, her gold vermeil jewelry clattered as she walked over to a casket to cosmetically prepare a body. We were not introduced. Jimmy merely nodded in her direction and said, "That's our lady attendant."

I walked over to where the woman was working and inquired politely if I could watch her make up the body. She whipped around to face me, put her hands on her hips, glared momentarily and then snapped, "Get the fuck out of here, kid!"

Mortified, I ran back into the office and told Jimmy what had happened.

With a dismissive shrug, he said, "Let Tilly do her work and leave. Don't bother her."

"I wasn't bothering her. I just wanted to watch," I explained.

He continued his paperwork without looking up. I knew our conversation had ended.

Not surprisingly, this brief, first encounter with the lady attendant left a bad taste in my mouth. On Tilly's subsequent visits, I stayed out of her way, but it seemed I could not stay out of her thoughts. She personified the adage, "Those with the emptiest lives have the loudest voices." As time went on, her jealousy turned into a warped obsession. Later, I learned that she had concocted two of the most improbable tales about me I'd ever heard in my life.

There was the "Alexandra desperately seeking an apprenticeship" story in which I'd allegedly slept with a funeral director in exchange for his coveted sponsorship. As the story had it, this man's wife came home to find us making passionate love in their bed. This infidelity sent the wife hurtling over the edge of sanity and caused her to be confined to a mental institution for the rest of her days. Of course, I did not get an apprenticeship with his firm.

The irony of this tale was not that the funeral director and I had no more than a cup of coffee together while discussing my possible employment, but rather that he'd been divorced long before I was ever born. The fact that he had no wife was a detail that mattered not at all as this tale made its way through the industry.

Then there was the infamous "Atlantic City" story. Supposedly, I'd bedded twenty-seven men (how she had arrived at that figure I'll never know) on a five-day jaunt at a funeral directors' convention.

Believable? Hardly. At least not to sensible, rational, educated people. But to funeral directors, it was just the thing they loved to believe, perhaps to indulge their often extreme voyeuristic tendencies.

At first when I heard it, I laughed at the absurdity of this tale. Then when I realized that other people actually took it seriously, I balked, making clear that it was just so much nonsense. Innocent or not, I was reprimanded by one of her accounts, who made it clear I was in some way responsible for the gossip.

"Why should she say those terrible things? You shouldn't have gone. Your presence alone gave her the opportunity to say things. If you weren't there, she couldn't say anything," the man told me.

I didn't know then that these tales would follow me, marking me in a most negative way. Later I winced as many undertakers pointed fingers at me and said loud enough for all interested to hear, "She's the one who was with twenty-seven guys in Atlantic City."

I tried to take the high road, never confronting this obviously disturbed woman who had interjected herself, unwanted and unwelcome, into my life. Unfortunately, my silence was interpreted by some as a tacit admission of guilt. Nothing could have been further from the truth.

Though Tilly and some of the others found me to be prime gossip material, these were exciting times for me. I was the young, typically enthused, fascinated, funeral-school candidate, sharing all the morbid questions laymen have.

Each morning I awakened to a new experience. Would we have any funerals that day? And if so, how many? What did this person or that die of? How old was he or she? What would be worn for the viewing? Where would the burial be? Would a lot of people visit? Which casket would the family select? Could I help with everything? *Oh please*, I thought hopefully, *let me help*.

When Jimmy did allow me to assist, I was in my glory. "Could you grab an arm while we put on his jacket? Could you put her jewelry on? Would you comb his hair?" were just some of the requests I obliged gratefully. To me, they were all part of learning this vitally important business.

When things were slow around the funeral home, I whiled away the afternoon reading *American Funeral Director* magazine, intrigued by the articles about funerals, cemeteries and all things death-related across the country. Although such breaks were often welcomed, I preferred it when we were busy so I could continue to hone my skills and learn new ones. I especially looked forward to the ride into lower Manhattan with Jimmy when it came time to file a death certificate. We had to file in the city's Department of Health building, where funeral directors of all ages, shapes and sizes, dressed in their ubiquitous black suits milled about and greeted one another effusively. Yet, despite the cheerful tones of their voices, some of their comments were none too friendly. I was particularly confused by the wall at the burial desk, which was covered by scrawled epithets. It was not in keeping with the dignified image of funeral directors that I'd previously had. By reading the often obscene messages on that wall, I learned who was screwing who, who was gay, who was a drunk or a drug addict. And I thought I'd left high school behind me!

Eventually, the Department of Health posted an official-looking sign ordering us not to write on walls. A less official sign was taped beneath. It read: "Funeral Directors who write on walls should be barred from the profession."

Over the course of my employment at his funeral home, I began to notice Jimmy's business was declining. As time went on, I found out he had a gambling problem and wagered heavily on sporting events, from ball games to horse racing. Jimmy and I began to spend more and more time at the racetrack, crossing paths with a number of unsavory characters. Some of these men, familiar to me from the funeral business, were more than happy to befriend me and some were certainly more aggressive in their flirting than others.

Early one evening, plagued by a severe headache, I went upstairs to the apartment and fell asleep. Some time later, I was awakened by a heavy body on top of me and started to scream. I felt a hand quickly cover my mouth. Dumbfounded, I looked up and stared into the face of Jimmy's hearse driver, Ernie. The short, heavyset man was at least thirty years my senior and reeked of liquor. He took repeated swigs from a bottle of Scotch, interspersed with slobbering kisses all over me. I felt powerless. Before that evening, Ernie and I had never said more than a few polite words to one another, all in the course of business or at the racetrack. But that night, in the dark room, that drunken man begged me to have sex with him, even offering me a large sum of money for the experience. He told me repeatedly that he was wealthy and would take care of me if I cooperated. Frantically, I managed to free my hands and clawed at his face with my long, sharp nails. Inflicting temporary pain, I managed to slip out from under him, then ran down the stairs and out the door.

I never spoke to Jimmy about this incident until much later, since he was supposed to be good friends with Ernie and I was also afraid of losing my job. When I did tell him, Jimmy merely shrugged it off, seemingly disinterested. I should have learned then and there that true friendships in the funeral business were rare, and opportunistic relationships served many of my peers much better.

After a year or so the funeral home was sold. We went our separate ways. For me, it was on to jobs in two more funeral homes while continuing to attend college, but not before a brief interval when I picked up and dropped off money for Larry, a bookie who knew Jimmy. Not your usual after school job, but as a teenaged girl, I was the perfect foil. Who would suspect me? It never occurred to me that what I was doing was illegal and potentially carried a jail sentence. All I knew at the time was that it was the easiest money I had ever made and it seemed exciting. I felt a bit like Virginia Hill, the girlfriend of mobster Ben Siegel, who had been a courier for the mob and about whom I had recently written a college term paper.

This foray into the underworld culminated in a trip to Las Vegas, where I delivered a substantial amount of cash to a well-heeled customer. However, what I didn't know when I set off on the trip was that the customer in question thought I was more than just a courier—he thought I was sort of a gift for him and he expected we would sleep together. That was not going to happen! I left Vegas upset and angry that I had been set up in such a way. Leo didn't think it was a big deal and laughed it off. But I couldn't, so I severed our business relationship. In retrospect, I see how painfully naive and inexperienced I was.

Although my courier days were over, Benny, one of the bookie's customers who owned a local bar came over to me when I went to make a last pickup. "Could you do me a big favor tonight, Alexandra, and tend bar?" he asked. "My barmaid just called in sick."

"Tend bar!?" I was aghast at the idea. What did I know about tending bar? Plus, I had begun to work part-time in one of my old acquaintance Fred Passarella's funeral homes and was concentrating on learning more about the funeral business, not to mention how tired I was between attending school and working.

"It's easy," he explained. "These guys are shot and beer drinkers. You won't have to make any fancy drinks."

Reluctantly, I agreed. I was living in my own apartment and had been supporting myself since I'd entered college. Since I had no contact or financial assistance from my adoptive parents, money was a constant problem.

I ended up tending bar for several months, hating every minute of it. I tried to do my homework and ignore guys when they hit on me. Oddly enough, the ruder I was to them, the better they tipped me.

The bar owner seemed always upset with me, admonishing me to be nice to the customers. But I couldn't bring myself to flirt like the other girls. I found it demeaning to be called a barmaid and I was insulted by the presumption that girls did this work to meet guys. I didn't think the kind of guy likely to come into that bar would be someone I'd care to meet.

However, one night, a tall, heavyset, well-dressed man in his late twenties pulled up in front of the place in a spanking new Lincoln Continental. He came in and disappeared into the back room for awhile with the owner. Afterward he sat at the bar and ordered a drink. Then, like some other customers, he made a pass.

"Listen, I'm not interested, so save the spiel!" I told him as I slammed his drink down in front of him. I made up my mind then and there I would quit this job real soon.

The man drank his drink and left wordlessly. Under his napkin, he'd left me a hundred dollar tip.

The next time this fellow came back, he ordered a drink but didn't flirt. Instead he told me his name was Vito. "You're nothing like the other girls here," he said in a deep baritone. "Why do you work here when you obviously can't stand it?"

"Rent and tuition!" I shot back at him.

Vito came back several times, each time leaving an outsized tip, each time acting like a gentleman. The last time he asked me on a date.

I said no. He accepted the rejection graciously and told me I could get in touch with him if I ever changed my mind. He gave me his telephone number. Several months later, I had a change of heart and called him. We began to date. In the meantime, I had begun work in yet another funeral home.

My next boss, like my first, came with his own set of problems. Unlike Jimmy, this new boss didn't gamble. He drank instead. Tom drank at lunch, drank at dinner and, if I'd been there in the morning, I probably would have witnessed him tipsy after breakfast—possibly a little vodka mixed in with his orange juice. A small, thin man who was sensitive about his receding hairline, Tom wore a toupee which I immediately detected and favored polyester leisure suits as his mode of dress. Given to dispensing repetitive instructions when under the influence—which was most of the time—he repeatedly buzzed the intercom next to the receptionist's desk in the funeral home from his home next door. With each successive buzz, his words became increasingly slurred and more difficult to understand. Ever polite, I kept assuring him, "I have done the ordering for tomorrow's funeral, you don't have to be concerned." This consisted of calling the church to schedule the religious ceremony, the cemetery to open the grave, the livery company to order the hearse and limousines and any other incidentals which might be necessary. Each time, seemingly satisfied the calls had been made, he'd hang up only to buzz back within fifteen minutes and ask the same questions again. By the time my shift ended at ten o'clock, I was always exasperated.

I tried hard to find something to learn at this job, but Tom, most of the time, was too inebriated to teach me. Just as Jimmy's business had diminished as his gambling problem increased, Tom's business, too, was swiftly declining. At best, this funeral home was a good place for a student to do one's homework—it was nice and quiet. And Tom's funeral home grew quieter still, as I continued to work there while waiting for an opportunity to move on.

One evening, I needed to go back to Jimmy's funeral home, now under new ownership, to retrieve some school books I'd left behind. Walking in, I was met by a tall, slim, bearded man with a distinguished look more often seen in the world of art or academia. He was so engrossed in his project—painting a large mural of a soothing seascape across the lobby wall—that he took no notice of my presence at first.

"Who are you?" I asked curiously.

"My name is Peter Provenzano," he answered as he whipped around to face me, apparently startled at being interrupted.

"What are you doing here?" I asked, despite the fact that the answer was obvious.

"Redecorating this place for the new owner. And may I ask who you are?"

"I'm Alexandra Mosca. I used to work here. I left some text books and I need them."

Since the staff had left for the day, Peter offered to accompany me into the basement where I'd last seen my books. Unfortunately, they were gone, as were all other remnants of the previous ownership. Sensing my disappointment, Peter asked me, "Are they that important?"

"They were Jimmy's...the previous owner's books from embalming school. He said he wanted me to have them if I ever decided to go to school for funeral directing myself."

"You want to go to funeral school?" he inquired in disbelief. "Why in the world? You're more the model type."

"Well, thanks, but I *am* very interested in this business and I think I want to go to embalming school."

"What a waste, a girl with your looks."

"I don't think it's a waste at all," I said. Then, feeling embarrassed, I quickly changed the subject. "Do you mind if I watch you paint a little?"

"Not at all."

I watched with interest as Peter made the canvas come to life. His seashore scene looked so real I wanted to walk right into it and take a swim. A considerable amount of time passed until Peter put down his paints and brushes. "Why don't we go to the diner next door for a cup of coffee? he asked, smiling at me.

We sat in a booth at the diner and I drank my coffee rather self-consciously as I realized Peter was studying me intently.

"Why are you staring at me?" I finally asked.

"I've been studying your face. I'm staring at the woman I'm going to paint."

"You want to paint me?" I was bewildered.

"Yes. Portrait painting is my specialty."

I was skeptical at first, thinking it could be a unique pick-up line.

"I'll ask my *boyfriend* what he thinks."

As if reading my mind, Peter responded, "I'm not trying to make a date with you. This is legitimate. If you have some time to spare, come back to the funeral home with me and I'll show you some of my portraits."

I agreed and waited in the deserted funeral home lobby while Peter disappeared upstairs and returned, juggling a stack of paintings. Among the collection were movie stars who had been glamour girls like Farrah Fawcett, Jaclyn Smith, Cher and Loni Anderson. But balancing the glamour girls' collection were portraits of Presidents Nixon, Ford and Kennedy. Peter's talent for portraiture was extraordinary; I was convinced.

That same week I began to sit for Peter as he painted his first "Alexandra Portrait." I rushed to Peter's studio each night after closing up the funeral home when the evening visitation had ended. His brushes seemed to glide effortlessly across the canvas as I sat on the other side, unseeing, barely breathing, my posture stiff and straight, "holding the pose" as Peter instructed. Two weeks later, he was finished with the first portrait.

I sat waiting in anticipation of the unveiling. This time Peter came down the stairs with a large painting tucked under his arm, covered in cloth. Once uncovered, it revealed a very sophisticated, glamorous rendition of me in a long, white gown. I was quite impressed and flattered.

"I hope this is just the beginning," Peter said as he presented it to me.

And it was. I sat hundreds of times for him over the next dozen years, as his primary model. Soon the press picked up on what they considered to be a most unusual story. At first only the local newspapers took it up, then the story took on a life of it's own.

As time went on, Peter tried to encourage me to pursue other venues in the arts, but I reminded him again and again that I was going to be a funeral director.

I did not know it then, but it would be posing for Peter which would keep the balance in my life and save me from being consumed by the business of death. In addition to his art work, Peter had an intense interest in photography and we began to go on "picture-taking outings" together, beaches and parks becoming our favorite locations. It was on these jaunts that we would talk about my aspirations for the future, with Peter always trying to persuade me away from the funeral business. Needless to say, I wouldn't budge. With tenacity of purpose, I forged ahead with my ambition to set the funeral world on fire. But just in case, I continued to model for Peter on the side.

The posing was going well, but not so my relationship with my boyfriend Vito, the man I had met while bartending. Although he owned several legitimate small businesses, the truth of how he really made his money was more sinister. I was blind to it at first, but Vito, beneath his low-key, pleasant exterior, was a *wiseguy* and dating him came with it's own unique set of problems. Our relationship may have been exciting, but there were darker aspects to Vito which, during the next months, I began to see. Vito's lifestyle, although I didn't know it then, typified mobsterhood. He was generous to a fault and spent lavishly on me. We went to all the best places in Manhattan, ate the finest food and drank the best wine and the most expensive champagne. He indulged my passion for shopping, often buying me something pretty to wear when we went out. We were forever running into "friends" of his at restaurants, concerts and social clubs—friends who would send drinks to our table along with good wishes. He loved to show me off. On the other hand, he hated the fact that I worked and especially that I worked in a funeral home. He didn't think that was progressive...just weird. And he was very jealous. So jealous, in fact, that my posing for Peter was becoming a harrowing experience.

One night Vito waited in a restaurant parking lot where Peter and I were having dinner, ready to have it out with Peter.

"He's exploiting you," Vito screamed at me as he lunged for Peter.

Before he could grab Peter, I got between them and told Vito that he had no reason to be jealous and that I was going to continue to pose for Peter whether he liked it or not. Insulted, he stormed off in a huff. After that, he refusing to acknowledge Peter's existence. It was easier for both of us that way.

Despite Vito, as time passed my friendship with Peter deepened. I continually sought his counsel. He had an innate sense of people and could size up their true motives in one meeting. He more than made up for my inability to judge people's characters. He became my chief confidante, friend and support system.

Although it would be some time before I enrolled in mortuary school, I was already saving a little money toward that goal while attending college and working two and sometimes three jobs at a time. I was already full of big dreams, planning the funeral home I hoped one day to own. I planned it down to a precise location on Francis Lewis Boulevard in Bayside. At the time, a Scaturro's Supermarket occupied the site. *No problem*, I thought, *I'll buy it*. I'd read in the funeral trade journals that supermarkets were the perfect buildings to convert into funeral homes. They were usually all on one floor which made it easier for the disabled, plus people, research had shown, did not like going downstairs in a funeral home.

In my fantasy, I would commission Peter to paint a mural in each chapel, each reflecting a different ethnic theme. Owning to the ethnic composition of the neighborhood, I would be sure to have Italian and Greek murals. I even went so far as to go to the planning board to get a breakdown of the neighborhood's demographics. Next, I made a list of possible financial backers, an essential element to opening the business.

Someday, not in the too distant future, I hoped, there would be a grand opening, as was the custom for new funeral homes. I would wear a white, Grecian-inspired, one-shoulder silk gown. Champagne would flow, my full-length portrait would hang in the lobby and the room would be filled with important people. I would be the toast of the town. Before too long, business would pour in. Everyone would want to hold his or her loved one's funeral at the newest, most stylish establishment in town. I would be benevolent and not put the other funeral home owners out of business by taking all the business. Perhaps we all could be friendly competitors. I romanticized being a funeral director so much, I began to wonder if actually being one could ever match my fantasies.

CHAPTER 2

A Hypochondriac's Worst Nightmare

"Looking forward to meeting you," began the greeting letter from the American Academy - McAllister Institute of Funeral Service, New York's premier mortuary science school.

I read on.

"Please remit your tuition for the school year, in the amount of $2,500.00."

I promptly sent in what for me was a considerable amount of money, partially saved, partially borrowed on a student loan, with the happy thought, *It won't be long now!*

Proudly, I carried that letter in my purse for several weeks before school began, showing it to friends, relatives, co-workers and anyone else I met. I held my head high, overjoyed to have been accepted to the private school that the most important New York funeral directors had attended. Many of the same instructors were still at the school and I would have the benefit of their experience. Even though the State University of New York at Farmingdale, LaGuardia Community College and St. John's University had all begun to offer mortuary science programs in New York, McAllister (as it is commonly called) is, and always has been, considered the preeminent mortuary school.

When the first day of school finally arrived, I awakened hours before dawn. With my excitement growing, I eyed the new dress which hung on my bedroom door. I spent considerable time getting ready, wanting to make a good impression on my new instructors and classmates. After brushing my hair until it gleamed, I decided that I was as ready as I'd ever be and began my journey to school. No small feat, since I had never before driven a car in the hustle-bustle of Manhattan traffic.

McAllister was located on the fourth floor of an unimpressive office building on Park Avenue South in midtown. The urban location left the school open to much ridicule by students looking for the sprawling, tree-lined campus depicted in its catalog. A majority of the students came to school dressed in their Sunday best. Suits and ties were as common for the young men, as dresses were for the few women. A preponderance of students wore black. The formality of this first day set the tone for the remainder of the year. Though most people embraced casual dress, we budding funeral directors differed by accepting without question an outward conservatism in dress and demeanor. In fact, this was just one of the things which set us apart from other students our age. In general, our politics were conservative and low-key. No marching for causes or rebelling against the establishment for us. If I felt different in certain ways, the ideology and socio-economic background I shared with the others allowed for a commonality.

Students eyed each other curiously. Some knew one another from the funeral industry; many of their parents were colleagues. Immediate cliques formed between them, making those of us who had no ties to the business feel like outsiders. There was another discernable difference between the children of funeral home operators and those of us without family ties: the way we traveled to school. We came to school on buses, subways and in car pools. They traveled in new sports cars, Cadillacs, family limousines or by car services. Some even drove to school in hearses and flower cars.

Congregating in the coffee shop on the ground level of the building before and between classes, the young men and women with families in funeral service bragged to one another about how much business their families' funeral homes did and about the big salaries waiting for them after they completed embalming school. They glanced disdainfully our way, wondering out loud just where we, without family contacts in the business, hoped to ever find jobs. It was clear they considered us interlopers. And it became just as apparent that inherited wealth often spoiled those waiting for their due.

Funeral service has been traditionally thought of as consisting only of family-owned businesses, handed down from generation to generation. However, things had begun to change. Insidiously at first, then openly, corporations were buying up the small "storefront" funeral homes in New York and other states. My classmates seemed oblivious to these changes despite some smaller local funeral homes closing their doors and the number of corporately owned funeral homes increasing.

Although there was a preponderance of the offspring of funeral business families in the school, there were also many children of funeral directors who were not choosing to go into the family business, opting instead to educate themselves for and pursue other careers. These factors combined to explain the new group of young people without family ties entering the field.

More than two hundred students were enrolled in that September class, only five percent of them female. The majority of students were from the New York City area; students from Pennsylvania, New Jersey and Connecticut comprised the rest. Because of the large enrollment, we were separated into two classes and for the remainder of the day we all participated in orientation.

The school was headed by two men in their seventies who had once run separate embalming schools. Dr. Otto Margolis merged his school, the American Academy, with the McAllister Institute run by Dr. John McAllister. Neither of these men were funeral directors. Rather, they were educators and stern disciplinarians, considered relics by their students. It was their fervent hope to elevate the status of funeral services through education. Both men insisted on a well-rounded education apart from mortuary studies; science versus sales techniques. Not only would we study embalming, the history of funeral service, funeral service principles and restorative art, but also the so-called hard sciences, including anatomy, microbiology, chemistry and pathology. These classes were taught either by qualified professionals or funeral directors who had become instructors. The goal was to enable us to speak knowledgeably and proficiently about our field.

A new eighteen-month program was implemented the year I attended McAllister for students who had not attended college prior to mortuary school, resulting in an especially heavy enrollment. I was enrolled in the twelve-month program, having three years of college behind me. The end of the program, however, seemed eons away from that first day of orientation.

I settled back in my seat as Carl Bitterer, an instructor in a crisply pressed white shirt and black tie, called on each student in the room and asked the pointed question, "What made you choose funeral service?"

Surely this was a most unlikely career choice for those of us without family in the business. To say you were interested in working with the dead would seem plain weird to many.

I doubted anyone was going to answer, "I always wanted to be an undertaker when I grew up" or "I played funeral director as a child, burying my Barbie dolls in shoe boxes."

In those without family ties to the business, Bitterer indicated, the funeral service bug usually bit after some kind of exposure to a funeral director or by a profound, indelible experience at a funeral one had attended or because of being exposed to and affected by death.

However, that day in class, two answers reoccurred over and over again.

"My father owns a funeral home."

"I want to help people."

After someone had offered that second reply, a wit in the classroom shouted out, "If you want to help people, join the Peace Corps."

However, there were also those who believed that they were honoring a "sacred calling." They claimed they had been guided by a higher power to do this work. One student, when called upon, pointed up at the ceiling and told us, "This is what the Man upstairs wants me to do."

Amused titters were heard throughout the room, although the terms "a calling" and "sacred duty," were incorporated into much of our school material.

Yet, it wasn't easy to know what to answer. "I'm here for the money," would have been the honest response for many. Such unwelcome candidness, however, would have been held in contempt, even by like-minded students. A few of the group admitted they had never seen a dead body and were curious. A couple of them had not even been inside a funeral home. We immediately were suspicious of them and kept our distance.

One tall, thin young man with a pasty complexion, wearing a rumpled black suit evoked images of "Digger O'Dell" the friendly undertaker from an old television program, *Life of Riley*. Another ungainly boy seemed so weird that he instantly earned the nickname, "Igor," as in Frankenstein's assistant. We were convinced he was headed for some weird behavior; necrophilia couldn't be ruled out, we mused.

The late afternoon, September sun streamed through the window as I listened to my classmates answers, trying to sort out my reasons, wanting to be able to reply honestly to Mr. Bitterer's question when my turn came. But my motivations were too complex and personal to explain to this alien group. How could I tell them that I'd always wanted to explore my own mortality and the meaning of death as it related to my mother's death in childbirth. How to explain that I liked church and ceremonies, pomp and circumstance; that I found cemeteries peaceful and calming, that I was inherently empathetic about the suffering of others and that I was looking for meaning and purpose in my life? And, on more concrete notes, that I wouldn't mind the money and prestige and I always loved a challenge.

I decided that I could not share any of these reasons, at least not that day. I settled on a safe, mundane answer. "After working in a funeral home for a few years while attending college, I developed a keen interest in the business and want to become a professional in it." That said nothing! Well, nothing in detail.

After each student had been questioned, Bitterer went on to outline the year ahead. The school year was divided into two terms. "The first term you'll concentrate on your academic studies, learning from your textbooks. You will be given a taste of the standard sciences, anatomy, chemistry, biology, microbiology and pathology."

Pathology was the only hard science which interested most of us. We were more enthused about our social science curriculum, which bore intriguing names such as Funeral Service Principles, Restorative Art, Counseling and Death and Dying. A percentage of students were expected to be weeded out by the end of the first quarter. "Some will not maintain the 75 percent average and others' initial interest will wane," our instructor assured us.

Mr. Bitterer told us, "You will begin your second semester with a smaller group as you put embalming theories into practice at the morgue in the infamous Bellevue Hospital. Your subjects will be the unclaimed bodies of New York City's indigent." These embalming sessions would continue biweekly until graduation, he told us. This phase of our curriculum elicited a number of interesting questions, mostly from the students without family in the business.

"What kind of shape are these bodies in?"

"Can we catch anything from them?"

"What happens to the bodies after we finish embalming them?"

Other mundane topics covered at the orientation were absences—there weren't to be any unless it was a dire emergency and you returned with a note from your mother (some students were over thirty); the discipline book—in which students who misbehaved would find their names; the dress code—no jeans; the behavior code—no drinking or drugs (as if this needed to be emphasized) and, finally, the abbreviated schedule for the remainder of the week.

During a brief break, the whispered conversation among the students was that the tests had not been changed in years and were for sale from the last class.

"Any questions before we end for the day?" asked the instructor.

There weren't any. Everyone was anxious to leave.

"Dismissed," Mr. Bitterer said with a small smile. "Be here nine sharp tomorrow morning. We will have abbreviated classes."

Students hastily left the building, eager to enjoy the remainder of the warm fall day. I headed for my receptionist job at the funeral home, feeling a profound satisfaction at having made it this far. On the drive home, I couldn't help but reflect that the day had been reminiscent of my first day of high school. This seemed peculiar after intense college studies. There was a giddiness in the air that belied the serious tone of our purpose. Still, I was looking forward to the year ahead.

The next day, we briefly sampled each of our classes and were given an overall view of what each class would encompass.

Death and Dying, the first class of the day, was a subject I had previously taken and done well in at college. It was a serious, heart-rending, class which covered numerous aspects of death, including terminal illness, the grieving process, death in literature, death in the media, death and society and funeral customs. The subject forced you to examine your thoughts, fears and curiosities about life, illness, old age and death. In the college I attended, the course had been taught by a sensitive, caring professor and we all learned lessons in living.

Our next class, Restorative Art, promised to train us to reconstruct body parts such as noses, ears and chins, out of wax, to enable accident victims or corpses disfigured by disease, to be viewable. We were to learn about facial markings, parts of the closed eye, lip lines, parts of the mouth, forms of the nose, shapes and sizes of the ears. Hair restoration of the head, eyebrows and moustaches would be included. We would further study how to mask abrasions, burns, fractures, punctures, pistol and rifle wounds, stab wounds, discolorations, scars and the dreaded "skin slip"—separation of the epidermis from the derma—and closing mouths with buck teeth.

Even the situation of decapitation would be reviewed, eliciting both laughs and gasps from the class. Our restorative art textbook, written by an embalmer and former instructor assured us that "the severance of the head from the body is less difficult to restore than it might appear, unless the facial bones are badly mangled. Supposedly, with the aid of a metal rod, fine wire, splints, sculpturing wax, some careful suturing & certainly some masterly ability, a head could be successfully reattached to make open casket visitation possible.

A final instruction would be on the proper and careful use of a hypodermic needle used to "tissue build"—fill in sunken, emaciated tissues with a liquid colloid, a chemical which becomes gel-like when injected, recreating natural facial contours.

Most of the class seemed almost fiendishly interested in correcting such anomalies. There was much cross conversation and musings on just how many head-on collisions resulted in decapitation.

"Jayne Mansfield was decapitated!" one dark-haired man called out.

"Yeah, did they put her head back on?" questioned another.

"Probably not; the embalmers weren't skilled AAMI graduates," jested our teacher. He went on, "If time permits, we will also touch on the application of mortuary cosmetics." Restorative Art certainly seemed like it was going to be a voluminous subject.

Our next class was Funeral Service Principles taught by Todd Owens, a former student. This course dealt with the fundamentals of the business: caskets, casket selection rooms, a brief history of the funeral industry, types of funerals, different funeral customs, funeral merchandising, funeral terminology and definitions, marketing strategies, advertising, necessary equipment for the funeral home, and the layout and furnishing of the place. We were also advised to "sit on the same level as your clients, without a desk between you, so that if called for, you may touch or have physical contact with the bereaved family." A well intentioned gesture perhaps, but open to much misinterpretation.

"Where do we touch the widows?" a student called out.

"Depends what they look like," shouted out another, sending the class into gales of laughter.

"A pat on the hand or a quick hug will suffice," our instructor cautioned seriously. He also wanted us to be aware of the nuances of terminology. This was important in our field, where offense might be taken when none was meant.

"Do not answer the funeral home telephone by saying 'Good morning or Good afternoon.' It is none of those things for a person calling a funeral home," he told us, adding vehemently, "and never refer to the body as 'it,' as in 'where is *it* now' or 'where did *it* die.'"

Eventually, we role-played the making of funeral arrangements and Mr. Owens suggested that it was best to make the funeral arrangements, if possible, in the home of the family. "Most people find a funeral home to be a frightening and intimidating place. Usually, people feel more comfortable arranging a funeral in the security of their own homes." He went on to say that since casket selection is the most difficult aspect of a funeral arrangement, many people are reluctant to enter a room filled with them. To that end, a catalog of casket photos makes the experience less painful and awkward.

Mr. Owens detailed other areas the course would cover, including funding for businesses, clergy relations and a comprehensive explanation of caskets, including types, colors, gauges, components, handles, hardware, interiors, types of seals, exterior finishes, upholstery material, and padding materials, as well covering vaults, grave liners, and transfer containers.

We were also reminded that the funeral business is "based on sentiment and religion" and that such money-saving tips as curtailing flowers "showed a lack of sentiment," as did omitting any aspect of merchandise for sale.

The initial session ended with Owens reciting the ten reasons bereaved families call on a particular funeral home.
1) Previous service – approximately every thirteen years.
2) Reputation of firm – keep up a good reputation.
3) Recommendations – clergy being the best.
4) Location.
5) Good signs.
6) Good lighting.
7) Church affiliations.
8) Cleanliness.
9) Parking.
10) Furnishings – The current trend is for funeral homes to be decorated more like a home.

"We will cover each of these topics in detail throughout the year," Owens assured us as we filed out of the room and headed to our next class, Pathology.

Pathology, I thought as I settled into my chair, *will be one of our most interesting courses.* It was taught by Dr. Roberts, a kindly, retired medical doctor. What I didn't realize was that it would also turn out to be a hypochondriac's worst nightmare! There were so many diseases that caused death, most of us had never even heard of half of them. And by the end of this brief, introductory class, many students thought they were showing symptoms of at least one.

"The purpose of this class is to acquaint you, as funeral directors, with the various diseases with which you will come in contact. It will also enable you to read, understand and explain to a family the cause of death written on the death certificate," Dr. Roberts explained.

"For instance," he continued, "upon encountering a person who has been stabbed, it would be preferable if you could phone the medical examiner and explain that there is a knife wound in the lower left quadrant of the deceased's back, rather than, 'He's got a knife stuck somewhere in his back.'"

Students listened intently as the doctor listed terms readily found on death certificates: edema, abscess, embolism, hematoma, idiopathic, toxemia, trauma, virulence, septicemia, lesion, hemorrhage, hydrocephalus, etiology, congenital and anasarca. I suspect the unusual attentiveness of the class was a deep-seated belief held by many of my classmates that funeral service was a quasi-medical profession. In fact, among us were two twin brothers, Anthony and Michael, who had been pre-med in college, settling on embalming school only after being unable to gain acceptance in a medical school. As well-versed as some of our professors, these boys spent many unselfish hours tutoring classmates.

Then it was on to our embalming class where some very important points were made, not only about practical embalming, but about the personality requirements of embalmers and related theories of behavior.

Joe Cardone, our instructor, was a seasoned embalmer who spoke with a heavy New York accent. He ordered us to write the following tenets in our notebooks and chided us to "Remember them and keep them with you." These were our "Embalmer's Commandments:"

1) Wash your hands after placing the body on a stretcher during house removal.
2) Ask to strip the bed if necessary.
3) Your duty is to terminate infection.
4) All infectious diseases multiply after death and before embalming.
5) You are protecting the public health and environment.
6) Sanitation begins at the removal and continues to the funeral home.

7) Embalming may occur in hospitals, homes, convents and monasteries.

8) Embalming renders a body impervious to chemical processes.

9) People who are morbidly curious are sick.

10) The funeral business is built on sentiment.

11) Everything you do should have an aura of reverence.

12) Don't say "it" when referring to a body.

13) Most funeral directors are conservative, dignified and morally upright because they have to be and they get used to it.

14) Be genuinely sympathetic and keep quiet.

15) Remember the adage: "There is no grief like my grief, no sorrow like mine."

16) Be efficient.

17) It is unethical to divulge any confidence that is revealed in a funeral home, including malformations of the human body, such as tattoos, gunshot wounds and scars, the evidence of hermaphroditism, etc.

18) We *displace*, not *drain* blood.

19) The main reason for Egyptian embalming was religious. Non-religious persons dispute this, so be clinical.

20) Get the body as soon as possible after death. Embalming will be easier.

21) Next of kin may legally watch embalming. But why would they want to?

22) It's not always necessary to sew the lips together.

23) Disinfected blood goes down the sewer system and is no more dangerous than the waste of a sick person who is going to get well.

24) Ethnic values must be considered all the time.

25) Don't mention the aspiration procedure when pressed to explain embalming.

26) When the families need you, they will understand your function.
27) Never guarantee embalming.
28) You judge a civilization by the way they care for their dead.

Painstakingly, I jotted down every word, as if it were gospel.

"Any questions?" Cardone asked after he finished dictating his list.

Almost every hand in the room shot up. There were myriad questions.

"Does the blood really go down the drain and into the sewer?"

"Yes."

"Why can't you guarantee embalming?"

"Because embalming is dependent on a number of factors. The skill of the embalmer, the ground conditions, the type of casket selected and whether or not that casket is enclosed in a vault."

"How do the lips stay closed if you don't sew them together?"

"There are several options. A tack gun, which is sort of a stapler for mouths. Lip cement or plain old 'crazy glue.'"

Seems we'd just learned the 102nd use for that household product.

"Do funeral directors still embalm at home?"

"In rare instances. Though it does take place in convents when embalming nuns."

"Are people really allowed to watch embalming?"

"The law says they are. Now, you all have valid questions and I will answer each one in the days to come," he said, seemingly heartened by the interest shown by the class.

Cardone went on to explain that, "Embalming is the cornerstone of this industry. Without a properly embalmed body for viewing, we wouldn't need a funeral. The Department of Sanitation could do our job and we'd all be out of business."

The allusion to the Department of Sanitation elicited giggles.

"The body is the star of the show, not the casket, flowers or chapel decor, not even the funeral director. No matter how much you know about the history of funeral directing, anatomy, chemistry, types of caskets or this newfangled idea that funeral directors should be 'grief therapists,' never forget that you've failed at your mission if you cannot turn out a good body for the visitation. Everything else can be perfect, but if the family does not like the way the body looks, you've lost them!" Mr. Cardone declared passionately. "In other words, the most important person at a funeral is the dead guy. Everyone understand?"

We all nodded in unison.

"Good. The most important class you take here is mine. When I finish with you, you will know everything there is to know about embalming or you won't graduate."

We sat in silence.

"I've given you a lot to take in today, I know. But before we wrap up, I want you to copy down the non-legal definition of embalming." He turned to the blackboard and wrote:

Embalming is the process of chemically treating the dead human body to reduce the presence and growth of microorganisms, to retard organic decomposition, and to restore an acceptable physical appearance.

"And don't you ever forget that!" Cardone admonished as the class ended.

Crammed into our already full schedule were both The Psychology of Funeral Service and The Sociology of Funeral Service. It amazed me how courses commonly taught at universities could be refocused to relate specifically to the funeral industry. My notebooks were full of information as the school day ended.

Jostling our way into the crowded elevators, classmates joked and laughed about much of the data we had been given.

"'Morbidly curious people are sick!'" mimicked one fellow.

"When do we have to start acting morally upright?" another asked, mockingly.

As the elevator doors opened on the main floor, we all piled out.

"You got a car? Can I drive you home or something more?" one fresh guy called after me.

"I have a ride. Thanks anyway," I answered, as I walked toward the parking garage, several blocks away, to retrieve my car, as did a number of my classmates. My car was old and not too pretty, but it ran well. At the garage a few of us got to talking about where we lived and I decided to join three guys from Queens County in a car pool. Their cars were no better than mine and taking turns and sharing expenses would make the commute more affordable for all of us.

We soon learned that if we got into the city early enough and sat in the car until nine o'clock, a coveted, metered parking space could be ours. We would take turns feeding the meter every hour throughout the day. We didn't realize at the beginning, but appropriating a parking meter was tough work, sometimes bordering on dangerous.

Driving in alone one morning when I had to go to work right after class, I spotted an empty space then hurriedly attempted to park my car in it. As I put the car in reverse and began to back into the spot, I heard the screeching of tires and saw the flash of a long, black hearse trying to pull into the same spot, narrowly missing a collision with me.

"What the hell are you doing?" I demanded, shaken, recognizing Buttons Guarino, the school bully. He was the son of a well-known funeral family.

In a flash the tall, blond-haired young man jumped from the car wielding a baseball bat, threatening to shatter my windshield.

More angry now than scared, I reached behind the seat for the tire iron my boyfriend insisted I carry. I got out of the car brandishing it before me.

"Not if I don't break yours first!" I shouted back, trying to match his menacing tone.

"You're a broad! You wouldn't dare!" he exclaimed in utter shock.

"Try me! Now get out of my space!"

"What a way to act! Shame on you!" Buttons shook his head as he got back in his car and pulled away, tires squealing. Ironically, I had earned his respect and for the remainder of the term he watched out for me. But his temper was still evident in his encounters with others. Years later, I was not surprised to learn of Buttons' murder. And a gruesome death it was. His throat was slashed as he sat on a park bench in Brooklyn.

CHAPTER 3

Gender and
Other Differences

Despite my passion about educating myself for my future career, the school days which followed often made me feel · like an outsider. Cliques formed among my classmates; undertakers' offspring banded together along with the "hangers on" from the non-family group, convinced their subservience would land them apprenticeships with the objects of their devotion, when school ended.

Young men without fathers in the funeral industry also bonded, making a fact of embalming school life and funeral service life-to-come particularly glaring. To make matters worse, the solidarity I'd envisioned, even longed for, simply did not exist among the small group of female students.

Chances were another female funeral director and I would never go move a body together or even have a drink together after work. It was a distinctly male world. The females in school became instant adversaries. An uneasiness and competitiveness hung heavily between us and I could never really understand why. We were all there for the same purpose—to become funeral directors—or so I thought. However, one of the instructors swore that a young woman in our class was there to get a husband. She did, dropping out of school immediately following her engagement. Given our small number and the patriarchal, sexist nature of the funeral industry, it would have been to our advantage to pull together, not apart, as we did. Especially since it had been made clear to us early on by some of our instructors—all male—that females were merely tolerated in class. Although most instructors treated us courteously, the prevailing attitude was amusement that we wanted to do "a man's job." That women might be more sensitive and more conscious of funeral aesthetics, was the only nod to our potential involvement. Mortuary school held limited expectations for women.

As for me, the men singled me out and showered me with attention, even electing me interim class president. Of the small number of females, it seemed I was considered the most attractive. However, my popularity with the male members of my class only further alienated me from most of the other women. Nancy and Wendy, two friendly and mischievous sisters from Clifton, New Jersey were the only girls to befriend me. Although their father owned a successful funeral business, they did not possess the elitist snobbery I saw in the other children of owners. Most of the other girls ignored me, occasionally looking my way with scowling expressions, and one, Martha Ann, the jealous and haughty daughter of a successful Queens undertaker, was downright hostile. Overweight, and unattractive, she dressed like a man and had a particular dislike for me, tossing insults my way at any opportune moment. As I was leaving the building at lunchtime one day, Martha Ann cornered me and demanded in tones dripping with sarcasm, "Who's taking the princess to lunch today?"

Hoping to put an end to her verbal abuse, I countered with my own sarcastic comment. "I haven't decided yet. But it's a good thing your daddy has lots of money, because if you waited for a guy to take you to lunch, you'd starve."

Nancy and Wendy, never far from the action, laughed heartily as Martha Ann's pale skin reddened in anger. Her rude behavior continued. I suspected her hostility was the result of being considered not only the "ugly duckling" of our class, but knowing others joked that she looked like a guy. In our most unenlightened universe, a woman's sexual orientation was open to speculation and reason enough to make her the butt of jokes.

The school year moved along. When we weren't reading about death or learning the skills needed in the business, we spent many class hours watching movies about terminally ill patients heroically vowing that they were ready to die, but of course, not before first making their own funeral arrangements. I often found these movie shorts quite depressing and could not help but take those images home with me. Yet many of my classmates thought the movies were a hoot. Peels of laughter filled the room as we watched some of the films, sounding as if we were watching Mel Brooks comedies instead. This made me wonder why psychological testing wasn't a prerequisite for admission to our school.

In Restorative Art, the class which was supposed to teach us to recreate body parts, many of the guys played jokes, constructing women's body parts or men's exaggerated genitalia, throwing wax across the room at one another and strategically placing wax on chairs to be accidentally sat upon. Oddly enough, I soon realized that many of my classmates were morbidly afraid of death and reacted in infantile manners to our death studies so that they would not be teased or made fun of. Even Dr. Roberts' emotional disclosure that he had just, "lost his mother," was greeted by a number of my classmates chorusing, "Maybe you'll find her."

As the year progressed, Funeral Service Law, Standard Accounting and Grief Counseling were added to our course load. In Funeral Service Law we were familiarized with the legal terminology of death such as the difference between clinical death—also called "legal death" which is marked by the cessation of cardiac and respiratory activity—and cellular death—a lack of oxygen to the cells after the blood stops circulating. The legalities of taking custody of a dead body and the legal order of kinship, were also covered in the class.

In order to turn funeral directors into "grief therapists" or "grief counselors," we play-acted very elaborate scenarios in which bereaved families, after completing funeral arrangements, turned to the funeral director. Of course, we were not therapists; our wisdom was gleaned from one short year in embalming school, but we were supposed to help assuage grief. Supposedly, the funeral director had the ability to understand, comfort and console; he (or she) was all-knowing. I wondered how we would become so wise from our smattering of psychology courses, when some psychologists did not achieve this same expertise after many years of training.

The motivation behind funeral director as "grief therapist" was to elevate our status in the eyes of the public into that of a more learned professional who not only sold merchandise and provided a lasting memory, but also helped to start healing the minds of mourners. This idea seemed noble to some, but unrealistic and grandiose to me. We were not given the knowledge one would need to perform in that way, nor did we have the training or education to hold ourselves out as such. I seriously doubted that the general public wanted to be counseled while making funeral arrangements. Surely, I thought, the sale of merchandise conflicted with the professional tone the industry was attempting to portray. The age-old conflict between my colleagues was whether or not the funeral industry was a profession, but the sale of merchandise precluded that definition. At best, we could agree on the term "quasi-profession."

Six months into the twelve-month program, I seemed to have more questions than answers. Perhaps this is how the school meant it to be.

My social life, however, was full. I had gotten engaged to Vito, who presented me with a beautiful diamond ring. I also spent hours posing for Peter as his portrait model. But at times I felt too powerfully involved with school, my job at the funeral home and the entire business of death. It didn't help that one of our instructors began each and every class with either the observation that, "Everyday, we are one day closer to death," or "We are all dying everyday." The inevitability of death was a constant theme and for me, being born in the way I was, which ended in my mother's death, it was a lifelong one.

Anxious to begin the career of being a "real" funeral director, I wished that I could be magically transported to the last day of school. Realistically, I knew I had to endure another six long months before the reward of graduation.

The phrase, "The funeral business is based on sentiment and religion" was drilled into us constantly. I sometimes heard it in my dreams. We were encouraged as to our opportunities in the industry and a rosy picture was painted of the job market. The school even offered to place the students.

The sales techniques stressed by some of our instructors were geared toward selling the highest priced merchandise possible. Caskets were always described in terms of the protection they offered from outside elements. The higher the price of the casket, the more protection, the more value for your money and—a most insidious implication—the more a family cared about their loved one.

We were cautioned about our public demeanor; it ought to be conservative and low key. We were told to be ever mindful that the public was watching us and that they were all potential

customers. In fact, we were told to see everyone as such. Controversial behavior was anathema! I had no way of knowing then that
I would be the one student in our class whose behavior would be
considered the most controversial ever. Even the matter of drinking in public was covered by one instructor. However, my own
experience conflicted with the advice. I'd already known a number of my colleagues to imbibe heavily and in public.

"Don't go out and get drunk in public because if someone
drops dead in the restaurant or a family member of the restaurant staff dies, they will not call you for the funeral," said one
instructor.

"Be nice to everyone. See all people you meet as potential
client families. But remember, no matter what you do, you cannot raise the death rate," he declared. I think that was supposed
to be a joke!

One of the most affecting parts of the year was our biweekly embalming sessions at the Bellevue Hospital Morgue.
Many of my classmates looked forward to this. The feeling being,
"At long last we're going to work on real dead bodies, rather than
just read about them." This experience also weeded out those in
the class who only wanted to talk about death but not touch it.

The Bellevue Hospital Morgue offered us their facility
and their unclaimed, indigent bodies on which to practice our
embalming. When we were through, the bodies would be transported in cardboard boxes to Hart Island, commonly known as
Potter's Field, for burial "en masse" by the prisoners who were
incarcerated on the island.

Every other Wednesday, my class peered into the small
morgue window to get a look at what was awaiting us on the
table. Some were reluctant to open the door. It was not so much
the sight of the emaciated, often frozen, dead bodies—some dead
for several months—which really made us hesitant to enter, but

rather the sickening stench of rotting flesh. *"Eau de Bellevue,"* we called it mockingly. In that room, breathing proved difficult.

Inside the dark, dank room, our class was split into groups of ten and, armed with our personal embalming kits—consisting of a scalpel, scissors, forceps, a needle, suture and an aneurysm hook—we huddled around the table. Our embalming instructor, Mr. Roberts, asked each of us to locate a particular artery, raise it with our instruments and attach it to the embalming apparatus. The clatter of steel instruments hitting the table reverberated throughout the large room, muffling the constant chatter.

"You raise the right axillary artery," he told Carol, a primly dressed, redheaded girl who had been trying to disappear into the background.

"Me?" Carol asked meekly, looking aghast at the partially decomposed corpse on the table, parts of his face eroded, a gaping hole where his nose had once been.

"Yes, you."

"I don't think I can," she answered, her facial expressions running the gamut from disbelief to disgust.

"I don't think you can either. That's why I called on you. What are you doing here? Looking for a husband?"

"No, I want to be a funeral director," Carol responded unconvincingly.

"Another cupcake wasting the class's time," Mr. Roberts muttered through clenched teeth.

Carol burst into tears, bolting out of the morgue, never to return. This class clearly was not meant for the faint of heart.

Without missing a beat, the embalming instructor repeated his request to another student, a male this time and one who was proud of his embalming experience.

"And what do we do if a body moves on the table?" Roberts asked gravely.

"Call the M.E.!" shouted several students in unison.

"Wrong answer!"

We looked at him questioningly.

"Whack the body over the head or you'll lose the call!"

After a momentary silence, the class began to laugh, as it registered that this is what passed as funeral director humor.

But jokes aside, Mr. Roberts tried his best to drive home the point that embalming was a potentially perilous act. He read the following warning to us:

"Within every body, there is a potential danger of infection from some microbiologic source. At death, that body becomes a culture media and a source of contamination. Hazards increase due to conditions surrounding any given form of death."

A number of students had embalming experience and were eager to show off their skills. Others fought back nausea as the stale odors of decay, rotten flesh and formaldehyde combined, while a few were unable to fight it off. One girl fainted and some remained in the background, unwilling to participate. It was obvious these students had never even seen dead bodies before and clearly did not have the stomach for this kind of work. This was not a place for the thin-skinned. I wondered to myself why it was not mandatory for embalming school applicants' to have seen a dead body before being accepted to the school. Furthermore, it didn't seem to make sense on the part of the applicants. How could they possibly know that this was what they wanted to do? These people must have been lured into mortuary school by the myth of high pay in the funeral industry.

Much of the inattentiveness in the morgue could be attributed to two factors: the practical exam for licensure had been abolished—a bad move—and many of my peers had no intention of ever embalming, a fact about which they were proudly vocal.

As for myself, I knew that when I was hired as an apprentice, I would be required to embalm. I made the choice to roll up my sleeves and get down to business. Besides, I wanted to learn embalming. It was, after all, a necessary skill in our business and an art of sorts, one which very few mastered. I listened carefully to our instructor and when called upon to isolate a particular artery, did my best to search in the tangle of veins, muscles and tendons for the artery requested. Slicing through the partially frozen flesh, with my brand spanking new scalpel, I watched as blood spurted out, staining my plastic gloves.

"I've got it!" I called out to Mr. Roberts, upon my successful find.

"Good girl!" he responded, his head nodding in approval.

Our last school quarter began in July and the summer heat intensified our moods. Many in the class fought often and easily with one another over parking spaces, test papers, job possibilities, friends, family ties... anything that rubbed them wrong at that moment. When they weren't fighting, a malaise prevailed, broken up from time to time by water pistol fights or childish pranks. One clown let several pigeons loose in class, causing our seventy-year-old microbiology teacher to clutch his chest and gasp for air. I looked around the room and thought how sad it was that these people were our future "caretakers of the dead." I hoped they would mature quickly.

At last September arrived, along with final exams and the dreaded National Boards, a preliminary to our apprenticeship and licensure. My classmates and I had discussed our seating plan and how we would share answers for the last time. However, the morning of the exam, one of our proctors had other ideas.

My Restorative Art instructor was one of our proctors. He and I had never gotten on well and he gleefully announced that he had a "special" seat for me: alone and in front of the class.

Although I'd been on the honor roll throughout the school year, I was panic-stricken, needing the security of someone else's paper with which to compare my answers, just in case. I was most afraid I'd draw a blank, but it didn't happen.

I answered every question to the best of my ability and felt reassured. That night I attended our school's dinner dance, which was held at Terrace on the Park, the site of the 1964/1965 World's Fair.

Dressed in our party finery, we danced, drank and made merry, thrilled that the year was over, feeling important and accomplished. We were all anxious to get on with the business of being funeral directors. Blindly optimistic, we looked forward to working in the industry; certain we were going to make a big difference. That night we all shared the overriding feeling of having achieved a major goal. Nevertheless, we couldn't be sure, because we had to wait to see if we passed our exams.

Within a month all our grades were recorded. I had passed. The future lay ahead and I was eager to grasp it.

CHAPTER 4

You Don't Look Like an Undertaker

In order to become licensed as a funeral director in New York, you must spend a year as an apprentice, after your schooling has ended. However, the year I graduated, to my dismay, there were almost no apprenticeships to be had. Doggedly, I applied to every funeral home I could, near and far, for a job.

Nevertheless, a few weeks after school finished, I was still frantically looking for an apprentice position. Although I was working at two funeral homes as "floor help"—the common industry term for receptionist—neither place would agree to keep me on in an apprentice capacity. In desperation I offered to work for free, as I had heard a number of other people were doing, just to get my license. Even that did not seem to be an inducement to potential employers.

By then I had confirmed what my early work experience and gleanings from school had taught: female apprentices were not welcomed. Rather than seeing the benefit of a woman around the funeral home, women were, for the most part, seen as a hindrance to the work at hand. In fact, I now found there was a code of silence which, in effect, did not let women looking for apprenticeships know a job was available. During the next weeks, I experienced it first hand several times. When information leaked through to me about one job opening, I hurriedly rushed to the funeral home only to be told there was no job. Days later I found out the position, which I had been told never existed, was now filled—by a male.

"You don't look like an undertaker!" is a phrase I got more than sick and tired of hearing. It was true, I guess. I never did look like an undertaker. Then again, what does an undertaker look like?

As sophisticated as society has become, one likeness still comes to mind: that of a man (never a woman) personifying the "Grim Reaper." Nobody looks like that in real life. It's merely an image the public has foisted on the industry—or vice versa.

When I tried to emulate my peers, I came off rather theatrically. And the dramatics made me feel insincere. Perhaps I worried that the general public had become so brainwashed, theatrics were what they had come to expect and the difference between honesty and play-acting could no longer be detected. Still, I wanted desperately to fit in and gain the approval of my colleagues.

Admittedly, I rebelled against the traditional black garb as everyday attire, opting instead for stylish dark skirts, subtly colored silk blouses and spindly high heels.

My long dark hair was another matter. Regardless of how hard I tried to keep it in place, it always seemed attractively tousled, unwittingly inviting unwanted caresses by associates. Finally, in an attempt to conform, I cut off my waist-length hair. I cried for weeks, feeling the loss of a characteristic part of myself.

In the funeral business, I came to realize, conforming is everything. That is, the outward semblance of conforming is what counts. I was a young woman trying to do a job I believed in, not play a role right out of popular fiction. Yet try as I might, I already was being labeled "too sexy" and "too controversial."

During my search for employment, I met many funeral directors. A feeling of longing to be one of them overtook me. I wanted to be successful and a leader, too. I was mesmerized by the power I thought they wielded and I admired their looks and their lifestyles—the expensive designer cut of their clothing, the jewelry, the limousines, the expensive dinners, the cash flowing. I felt by becoming a funeral director, one would be respected in the community and do a service for mankind, as well as, I thought, make a fortune just by mastering that steadied look of compassion. But I knew I wanted to be more than just a caricature of a funeral director.

With the exuberance and vision of youth I wanted and was committed to making a difference in my business. I was really going to help people, not just snatch their cash away in the guise of arranging a more "meaningful" funeral, i.e. the more you spent, the more significant the funeral and the more you loved the deceased. And if you spent enough, perhaps death could become optional. In fact, I did not want to make my living out of the misery of others. I wished funerals could be less costly. I fantasized that I would be the one to make this so. Perhaps I could find a way to have them subsidized by the government or by a universal insurance.

I hoped virtues I held dear, such as honesty, sincerity, compassion and integrity would prove to be valuable assets. I always treated people as I'd wish to be treated in similar circumstances. And I felt as a woman I could bring sensitivity and compassion to a difficult time in people's lives.

Yet, as I learned about the stagnant and unprogressive ways the funeral business tried to keep women in their places, I felt discouraged. To file a lawsuit on discrimination would have been to dig one's own grave. It was silently understood that you didn't make waves if you ever hoped to work. Word traveled easily and blacklisting was quite common.

At any rate, I was not a feminist. I did not want to emulate the male role. I always dressed in skirts or dresses for work, make-up on, hair styled. And I believed women had traditional roles to fulfill in life, that they were nurturers by nature. Feeling as I did, I could understand funeral directors who resented women's entrance into the funeral business. They thought we would usurp their positions in what had always been the traditionally male field of funeral directing. They also thought women were not up to the job. On the other hand, I had always felt comfortable in accepting certain roles that were traditionally fulfilled by men. I believed women could aspire to the heights of business and life as yet uncharted. I vowed to become a funeral director yet I knew and expected people would lean on me. I journeyed on, ready to break new ground.

Working with a list of funeral homes which included the five boroughs of New York City and Long Island, I visited or telephoned each. And what a learning experience that was!

I visited funeral homes that came in all shapes and sizes, depending on the years they were built and the laws by which they were governed. The older funeral homes were usually nothing more than small, box-like buildings with one chapel. They did not contain an embalming room and the decor was antiquated, dreary, dark and heavy on the velvet. These funeral homes, commonly called "storefronts" fell under the "Grandfather Clause" of a law which was passed in New York State in 1968. After this time, new funeral homes had to adhere to stringent regulations in order to open. These regulations mandated an embalming room, even if it was not to be used, a separate arrangement office, off-premises loading and unloading areas and a specific square footage requirement. Added to this was a requirement of not less than seven parking spaces. Obviously, these new requirements were costly and prohibitive for entrepreneurs. The storefronts were permitted to operate and even to be sold as funeral homes as long as the new owners kept the existing business registration and funeral home name. If they did not, the funeral home would no longer be permitted to operate unless it was brought up to the new industry standards.

While the vast majority tended to be relatively modest, mom-and-pop operations, some funeral homes were spacious and elaborate. Often the demographics of the locale determined the decor. Certain funeral homes were understated and serene, others were blatantly ostentatious. In Catholic communities, statues of religious saints, often life-sized, dominated the interiors. Lobbies were filled with religious articles, including photos of popes, bishops, cardinals and the funeral director posing with his parish priest. This decorating style could be best described as "early Apostolic." It was this style of decorating that has made funerals and religion synonymous in the minds of the public, a view some funeral directors capitalized on. *Come to our funeral home. We're the most religious!* they seem to be shouting.

Because of the heavy interaction between funeral homes and houses of worship, the mistaken belief that funeral establishments are endowed with some sort of clerical respectability has arisen. We are, for business reasons, allied with the clergy in the complete funeral package. But we are certainly not the clergy. A religious bent is not a prerequisite of the job. Yet some funeral directors swore their vocation was "a calling."

Funeral homes and their directors usually have a religious affiliation, advertise as such and donate to their churches or synagogues. Often a clergyman will recommend a certain funeral home and though this is kept hidden, sometimes a contribution or even a kickback is offered and accepted.

Just as a funeral home is often located near a church, a florist, too, will many times set up shop close by. Funeral flowers are a big business and, as I gained more experience I came to see, a big waste, as more and more cemeteries strictly limit the amount of flowers they accept, some accepting none at all. Florists routinely offer kickbacks to funeral directors who push their floral pieces, supplying them with catalogs depicting every conceivable funeral arrangement. In these books one can select from bleeding hearts, broken hearts, Gates of Heaven, casket pillows, slumber blankets, bibles, clocks identifying the time of death, crosses, archways and even ethnic variations, such as shamrocks, national flags and sentimental favorites—like dogs, cats, cars, etc.—recreated in flowers. Many of these floral pieces cost up to one thousand dollars. Unfortunately, rather than discourage a family or advise the members to chip in together and limit the amount of flower pieces, some undertakers will encourage big sales to increase their commissions.

In the funeral business location is everything! To be centrally located is to be blessed. The address is of paramount importance to families in their selection of a funeral home. In fact, this concern usually supersedes all others, including reputation and price. So illogical was this choice yet I could almost envision a family explaining, "We selected the funeral home on the boulevard because of its location and parking. The poor reputation of the proprietors is of no consequence."

Of course, adequate parking facilities help, but usually are not essential in cities where there are parking lots nearby or a vacant supermarket or shopping center parking lot within walking distance in which to park cars.

Once inside the chapel (reposing room) there is little discernable difference between rooms in other funeral home buildings. All chapels are composed of essentially the same elements; industrial carpeting, folding chairs, torchieres, eternal flames, now electric rather than burning candles, a cross, crucifix or Star of David at the head of the room, a casket bier to rest the casket on, a prie-dieu and often lithographs or inexpensive prints decorating bland walls. Of course, within their similarity, there are also varying degrees of quality and wear and tear, with some rooms renovated more often than others. One funeral director I called upon summed up the social nature of funerals quite succinctly. "Some people come to funerals for a night out, to socialize. For them we're like caterers without the food and music."

I'd gone to school, but I was getting quite an education about what the various funeral homes had to offer. Unfortunately, I was making no progress on the apprenticeship front. Rejection loomed around every corner.

The funeral directors' reasons for not hiring me became a familiar refrain. "Women can't lift and move bodies out of homes, go into dangerous neighborhoods, won't be able to stand the pressure and are too sensitive." Also, "My wife or girlfriend (or maybe both) would not like you around. And you would be a distraction to the other workers."

Making the rounds of the various funeral homes, hoping to be hired as an apprentice, became more frustrating and demoralizing as time wore on. Many of my encounters left me close to tears.

Although I was always anxious to convey my interest in the funeral business to the boss, the interview often took a sharp turn from funeral-related matters.

"Are you married? Do you have a boyfriend? Would you like to have dinner Friday night?" became questions at which I cringed. I could see that employing me was the last thing on such men's minds.

I politely declined their offers, risking alienating future contacts. And I was ever-mindful that these funeral directors, with a word to a colleague, could prevent me from working elsewhere in the industry.

Most of the interviewers did not seem to care much about my embalming experience or my familiarity with funeral service work, given my employment history within the field. They seemed unable to get past the idea of an attractive woman wanting to be a funeral director. I was keenly aware that my gender was working against me.

I felt encouraged during one interview as the owner proudly gave me the grand tour of his newly-renovated funeral home. He was particularly proud of his state-of-the-art embalming room. Leading me inside, he explained his new embalming machine to me. I expressed my interest in the embalming procedure, which was, we agreed, the cornerstone of our industry. I thought, *Here's a man taking me seriously at last*, until he leaned against his spotless, white tiled walls, stared at me and began to think out loud:

"But if I hired you to embalm you would get blood and guts all over you. You wouldn't look pretty anymore. You could ruin your nice clothes. You could even catch a disease," he said.

Not wanting to encourage this line of conversation, I remained silent.

"No, I can't hire you. My senses would be offended if you somehow became marred for life in my embalming room."

"Thanks for your time. I'd better go," I said nervously, as I turned to leave.

"You're welcome. Come back and visit anytime," he said in farewell.

I decided he was either a crackpot or putting me on.

On a subsequent interview a heavyset man told me that if he hired me, it wouldn't much matter whether I became proficient at embalming as there were "other things" I could do for him that men could not. His meaning was clear and I left his funeral home in a hurry.

During yet another fruitless interview, a man with owl-like eyes was blunt enough to tell me, "You don't belong in this business. It's a joke you wanting to be a funeral director. You'll just give the men ideas." So many of these men refused to take me seriously, dismissing me and my credentials altogether.

All in all, I received many offers for dates, but none for a job.

I began to wonder if I'd ever get my license. Things were not looking good and people in the industry were discouraging me. But that only made me more determined as I shrugged off rejection after rejection from major firms and smaller firms alike.

Meanwhile my fiance, Vito, was pressuring me to set a wedding date, but I was reluctant to do so.

"It would mean sacrificing my career," I explained.

"What career?" he asked incredulously.

Vito was a traditional man. He was ready and willing to marry me, with no expectations of my holding a job or contributing financially to the marriage. In fact, he preferred I did not work at all, viewing a working wife as a negative statement on a man's ability to provide. Money never seemed to be an issue, as he lavished large amounts on expensive dinners and gifts for me.

I momentarily wondered if I was making a mistake in my chosen profession, quickly decided I was not and then put the thought out of my mind. With steely determination, I continued my search for that elusive apprenticeship.

One particularly bleak winter morning, my mind on the interview I was headed to, I was stopped by the police for running a stop sign. I had never gotten a ticket before and ended up telling the policeman my job-hunting troubles. He tried his best to console me, but I still got the ticket.

My appointment that day was at a funeral home operated by a husband and wife in Corona, Queens, a once staunch Italian enclave, now changing and coping with increased crime. To me, it was a long shot. I hadn't had too much luck so far making a good impression with wives.

Arriving a bit late, I interviewed with the husband, John, a tall, transplanted Southerner with grey-flecked hair, who seemed glaringly out of place among the slick metropolitan New York funeral directors I had met so far. He had courtly manners and spoke softly. So softly, I had to lean forward to hear him. I answered his questions with a composure which belied my desperation for this job. But then I thought, *Why not go for broke?* Nothing else was working.

In a rush of words I told him, "I can't find an apprenticeship, time is passing quickly and I have been everywhere. You don't even have to pay me. Just let me work a year for you so that I can get my license," I pleaded.

"Sweetheart," he said in a gentle Southern accent, "I couldn't let anyone work for nothing."

He told me that he had to talk it over with his wife who was at their winter home in Florida. I thanked him and left. Although he hadn't made a commitment of any kind, I felt a glimmer of hope.

Driving only several blocks from the funeral home, I replayed the interview in my mind. *Is he seriously considering me? Or is he just another funeral director who said, "I'll let you know? but meant "Not on your life, sweetheart."* As I was going through a litany of questions, I sailed through a red light and crashed into a van. There was considerable damage to my car, but luckily I escaped with only some bruises and scratches. The damage to the van was minor and it turned out the driver was unlicensed and would not be pursuing me legally. Severely shaken, I called a friend at an auto body shop and waited alone in the cold for the tow truck to arrive.

The driver dropped me off at my apartment. Until then I had gone through the motions of getting the car attended to, but alone in my apartment, the realization hit me that because of my preoccupation, I had become a danger to myself and others. Also, still without an apprenticeship, I now no longer had the use of my car to continue my search. On top of that I now had a repair bill to pay. Disgusted and feeling sorry for myself, I wept and drank a good deal of wine. Finally, I drifted off into a much-needed sleep.

Over twenty-four hours later, I awoke to the insistent ringing of the telephone. It was Vito, who was alarmed at having called my number several times from out of town, getting no answer.

I confessed what I had so stupidly done.

"We'll talk later tonight when I get back from my trip," Vito said angrily.

When Vito returned, we talked, not agreeing on anything, as usual. He had made it clear throughout our relationship that he did not feel funeral service was an appropriate career choice for a young woman. He would admonish me not to discuss it when we were out socially.

"Forget this! Get a normal job! This will never work!" Vito shouted at me.

Not sleeping, eating sparsely, drinking and smoking, were taking their toll on me. I was growing thinner and paler and Vito was alarmed, as were other friends.

I wanted to go to Florida for a respite and Vito agreed I should, but he would not accompany me. We were fighting often and there was an ever-present tension between us which saddened me.

On a cold but sunny winter Friday, I went shopping with a girlfriend to buy some new clothes for Florida and to lift my spirits. We spent a pleasant day in Manhattan, the first relaxing day I'd enjoyed in months. Strolling through Saks Fifth Avenue, trying on newly arrived spring fashions, I forced myself not to think about the funeral business. It had been a week since I'd gone on my last interview. I hadn't heard a word from them, which was typical. All the potential employers said, "We'll let you know," but they never did.

Enjoying lunch at the Rockefeller Center Café, we talked about my upcoming trip. Getting away was the best thing I could do to relieve the stress. But the thought, *Is my career over before it has begun?* ran through my mind over and over. I thought about giving up. Then as quickly as it had entered, I put that thought out of my mind. I decided I would resume my search with renewed vigor when I returned from Florida.

Ladened with shopping bags from my excursion, I wearily turned the key in the door of my apartment. A ringing phone greeted me. I dashed across the room just in time to answer.

A soft voice, tinged with a Southern accent, responded.

"I was just about to give up."

It was John, the last man with whom I'd interviewed.

"Oh, hi John. I just got in from shopping," I said, trying to sound carefree, although my heart was pounding. *Please God. Let him have a job for me,* I prayed silently.

As was the case so many times in my life, God answered my prayers.

"I was wondering if you could drop by to talk about the job?" came the words I longed to hear.

"Sure...anytime...whatever you say...how about right now!?" I said in an excited rush of words.

"Come on over then."

"Thanks! Thanks John!"

I tossed the shopping bags on the couch and dashed out the door. I didn't want to give him any time to change his mind.

Fifteen minutes later I was parking my rental car in front of the Coppola-Migliore funeral home, a compact, one-story, red brick building, in Corona, Queens. The door was open and I walked into a lobby, which, even in the semi-darkness, appeared quite small.

I heard footsteps above me and a door opening, then John poked his head into the lobby. He invited me upstairs to the apartment where he lived with his wife and young son and offered me coffee.

I sat primly at the dining room table as John poured me a cup of steaming coffee. I didn't know it then, but that was the first of hundreds of nights I would sit at that very table, in the same chair, talking, drinking coffee and smoking cigarettes until the wee hours of the morning.

Before I had another chance to tell John how grateful I was, he began to tell me about the job. "Alexander (he would always pronounce my name in the masculine) this is a good opportunity for you. You'll learn a lot here. I'll work you hard, but you'll learn to be a good embalmer."

I listened intently as he continued, almost sounding like he was now selling me on the job. Of course, he didn't know I had no other choices and was trying not to pounce on his offer.

"We're all like family here. You know Bart. He works with us and is very happy here."

Bart, a happily married father in his early thirties, was someone I'd worked with briefly several years before when I'd been a receptionist in one of the local funeral homes. I liked him. A jovial guy, I remembered he'd lived on the beach after his first marriage had broken up, showering and dressing in the funeral home each day.

It would be good to see a familiar face.

"My wife, Rae, will be happy to have you here. You know, she's a funeral director and embalmer herself, so she'll welcome another woman in the business. She knows how hard it is for women.

At the mention of Rae's name, I felt uneasy. Her reputation, and everyone in the industry I was finding out had one, was in a word "tough." I wondered how she would feel about me. "John, did you tell your wife you hired me?" I asked with trepidation.

"I'm the boss, sweetheart. I make the decisions," he answered somewhat testily.

I realized I had struck a nerve and was immediately sorry for asking, feeling I'd offended my new friend.

The awkward moment passed and we went on to discuss everything under the sun before saying good-night—well past midnight.

"I can't wait to start my new job tomorrow morning. I'll be here early," I said enthusiastically, as John walked me out to my car.

"We're looking forward to having you."

The next morning, on the first day of my apprenticeship, I awoke unusually early, full of anticipation. I peered into my closet, wondering what to wear. Finally deciding on a black, mid-calf length skirt, white blouse, buttoned to the neck, black hose and a black bow in my long hair. The effect was sufficiently somber—I looked the part. Eager to begin my first day, I hurriedly drove to the funeral home.

The street was blocked by a hearse, flower car and limousines, so I parked several blocks away. As I walked toward the building, my first thought was that it looked different in the morning light. In my job search I had visited many funeral homes, some spacious and glamorous, so I couldn't help but make comparisons. This funeral home was quite small, both of its reposing rooms sorely in need of renovation and modernization.

The upholstery was worn, as was the dark carpet. Folding chairs were the old wooden kind, the wood scraped and scratched from years of use. Two letters of the sign were missing, spelling, oddly enough: FUN AL HOME. Nevertheless, I looked upon this place as my salvation…and it was.

Upon hearing me enter the threadbare lobby, John buzzed the intercom and invited me up to his apartment for a fast cup of coffee. When we came back downstairs, he introduced me to many new faces: the regular hearse and limousine drivers and an eclectic assortment of friends and neighborhood people who helped out around the funeral home. They all made a fuss over me.

When John started the funeral scheduled for that day, I watched discreetly from the back of the dark chapel as he said prayers, visualizing myself leading the large group of mourners. Afterward, John led the mourners to the church across the street and then on to the cemetery, leaving me to handle the telephone. Each time the phone rang, I quickly answered, hoping to take a "first call" (information on a death which has just occurred) on our pre-printed "first call" note pads. None came in that day. Instead, most of the callers asked who I was, not accustomed to an unfamiliar voice. When John returned he was surprised that we had not taken on any new funerals.

"Don't let this fool you. We're usually real busy here. Between our three funeral homes and my trade accounts, we hardly ever rest here," he explained.

"I'm glad. I want to work."

He offered to let me go home early, but I insisted on finishing out the day, still hoping to do some important work. I left disappointed.

Arriving for work the next day, Sunday, the funeral home was buzzing with activity. Several white *authorization for removal* sheets lay on the desk. "We have bodies to move right away," John said insistently.

John's mood was not laid back as it had been the day before. He was anxious to get the bodies out of the hospitals and into the funeral home. That was one of the first lessons he taught me: no matter what, take possession of the body. That way, in the event a family decides to go to another funeral home, you will at least get paid for making a removal and doing the embalming. As soon as Bart, my co-worker arrived, John sent us off on a removal together.

We were to move three members of the same family, who were killed in a neighborhood fire. I remembered seeing the news footage on television the previous night. As Bart, who still sported a neatly clipped beard since I'd last seen him, drove us to the New York Medical Examiner's building in Manhattan, we reminisced about the brief time we had worked together several years before and got re-acquainted. He seemed to know the funniest and worst things about everyone in the industry, who was who, who had alcohol, or heaven forbid, drug problems—major indiscretions in our most conservative industry—and who was sleeping with whom. He had me laughing all the way to Manhattan as he filled me in on the current gossip.

Approaching the building on First Avenue, I felt a strange sort of excitement and importance, as if we were on the most vital of missions. Sensing this, Bart handed me the affidavits to present. Then he deftly backed the station wagon into the narrow parking spot between similar removal vehicles. On the dashboard he placed a small cardboard sign which read: FUNERAL DIRECTOR ON OFFICIAL BUSINESS. He then opened the back of the car and slid out the "one man" stretcher, which he jokingly called the "one person" stretcher, since I'd also be using it.

"No sexism in this firm," he quipped.

This stretcher enabled a person to make a removal solo, as opposed to stretchers we also used which needed to be carried on both ends. I pushed as he pulled, following him up the ramp and into the building.

My first visit to the city morgue was an eye opener. I expected to see a pristine and orderly establishment. Instead, the New York Medical Examiner's building was a dirty, antiquated, seedy building with the foulest of smells. There were not enough freezer drawers to accommodate the overflow of dead bodies. As a result, bodies were strewn about haphazardly on gurneys, autopsy tables and on the floor. Most were covered with sheets, often blood-soaked, but some were not and those remains, limbs splayed about, were in plain sight.

Surveying the scene, I stepped gingerly around and over the bodies in my path to get to the man in charge. I looked down to see some sort of slime had accumulated on my new high heels, as the men working there stared at me. I tried not to gag on the smells and to be careful not to brush against anything, to avoid soiling my clothes. I wished I had some sort of protective gear on...something I could take off and toss in the trash later. Despite my disgust at the conditions, however, I forced myself to be professional as I handed the affidavits to the morgue man, who smelled faintly of gin.

"Sir, we are here from the funeral home to pick up the family killed in yesterday's fire," I said, trying to sound as official as I could. He peered at me through wizened, rheumy eyes, a faint look of amusement on his face. He seemed unaccustomed to being called 'sir.'

"Missy, you mean the post toasties. They're over there," he said, pointing behind him.

I looked in that direction.

"Yo! They're here for the post toasties!" he shouted to another morgue man.

I looked at Bart and raised my eyes quizzically.

"Over here!" bellowed the other man.

Lying on the filthy, cold, cement floor, wrapped in soiled sheets, were the charred remains of what once were human beings. Their facial features and limbs were indistinguishable; they now resembled tree trunks felled by a fire. My breath caught in my chest. I'd seen any number of dead bodies before, in various states of decomposition, but nothing had prepared me for this. They were so grotesque that I could only glance at them and had to look away.

Bart lowered the stretcher and with the assistance of the morgue man, placed the first body on the stretcher. They then repeated this motion with the other two bodies, placing them on the alternate "two man" stretchers. I carried one end of the stretcher out to the car. After giving the morgue men their gratuity, we were on our way back to the funeral home. In the car, I brushed at my clothing.

"What are you doing?" Bart inquired.

"Trying to get the germs off," I answered, continuing to brush, "I can't wait to get these clothes off and take a shower."

"You'll get used to it," Bart said knowingly.

"I don't think so," I said quietly.

John was waiting for us when we returned. He instructed us to box the bodies and then together, we were to embalm a body he had moved out of a house.

We drove the ten blocks to a smaller funeral home building which housed our embalming facility. The room was old and musty. Dank odors wafted up the stairs when the door to the preparation room was open. Ventilation was impossible as the windows refused to budge. Furthermore, there was no elevator in the building. We had to carry each body we brought in down a steep staircase.

"Can you do this?" Bart asked, eyeing me skeptically.

"Sure I can," I assured him, trying not to let nausea overwhelm me.

Bart lifted one end of the stretcher and instructed me to lift the other side. One of us would have to go down backward... and it wasn't going to be me. Even going down forward, carrying a stretcher with a dead body, was terribly difficult. There was much truth in the term, dead weight. Wearing high heels didn't help!

"Wait! Let me take off my shoes."

Without my high heels on I had firmer footing and slowly we lugged one body after another down to the cramped, unventilated embalming room. Out of breath, I sat down on a chair.

"Let's just rest for a minute."

"Too much for you?" Bart asked.

"No! Not at all. I just didn't expect to carry bodies up and down stairs. I thought all funeral homes had lifts or elevators."

"They don't. You have to get used to this if you want to be an embalmer."

"I can do it." I took a deep breath. "I just need a minute. Okay, let's finish our work," I said, jumping up, not wanting Bart to think a woman couldn't hack it. I felt strongly about pulling my weight. And what I lacked in brawn, I would make up for in a positive attitude.

Together we placed each body into a cardboard "morgue" box which would serve as its temporary resting place until we transported them all to the crematory. An ironic fate for people killed in a fire.

Wearily, I eyed the form lying on the porcelain table, awaiting our embalming services. After donning rubber gloves, I helped Bart remove the clammy, plastic wrapping, uncovering a large male body with thick gray hair and a moustache, who looked to be about sixty years old. Then, we removed the tie which served to temporarily keep his jaw closed, as well as the ties which bound his wrists and ankles. Ties, which, much to the dismay of the embalmer, sometimes left deep indentations.

"Go ahead and show me what you learned in school," Bart offered.

"You mean you want me to embalm him?" I asked in surprise. "I thought I was only here to help."

"Just get it started. Raise the artery."

I picked up the scalpel, extending the deceased's arm to get to the axillary area located in the armpit. Gently, apparently too gently, I nicked his flesh with the razor. A trickle of blood appeared. I tried again, but could not seem to muster up the strength to make a deep enough cut. Bart watched my feeble attempts and then waved me out of the way.

"I'll take over from here. Watch me carefully."

Rather than making an incision with a scalpel as we were taught in school, Bart grabbed a sharp scissors from the cluttered tray of instruments and cut into the man's armpit. Blood immediately spurted out and coursed its way down the sides of the table and into the sink's drain, to be diffused into the fetid waters of the New York City sewer. He searched in the tangle of veins, arteries and tendons for the axillary artery, attached it to the tube connected to the embalming machine so the fluid could be introduced into the arteries, then similarly attached the largest vein he could locate, for drainage. With the whirring of the embalming machine, the embalming procedure had begun. And although my eyes stung and my throat constricted from the toxic formalin solution, I assisted Bart every step of the way, feeling like a nurse assisting a doctor in the operating room.

In spite of the gore, I was intrigued by the embalming. It was a challenge to restore a corpse to a more pleasing, lifelike state. Odd as it seems, embalming often enhances the person's appearance tremendously. It has always been thought of as the artistry of the funeral business.

More than an hour later, we were finished. Bone weary by then, we brought the body back to the main funeral home to dress the man and place him in the casket.

"How did she do, Bart? Does she have the makings of an embalmer?" John asked good-naturedly.

"I'd say so. She did good...uh...for a girl."

CHAPTER 5

It's a Tough Job, But Somebody's Got to Do It

The first few months of my apprenticeship sped by. I often worked every day of the week. Most of my time was spent in the embalming room working closely with either John or Bart. Since John and Bart were considered to be fine embalmers by the rest of the trade, I felt fortunate to be learning from two such skilled instructors. Under their tutelage, my own embalming skills began to be refined. In the beginning, it seemed a bit odd to begin each day staring down into the face of yet another dead body, but soon embalming simply became the work at hand. Once I made the mental adjustment, it no longer seemed unusual.

At the funeral home, we discussed dead bodies as freely and easily as auto mechanics might discuss car parts. Anything you do daily, it seems, quickly becomes rote, even death. Yet, in truth, there was no typical day. On some days, the deaths were routine, usually elderly citizens dead of cardiac arrest or artherosclerotic heart disease, the two most common causes seen on death certificates. Other days brought us victims of auto accidents, freak accidents, homicides, suicides, terminal cancers and rare diseases. I learned much more than I had ever wanted to know about the ravages of disease and what horrifying things could happen to the human body. Try as I might, I could not help bringing those images home with me. While the majority of the dead we tended were over the age of sixty-five, many were in the prime of life, some just entering adulthood and, sadly, others were children and infants.

However, as commonplace as embalming became in my daily schedule, a respect for the dignity of the lifeless bodies and the smallest details of the embalming process were ingrained in me. We were ever mindful that the body on which we worked was loved by someone. Our primary and supreme ethic as funeral directors was reverence for the dead. This belief remained with me throughout my career.

"Always cover their private parts! Even if you're alone in the room," John insisted. And we always did, retaining a sense of modesty. In the years to come, I was often revolted by the careless and disrespectful manner in which remains were handled in other establishments. Sometimes poor embalming outcomes were the result of employers attempting to cut costs by not providing embalmers with the proper tools. Embalmed remains decomposing in the casket, cosmetics sloppily and inconsistently applied, clothing wrinkled and soiled, hair unwashed and men's faces sporting razor burns from none too careful shavings were all glaring signs of incompetence. We referred to embalmers who did such sloppy work as "fluid pushers." Many bragged about how quick they could get the job done rather than about the quality of their work. Where was their pride? Embalming is an art and of primary importance at an open casket visitation.

"Learn embalming right! Then nobody can ever pull the wool over your eyes and you'll always be able to find work," Bart advised me as we worked together in the cramped embalming quarters, the radio blaring the favorite songs of the era. Several times an hour an ironically popular song, *Another One Bites the Dust* played and we couldn't resist singing along between giggles. I also laughed the first time I saw Bart light a match and hold it to the deceased's nose in order to clear away any stray nose hairs. It was not his action, which was a common practice, but the words to another song, *You Light Up My Life,* which he sang, that evoked my laughter. Bart took a lighthearted, jovial approach to his work, which was always top notch.

His advice made sense and I tried to be an eager and willing pupil, even when I was weary. I soon learned that in the embalming process there were "good" bodies and then there were "bad" bodies. The "good" bodies were otherwise healthy people who had died suddenly, usually from a quick heart attack. Dying healthy almost always ensured that a person would be a prime candidate for the embalming procedure, yielding a most successful outcome. A grim irony if ever there was one.

On the other hand, those dead of chronic or disabling illnesses usually were the most challenging cases. Prolonged disease often called for large quantities of medication to be ingested. Impaired circulation, occluded arteries and veins plus fluid retention made matters worse. These factors could negatively affect the embalming procedure.

Embalming is messy work. When embalming is explained by a funeral director to a family, we begin with the delicate phrase, "A small incision is made in an inconspicuous spot, under the arm, for example..." This is the ideal embalming situation, yet in reality not always the case. Sometimes a body with impaired circulation will need six such incisions and often they aren't small. When a six-point injection is used, incisions are made under both arms, on both thighs and in the carotid artery in the neck. Most embalmers prefer using this artery, as it is the largest artery for embalming and thus the easiest with which to work.

But there are cosmetic problems when dealing with women who would be wearing dresses which do not have high necklines. Because of this, John did not allow us to use the carotid artery. As a seasoned embalmer, Bart grumbled about this.

Watching John embalm, I thought he seemed possessed of an almost magical manual dexterity. The most unpleasant embalming is that of autopsied remains, as far as messes go. No matter how careful I was, even while wearing my plastic apron and surgical gloves, I came home everyday with blood and fluid stains on my clothing. The dry cleaners wondered out loud what I did for a living. I assured them I was not a butcher... not exactly.

When not embalming, we moved bodies from their places of death: residences, hospitals or nursing homes. Nursing homes were my least favorite as we often had to wheel a stretcher through a common room occupied by residents, who often reached out a bony hand, just for some human contact. I seldom moved bodies from homes, because of the ensuing problems— the main problem being physical strength. No matter how deter-mined militant women funeral directors wanted to be on a par with men, declaring they could do anything a man could do, a man remains physically stronger. Most women, and certainly that included me, are not equipped to carry a two hundred and fifty pound man down three flights of stairs.

However, I liked going out on the hospital removals and volunteered as soon as a call came in and the death certificate had been signed by a doctor. My daily jaunts to move bodies brought me into some of the most dangerous neighborhoods of New York. I was sometimes the only live person in a deserted hospital basement, walking the dirty corridors in search of both a dead body and a morgue man to facilitate the transfer. Grimly, I mused that if I met with foul play there, nobody would ever find me. Certain hospitals weren't as bad as others and I went to many of the same hospitals day after day and became a favorite of the morgue workers, who were eager to help me load the bodies onto stretchers. Of course, I never forgot to give them their three dollar gratuities.

Since there were few women funeral directors and hardly any were seen moving bodies out of morgues, I was quite an amusing sight for some observers. Petite and delicate, with waist-length hair, long manicured nails, high heels and form-fitting dresses, I traipsed through malodorous, seedy hospital basements, dragging stretchers behind me. Frankly, I would have preferred wearing jeans to move bodies out of morgues. They seemed the most practical thing to wear—working as I was in dirty hospital basements, but for some reason it wasn't considered proper.

Removals and embalming were a challenge, but I never minded the physical labor, because I was young and strong and my enthusiasm for the business acted like a spurt of adrenalin. But there were those times when moving bodies on Friday or Saturday nights, driving past couples elegantly dressed for nights on the town, that I felt fleeting twinges of envy. Wasn't I supposed to be doing that, enjoying my young life? I told myself I'd have time for all that someday. But first I had to do this important work I was convinced I had been fated to do. Nevertheless, the life of an undertaker felt very isolating at times, but it was the unspoken trade-off to which I, like many others in the field, had agreed.

Except for my low salary (so much for the public's perception of the vast amounts of money we earned), which netted me less than one hundred dollars a week, I was generally content with these early days of my apprenticeship. But that contentment was short lived.

Arriving for work one morning, I saw that the regulars were milling in the lobby. But nobody was laughing or joking as they had been on previous mornings. There was a nervous tension in the air. One of the limousine drivers whispered to me, "The boss is back."

"Who?" I asked, confused.

"Rae. John's wife."

"Oh good! I want to thank her for the apprenticeship," I said.

I had gotten used to John as my boss, but everyone whispered that Rae was the real boss.

Soon Rae made her entrance, marching down the stairs into the small lobby. She was a muscular woman about my height with blond hair styled in a retro bouffant. She seemed larger than life, commanding and controlling everyone and everything around her.

"Good morning Rae," the men said stiffly, in unison, standing at attention. Never before had I seen them so uptight. They looked as if they were going to salute.

Rae nodded perfunctorily to them then marched over to me.

I thanked her for giving me the apprenticeship, hoping for some welcoming words in return. None were forthcoming. She merely nodded, looking intently at me. As she walked away, she shouted over her shoulder, "Tell my husband I'm going around the corner for coffee."

She walked out as abruptly as she had walked in. One of the pallbearers opened the door and watched her turn the corner.

"The coast is clear," he said with relief.

"Is she always like that?" I asked.

"This was one of her good days," he answered.

The atmosphere around the funeral home changed markedly with Rae's return. It felt rather like occupied territory. John had been a laid back boss, patient in his instructions and gentle when mistakes were made. John, Bart and I leisurely lunched together when time allowed, talking about the business and exchanging funny anecdotes. When business was slow, he allowed us to catch up on personal errands, go home early or even tune in to watch *All My Children*, my favorite soap opera.

Rae, on the other hand, did not believe in idleness, going home early or even the concept of a lunch hour. She seemed to resent the staff during the days when we had no funerals going on, as if it were somehow our fault, and paid us grudgingly at these times. Where John had been patient, she was demanding, authoritarian and picky. I felt she resented not only my being hired when she was out of town, but my mere presence. She took every opportunity to make it clear that I would have to prove myself. A stern taskmaster, Rae criticized me at every turn, often within everyone's earshot.

"Can you believe the inexperienced, so-called help my husband hires and then has to train?" she asked a girlfriend in exasperation her first week back from Florida.

Sitting at the lobby desk a few feet away, I wished I could sink into the floor. This was not the way it was supposed to be. I wanted my boss to like me and apparently she did not.

I'd had visions of being treated as a professional. But my job duties, which had consisted of embalming, removals, funeral arrangements, now grew to encompass the family grocery shopping, baby-sitting the couple's young son and walking their dog. On one particularly grueling day, after having spent long hours removing bodies and embalming them, Bart and I were summoned to clean the funeral home toilets. "The cleaners didn't come in and we have a visitation scheduled," Rae told us in a voice that brooked no disagreement. Our embalming school slogan, "Enjoy The Prestige Of Being A Graduate," seemed ludicrous as Bart in a suit and tie and me in a silk dress and heels, kneeled over toilets, brush and scouring powder in hand. This was not what I had in mind when I attended embalming school. But I tried to please her. Each day when we arrived for work it was anybody's guess what sort of mood Rae would be in. Some mornings she would cook a huge breakfast and insist I come up and join her and John. Other morning's she did not speak to me at all or sent me out with her list of errands the moment I walked through the door. When she did this, I always grabbed the list and rushed out—anything was better than being around her all day when she was in one of her moods.

The mornings she did not awaken until eleven were briefly peaceful. But then, with predictable regularity, she appeared at the top of the stairs dressed in a worn, cotton house dress and barked orders or rattled off a list of disagreeable tasks. I felt I had to prove myself to her by executing them down to the smallest detail.

We looked to John for support on his wife's most ornery days. But he backed Rae. After all, he loved her and she was his business partner.

When she was agitated we looked for any excuse to leave the building rather than be subjected to her continual orders. We vied for the privilege of going out on a removal—the farther the better.

Yet, for all the censure she heaped upon us, I grudgingly had to admire Rae's self-confidence in her abilities and the way my own abilities were improving. I only wished some of that confidence would spill over to me. I believed my patient, self-effacing manner with bereaved families was an asset, but Rae felt others might see it as weakness and take advantage of me. "Strength is the best quality to cultivate," she insisted. "People often mistake kindness for weakness and don't you forget that!"

I headed for work each day wishing she finally would see that I was giving the job my all. Of course, with no other job in sight, I had no choice but to stick it out and little by little, I grew stronger. I began to realize that after my training, I'd be able to face whatever came my way in the industry. My idealism was being sorely tested, but somehow I was coming through. At that point, I wasn't sure if it was in spite of Rae or because of her.

Everywhere I went, I was questioned by people who were both awed and scared about the business I was in. There was an endless fascination about what I did.

"What made you get into this field?" was the first question posed.

"Aren't you afraid to be in the funeral home alone?" was a common second question. To which I gave the stock answer, "It's the living you have to be afraid of, not the dead. The dead can't hurt you."

"Well, it's a tough job, but somebody's got to do it," people often said, as they patted my hand in admiration. Then the questions continued;

"Do you really hang bodies on meat hooks?"

"Are the internal organs removed during embalming?"

"Do bodies move in the casket?"

"Do their hair and nails continue to grow?" Another scary myth.

"Do you really embalm dead bodies?"

Some of their ideas were bizarre. Death folklore abounded.

There's a story that has become part of the lore of the profession and that's been retold countless times whereby a body in a casket supposedly sat up during a wake. I've heard several versions of this story, with varying particulars—whether it was a man or a woman, young or old, where it happened and when—but anyone who told it to me was absolutely convinced that it occurred.

Even when I tried to correct these misconceptions, people persisted in their delusions. I'd never realized how many death-obsessed people there were in the world and how little factual information there was about our industry. Many people were not even sure what a funeral director was or what he or she did. They never equated funeral director with embalmer, though they are one and the same. To much of the public, a funeral director was that nice "Mr. Jones" seen at civic and religious functions, handsomely dressed, donating money to every cause in the name of the funeral home. An embalmer was an obscure concept—some nameless, faceless ghoul who stayed in the basement waiting for the next body to be delivered. And Mr. Funeral Director was always referred to as their "friend." So many families would come for arrangements, bragging that the funeral director was a dear "friend." For some reason it seemed prestigious to claim a personal association with a funeral director. When I'd convey this information to my bosses, they would often look at me blankly, unable to recall the family in question.

I could not go out socially without the evening turning to the topic of death, once I was introduced as a funeral director. But social evenings became less frequent as I spent more and more time working. I felt I had to show my bosses I could work harder and work longer hours than anyone.

My youth, I was finding, was not considered an asset at all in the funeral business. Families of the deceased seemed tentative about both my gender and age, not sure I could do the job. One night when I had to drive a grieving family to the medical examiner's office to identify a body, they commented, "Oh, you're driving us? Are John and Bart too busy?"

The drive was a bit tense. I tried to make conversation and be as comforting as I could, although I always felt that they were unhappy about being pawned off on an apprentice—and a female apprentice, at that.

At the Medical Examiner's office, the family members had to view the body from behind a large glass window. It was always sad and I felt inadequate to the task of properly comforting them, especially because I knew they would have much preferred John or Bart, mature, paternal types, to be with them. *They are what people look for in a funeral director,* I thought with a sigh. *Will I ever be able to fit the bill?*

John and Rae's funeral home was well entrenched in a Catholic neighborhood. And although it had one direct competitor, located across the street, there were a lot of bodies to be embalmed and a lot of funerals to be directed. My bosses directed most of them, wanting to be visible to the neighborhood people. It was every director's goal to direct—to be the star of the show.

More months passed before Rae told me I was to direct a Catholic funeral the next morning. I had looked forward to handling a funeral myself for a long time. In my daydreams my hair would be perfectly coiffed in a French chignon, I would wear a stunning, black designer suit and a string of gleaming white pearls around my neck to lend an air of sophistication. First, I'd stand at the head of the chapel and then I'd lead the mourners across the street and up the stairs of the church, seating them and genuflecting at the altar. However, as the time drew near, I suddenly felt terrified, not only of not meeting Rae's high demands, but of the task itself. I didn't have any designer suits—couldn't afford them on my salary—didn't know how to create a chignon, didn't own pearls, and couldn't seem to remember in my distracted state, the simplest Catholic prayers of my childhood. My mind had gone blank. I broke out in a cold sweat, my hands clammy. Somehow, I assured Rae I would be in at 7:30 A.M. to direct.

What to do? Who can help me?

I couldn't admit I'd had a sudden attack of stage fright, not to John and Rae, anyway. But I could tell Bart. Bart and I were becoming good friends. He had such an open sympathetic way about him that I didn't feel self-conscious. And he was very experienced and knew all about the business.

"Bart, I have a problem that I hope you can help me with."

"Sure. Anything you need, I'll be there for you."

"Thanks. I'm supposed to direct tomorrow."

"Congratulations! I know you've been looking forward to it."

"I was, but I can't do it."

"You can't do it?" he echoed. "What's 'it'?"

"Direct."

Bart looked at me incredulously. "You're kidding?"

"No. I don't know what to do. I can't stand in front of people and say prayers. I can't even remember any."

"I know the first time can be a little intimidating, but it's easy. Here's a quick study guide. For Catholics you say a little Hail Mary, an Our Father and maybe, if you're in the mood, a Glory Be. For Protestants, Jews, Greeks or most anyone else, the twenty-third Psalm will work in a pinch. Got it?"

I didn't get it. I looked questioningly at him.

"Right now I don't remember them," I said embarrassed.

"How can you not remember prayers you've been saying all your life?"

"My mind is a blank. What should I do?"

"You can write them down and read them."

"No. I'll look stupid. I know... Bart can we practice?"

"Practice praying?" He chuckled. "Okay."

"I get out of here at ten. Where should we meet for the rehearsal?"

We decided to meet at Flushing Meadow Park, the sight of the 1964 Worlds Fair. It was a warm, early spring evening. I got there first and waited in my car, the Unisphere looming large behind me. A short while later Bart drove up and got out of the car. He had some packages with him.

"I've brought some refreshments. Lemon ices and rum. You like frozen daiquiris?" he asked as I got out of my car.

He poured some rum into one of the large cups containing the lemon ice, inserted a straw and handed it to me, then did the same for himself.

"This will relax you," he assured me.

I took a sip, then several more sips. It tasted delicious.

"Now let's practice. Write down what I say."

In the dim light of a street lamp, I wrote his words on a crumpled piece of paper: "Before we leave for Mass this morning, let us join together in a brief prayer for the peaceful repose of - insert name- soul. We will begin in the name of the Father, the Son and the Holy Spirit..."

Bart took a deep breath and went on, "This is to be followed by the words to the Our Father, the Hail Mary, the Glory Be and then concluded by the words, Eternal Rest Grant Unto Him Oh Lord-May the perpetual light shine upon him-May he rest in peace. May his soul and all the souls of the faithful departed through the mercy of God, rest in peace.

"Then give them a few moments of silence. After that ask everyone who is driving or riding in their own car to step up to the casket, pay their final respects and go out to their cars. Then you call the limousine list—the most immediate relative last, like a husband, wife, child...whatever. Let them carry on for a few minutes, but not too long or you'll be late to church. Hand them tissues. Put your arm firmly around them and escort them to the door...or they'll never leave. That's it ... simple. Got it?"

"I think so. They never went over any of this stuff in school. Even though I have seen a lot of people do it, it's different when you have to do it yourself."

"I know you can do it; you want to go over the prayers?"

"Yes, I'd like that."

Together, between sips of the frozen daiquiri concoction, Bart and I recited the Our Father, the Hail Mary and the Glory Be.

Passersby looked at us curiously. We were becoming too tipsy to feel self-conscious, we did not immediately notice the middle-aged couple headed our way.

"May we pray with you?" the woman blurted out.

Bart and I looked at one another.

"Sure, why not?" he answered merrily.

I offered them some of our drinks, but they declined.

As the night wore on, I lost count of how many times we said the prayers along with the couple who had joined us. It was well past midnight when we left the park. Fortified by Bart's rehearsal—and the frozen daiquiris—I was confident I could direct any funeral.

However, at 6:00 A.M. the next morning, I awoke with a throbbing headache, still dressed in my clothes from the day before, pressing rosary beads in my palm. It was an effort to open my eyes more than partially. I felt disoriented, wanting only to go back to sleep, trying to remember where the rosary beads had come from; they were not something I usually slept with. Slowly, memories of the previous night returned. The rosary beads had been a parting gift from the lady who had prayed with us. Forcing myself out of bed and into the shower, I rubbed my bleary eyes, willing myself to "get with it" as beads of warm water beat down on my head. It was an effort to dress. *Drinking and directing just don't mix*, I thought and vowed silently, *I'll never do that again!*

Several cups of strong coffee later, I felt able enough to drive to the funeral home. I scooped up my rosary beads from the night table and put them in my suit pocket for good luck.

Driving slowly and extra-cautiously on the Long Island Expressway I gave the little speech and prayers a last dry run, telling myself I could do it.

Entering the funeral home, I heard the apartment door open above me and Rae call my name.

"I need you to do something for me," she said as she came down the stairs.

"Sure Rae," I said, trying to hide the fact that I was shaking.

"Hurry over to Dunkin' Donuts and pick me up two dozen doughnuts, mostly jelly and Boston creme and mix in a few others," she instructed as she tossed a ten dollar bill down the stairs.

"But Rae, I don't want to be late starting the funeral," I reminded her.

"Don't worry about starting the funeral. Just go get the donuts...and have a cup of coffee while you're there," she said watching me.

How could she equate the importance of directing a funeral with picking up doughnuts!? I thought angrily as I hurriedly drove to the nearest Dunkin' Donuts.

The long morning line seemed interminable, with customers selecting donut flavors as if this was a monumentally important decision. At last it was my turn. I gave the order for the donuts and one coffee, which I sipped as I watched the young woman place one doughnut at a time in the box, seemingly in slow motion.

"Hurry up!" I snapped. "They're only doughnuts."

Putting down the coffee, I grabbed the boxes and dashed out the door trying to make it back to the funeral home quickly. Turning onto the funeral home block, I could see the mourners exiting the building, escorted by the pallbearers, crossing the street to church.

"Where were you?" one of the pallbearers called out.

"Picking up donuts for Rae," I answered, feeling silly standing there with the boxes in my hand.

"Well get rid of them and hurry over to church. We'll wait for you at the altar."

I darted into the funeral home lobby, tossed the boxes onto the desk and ran across the street to church, just in time to genuflect with the pallbearers at the altar.

That night when I thought about my embarrassment because of Rae's orders to pick up donuts, I couldn't decide if she had just wanted me to get away from the pressure for a few moments or if she was trying to pressure me more. I only knew that she was an unrelenting and persistent taskmaster, who kept pushing me. "How will you ever hope to succeed if you aren't the best?" she'd continually ask. Because of or despite her, I concentrated on learning everything I could about the business—that was what I was there for. Only that would make the constant prodding worthwhile.

There was so much to do and so much to learn. Although I'd envisioned myself working in a much more prestigious funeral home in a safer neighborhood, I had unknowingly been handed a valuable opportunity. The experience toughened me up for what lay ahead.

The ground I covered during my time with Rae and John was gritty; the streets mean. There were no sugar-coated experiences. I encountered many different violent modes of death. Like one I never forgot—the middle-aged man who suffered a heart attack while home alone with his pet German Shepherd and had his face eaten away by the ravenous dog, because it had not been fed in days.

"Did you order the Alpo-can corner casket for him," joked a colleague who telephoned looking for John, trying, as the men always did, to break the tension with humor.

That day, pale with horror, I didn't laugh. And what comforting words could you possibly have for parents in the throes of immeasurable, unknowable grief over the death of their sixteen-year-old daughter? The pregnant teenager had been struck and killed on her wedding day by an out-of-control car on a slick roadway. Her parents were following in the car behind her and witnessed the entire accident.

For a time we were known as the homicide chapel of Queens County, following a rash of murder victims buried by the firm. Killings seen on the evening news paled in comparison to the dead bodies I routinely saw on the embalming table. Preparing these remains were as much a test of stamina as of skill. Sometimes, seeing the victims of gruesome stabbings, gunshots and strangulations felt like more than I could bear. However, I steeled myself, as Rae instructed, realizing that if I allowed myself to dwell upon all the grief I saw around me, I would never reach my goal. In some cases, I had to utilize the same coping mechanisms as my colleagues. I tried to remain as emotionally detached as I could. After a while I understood that the gallows humor I heard all around me seemed to help, distancing me from the sadness and finality of death. Making death funny, at times, made it easier to deal with.

Although I grew worried that I would become as jaded as some of my colleagues seemed to be, I also developed a profound respect for human life. Walking through the oncology wards at Sloan-Kettering hospital in search of a death certificate made me cherish life all the more. "Don't sweat the small stuff," became my motto. I found myself growing impatient with the pettiness and nonsense of everyday life.

As time went on, Rae became harder and harder on us. None of us were spared her criticism as she sought perfection. Yet, I grudgingly continued to admire her. She was the toughest woman I'd ever met and, while a little femininity would have softened her, I came to realize she had to be twice as strong as any man. I hung in there, aspiring to the reward up ahead.

Whatever tasks Rae and John threw my way, I tried to master. Some I liked less than others. After the embalming process, the next important step was to cosmetize the bodies in preparation for visitation. Traditionally, because of the scarcity of women in the funeral industry, they would hire a woman who freelanced for the express purpose of doing this job. But as women slowly started to enter the business, any woman employed in a funeral home was expected to incorporate this task into her duties. Rae had been the one to do the cosmetizing and hairdressing all the years she had been in business.

"I want you to take over," she said. "So you need to watch me very carefully."

I sighed. Since my only concessions to hairstyles were washing my own hair, running a comb through it and "air-drying" under the moon roof of my car while driving to work, I was not anxious to learn. Besides, Rae was using words like "Italian curl," "spit curl," "banana curls" and backcombing—terms that sounded both foreign and silly to me. So I ducked this work as long as I could, until she confronted me one evening as I was about to leave the funeral home.

"Why are you leaving so early?" she demanded, as I tried to slip out the door.

"I'm going home. It's time to go home."

"Oh, no, it isn't. Not until that body's ready for viewing."

"What body?" I asked, trying to appear surprised.

"The one in there!" she said, pointing to the woman dressed in a pastel pink polyester "burial gown" and lying in a massive oak casket. Leading me by the hand into the room, Rae gave me some perfunctory instructions.

"They want her hair teased up with soft curls, a little wave over the right eye, pink lipstick and light blue eye-shadow." Then she turned to leave.

"Rae, wait. I can't do this," I said in a panic.

"What do you mean you can't do this? You should know how to do this by now. Yes, you can, sweetheart!" Rae said. She made the word "sweetheart" sound like a supreme insult. "And don't leave this room until you're done."

"What? I have dinner plans," I protested.

"So work fast," she said in dismissal as she closed the chapel door behind her.

I peered down into the chubby face of a woman I guessed to be about seventy-five. Her grey hair was thin and short. I touched her hair and recoiled. Oddly, though embalming did not affect me, the touch of a dead stranger's hair sent shivers up my spine. I took a deep breath and refocused. I waded through the old-fashioned cosmetics in the case on the table beside me.

Worse than the make-up, was the archaic curling iron. In an age of plug-ins, this long, tonged instrument needed to be baked in an oven until it glowed red hot. It reminded me of a barbecue instrument. I sat in a chair with my face in my hands while the iron heated, thinking about the ugly aspects of the career I so badly wanted. When I thought the iron was hot enough, I attempted to begin my work. Mimicking what I'd seen Rae do to test the heat, I clamped it around some tissues. Immediately they went up in flames. Instinctively I tossed the iron onto the floor beneath me, singeing the carpet.

"Oh no! Now I've burned the rug. Wait till Rae sees this," I murmured as I stomped on the still burning tissues. "This is not going very well," I shook my head dejectedly.

Turning my attention back to the body, I surveyed what I had to work with. The make-up part was easy enough, but the hair was another matter. Painstakingly, I curled a small section of hair at a time, singeing more ends than not. To remedy this, I trimmed them off, and then emulated the hair-teasing movements I'd seen Rae do so many times before. Time passed slowly as I curled, singed, trimmed, teased and sprayed the grey hair, section by section. When there was nothing more I could do to make her more attractive, I left the room to get Rae. Two hours had elapsed.

Rae's inspection of the body rivaled a military inspection. Finally, she turned to me and said, "You can go home now."

After all the work I'd put in, I had hoped for some words of approval like, *Well done!* I tried to take comfort in the fact that she would have kept me there all night if she hadn't approved. First thing the next morning I went into the chapel to see if Rae had re-done the body. She hadn't changed a thing. I knew for sure at that moment the work I had done passed muster. By then, I realized that words of praise were not in Rae's vocabulary.

Although the year proved arduous, it seemed to fly by. My apprenticeship was coming to an end. Physically and emotionally exhausted, I was, at last, to reach my goal.

Soon, I received the information that my pre-licensure interview was scheduled. As my boss, Rae was my sponsor and had to accompany me to the interview. Nervous, I asked her if she wanted me to pick her up for the trip into Manhattan.

"Pick me up? I don't know if I'm going," she responded.

I was stunned.

"Do you think you deserve a license?" she demanded, her eyes boring into me.

I refrained from speaking out loud the thought that ran through my mind: *I think I deserve the purple heart for working here.* Instead, I asked her how she could say such a thing, reminding her how hard I had worked, often seven days a week, and how much this meant to me.

"Well, I guess I should go. I'll think about it," she said in dismissal.

It was difficult to get through the remainder of the day. After leaving in tears, I called John, who promised to speak to her. The matter wasn't mentioned for the rest of the week. On the appointed day, after dressing with great care to make the proper impression, I went to the interview by myself, not knowing whether or not Rae would show up.

I sat in a waiting room with about twenty-five other young people and their sponsors. I was the only one alone. One by one, they were called into another room for their interview, until at last I was the only remaining candidate. The state inspector came out several times and asked where Rae was.

"Probably stuck in traffic. She'll be here," I answered with false bravado.

"We can't wait much longer," he said impatiently.

At the eleventh hour, Rae charged into the room, without making any excuses.

"Are you sure you're ready?" she asked.

I nodded, unable to speak. Nervous beyond words, I entered the conference room with Rae. The inspectors began to go down the list of questions:

"How many bodies have you embalmed during the course of your apprenticeship?"

"Can you explain arterial embalming?"

"Is cirrhosis of the liver an acceptable cause of death on a death certificate?"

I could barely respond. Anxiety, compounded by the uncertainty of whether she'd show up, had gotten the best of me. Rae answered most of the questions for me.

"Let her answer, Rae. She's the apprentice," an inspector chided.

"Cut the crap. She's been working for me. She knows what to do," Rae shot back.

And to me she commanded, "Write the check for your license fee, that's all they want. You passed!" she said authoritatively.

With my hand shaking, I wrote a check, as I looked timidly at the inspector. He shook his head, but said nothing. He had known Rae a lot longer than I and, despite her brusque manner, evidently had respect for her—or else he was totally intimidated by her.

I was still shaking as Rae and I walked to the elevator together.

"Thank you, Rae. Thank you for coming. This license means everything to me," I said sincerely.

"Well you've been trained by the best, so you'd better not disappoint me," she said. "If you do, I'll come find you and whip your butt. And one more thing," she said, pausing and fixing her brown eyes on me. "You're a woman in a man's world, so toughen up or you'll never make it in this business!"

Her parting speech was the closest she ever came to complimenting me.

CHAPTER 6

A Woman to Die For

"How'd it go?" Bart asked as we sipped our coffee together the morning after the interview for my license.

"Don't ask!" I said, cringing at the memory of the previous day and realizing I still had two more months to go before my apprenticeship was completed.

"That bad huh!?" he shook his head sympathetically. "Did she at least show up?"

"Yes."

"Well then, don't worry. You'll get your license. She trained you right; she just wants to see you sweat it out."

"Think so?"

"I know so."

I accepted Bart's words. They made me feel less tense than I had in weeks and once again I began making plans for my big future. When my fiancé gave me a new car as a gift, I actually applied for a license plate which read DOA - RIP. This prompted a fellow motorist to inquire, "Are you the coroner?"

And I couldn't resist naming my new, black Persian kitten, Morticia.

During our down time, which wasn't often, we passed the time having fun. Bart and I saw humor in unlikely places, even in the Mass Cards which our funeral home stocked and, like most others, sold to visitors. The absurd idea of dressing up as biblical figures saints and such, with our own faces peeking out of hooded robes and under haloes, made us collapse in peels of laughter. Would the purchaser recognize the funeral home staff on the Mass Card? We cracked up.

Attempts to poke some fun into our gloomy days, however, belied my increasing fears raised by the atmosphere of my trade. I began to see danger, disease and death lurking everywhere. My slightest twinge became an ominous symptom which, in my mind, signaled dire consequences. Every ache and pain was a sign of fatal disease. I pictured my demise in grotesque detail. These fears prompted increased visits to my doctor's office, where I would complain of phantom pains in every part of my body. If a dead body had it, I thought I did, too. Each and every imperfection on my body became cause for alarm: a freckle might be a melanoma, a cyst became a cancerous lump. As I suffered through this onset of hypochondria, poring over medical tomes, my coworkers found my health concerns humorous and ribbed me.

Despite their attempts to make me lighten up, I couldn't. One day, driving a minister back to his study after an afternoon interment, he started to tell us a story. "Just yesterday I was officiating at a very sad funeral," he began. "A young woman... thirty-three... liver cancer. She felt a pain in her side and was dead in three weeks."

"Three weeks!? How awful!" I shrieked in distress, as my hand went involuntarily to my side, to assuage the pain I was suddenly feeling in the area of my liver. Silently, I mused over just what a short time three weeks was. I hadn't seen some of my closest friends in the past three months.

After we dropped off the minister, Bart turned to me and in mock seriousness asked, "Would you like me to take you to Memorial Hospital for a liver scan?"

I shook my head, but my fears increased. To avoid such thoughts, I worked day and night. I volunteered for extra work and spent long hours removing and embalming bodies. The physical work took its toll on my body. I became thinner and constantly felt tired. After a spate of leukemia deaths, I became convinced I had that illness, as well.

I was so convinced that I scheduled a checkup and some blood work to be done. At the doctor's office, I studied my physician's face for signs that he too suspected I had some form of cancer. After the exam, he mentioned that I should call in a week for the results of the blood tests. Then he said that he suspected something was wrong…Unfortunately, I heard his next word as leukemia, probably because that's what I expected to hear. *I knew it!* I thought. Too stunned to ask for a clarification, I left the office in a daze and got lost driving back to work, sobbing all the way. By the time I got to the funeral home, I was distraught.

"What's wrong?" John said softly, "You look terrible." He put his arm around me.

"I have leukemia." I answered, unable to stop crying.

John looked stunned, but asked, "Is that what the doctor told you?"

I nodded yes. "That's what he thinks it is. I'm going to die so young. I always knew it."

John, Rae and Bart sat with me, talking about second opinions and thumbing through medical books to check out my symptoms.

For the next few days I cried all the time, thinking about my death and funeral. I didn't want to be dead at all and certainly not now. I was just beginning my career. I was supposed to bury other people for years to come. I supposed people would say how pretty I looked and how sad it all was. Unless the disease ravaged me beyond recognition and the casket had to be closed.

Naturally, I thought a lot about my funeral. How could I not?At that time in my life, I wanted a really big funeral with all the frills. I made elaborate mental plans. Rae would do my hair, which I wanted just as it was, long and straight, but nice and neat. And I hoped Rae would not have to put too much makeup on me. I wished to be dressed in a long white gown, as the casket would be fully open. As for the casket, I wanted the solid bronze with the glass cover. The one I'd seen mobsters buried in. Maybe they were the only ones who could afford it. I liked it for the protective quality of the bronze, of course, but also because I wanted to be under the glass cover. Sort of like a princess, but also so people wouldn't cry over me. Well, maybe no one would cry at all. Oh, Peter, Vito, Bart, John, Rae and some other close friends surely would be upset.

I hoped a lot of people would come. Maybe colleagues would come as a professional courtesy and for the spectacle of the whole thing...one of their own dying so young and all. I hoped people would send lots of flowers, preferably all white. White roses were my favorite.

Without doubt, the funeral Mass was the most important thing to me. We could have it across the street at St. Leo's; John and Rae would be co-directors. *I'd better pick the hymns*, I thought. My favorite was *On Eagle's Wings*, followed by *Ave Maria*. In church, I hoped there would be more than one priest on the altar and that they would allow some time for a eulogy. I wanted people to know some things about me and, since I had died so young, I wanted them to know what I had planned to do with my life.

As far as cemeteristure were concerned, mine had to be Catholic and I didn't like the thought of being underground; so my wish was to be entombed in a crypt—a private mausoleum would be my real wish, if I could afford it. St. John's cemetery was the perfect choice.

As grand as this all seemed, it was a step down from my original daydream of having a funeral with a horse-drawn carriage and procession down Northern Boulevard. But even so, my funeral sounded like it would be a beautiful event. Then the reality that I wouldn't actually be there to experience it hit me and I became overwhelmed with grief.

John and Rae didn't expect me to do any work. I came in but went to their apartment upstairs, laid down on the couch and watched soap operas on television. We all had lunch together and everyone tried to cheer me up, but I was convinced I was going to die.

Almost a week later, my doctor's secretary called. He wanted to speak to me. Trembling, I took the telephone and, before my doctor could speak, blurted, "I am not going to have chemotherapy. I don't want my hair to fall out, because I know I'm going to die anyway and I don't want to look ugly in the casket. That's not the way I want people to remember me."

There was a momentary silence on the other end of the phone. Then I heard my doctor's voice ask, "Chemo? What are you talking about? What do you think you have?"

I wondered why he was being so coy. "You told me I have leukemia."

Another silence, then laughter. "I'm so sorry. I should not be laughing. But I never said that. I said I suspected you were *anemic*. You mean you walked out of the office thinking that you had *leukemia*?"

"I'm not going to die?" I asked, stunned by the news. For almost the entire past week, I had considered myself practically dead and buried.

"One day you will, but not now, not from leukemia."

He treated me for anemia. One thing that contributed to my illness was the fact I hadn't eaten meat in almost a year after reading about how "healthy" a meatless diet can be. Healthy, indeed!

John, Rae, Bart and our new resident were all glad I was going to live, but not so happy that I had spent the week reading magazines and watching television while they all worked.

Nevertheless, this episode had been frighteningly real to me. All the fears I had managed to avoid, surfaced over that next week. One of the reasons I had become a funeral director was to conquer my fears about illness and death; I now found them heightened. Even after the leukemia incident, I overreacted to any minor physical symptoms, living in a state of constant terror. I felt myself getting more jaded and guarded.

My behavior, too, changed markedly as time went on. Obedient and undemanding as I had been at first, I began to rebel. When I disagreed with something or someone during the course of the workday, I asserted myself, harsh words flew and doors slammed. My temper reared its head. But, as strange as it may seem, that is what helped me stay the course in the funeral industry. It shocked people. I didn't look at all intimidating and had always bowed before authority, but now I was developing the toughness Rae had told me I needed. I hadn't grown up in a rough and tumble neighborhood where I'd had to learn how to fight, far from it, but I was learning it now.

Male colleagues had gotten used to regularly referring to me as *darling, kitten, baby doll* and *honey bunch,* terms other women may have been offended by but I found strangely endearing coming from them. However, this was in stark contrast to the "street" persona I sometimes found it necessary to assume and which served me well when dealing with some really nasty colleagues.

John, on the other hand, was ever patient and often sat with me over a cup of coffee explaining, "You have to learn to speak up for yourself, but you have to do it confidently and calmly."

That last part was hard. Refusing to continue to be intimidated by others or daunted by circumstances, I began to stand up for myself more and more, with words and actions that I hoped would signify that I was not a pushover. However, I was often conflicted about my new behavior. It was not only John's advice but I had been raised strictly, to have good manners and respect my elders. Well, now my elders were my colleagues and, at times, they weren't being very respectful to me. Tilly Fox, the lady attendant I had met when I first started out, continued to be obsessed with me and every aspect of my life. She talked about me all the time, making up embarrassing stories as she went along; stories that people passed along to others, making me look very bad. This woman had become more than a nuisance. I tried to explain to people that I did not really know her and had barely ever spoken more than two words to her, but they didn't seem to believe me. What I still didn't do however, was confront her, because I continued believed she was too disturbed and that dignifying her gossip with any attempt at lucid conversation would be an exercise in futility.

In other cases I gave as good as I got, but, unfortunately, the very same traits which helped me survive, caused me to be labeled as difficult, temperamental, even spoiled, at times. Spoiled!? *By whom?* I wondered. I soon learned, but never could understand, why unrestrained anger is not acceptable in women, as it is in men. Especially since Rae, one of the strongest women I'd ever met, had one of the worst tempers I'd ever seen.

"Patterning yourself after Rae is probably not a good idea," Bart advised.

"I'm not patterning myself after anyone. She's just taught me not to allow myself to be ground into the dirt," I said.

At work I was given more and more duties. I embalmed corpse after corpse, at times repelled by what could happen to the human body. The decay from illness and the destruction from accidents were often staggering. Some remains barely resembled human form. I wondered how people, ill with a disfiguring disease, could bear to live their final days in such states. Often I shut my eyes, but those awful, horrific images remained. They became seared into my consciousness. My work also caused me to reflect on the vagaries of life: one moment you were here, the next moment you were not. I was very sure of one thing though: most twenty-two-year-olds were not thinking such thoughts.

I began to recognize, if I had not fully before, that it was an awesome responsibility to care for the dead. Families depended upon funeral directors and entrusted us with their loved ones. This was truly a sacred trust. The eternal question of *Why do good people suffer?* was often posed. Families seemed to look to us for answers—answers we couldn't give them. In the midst of tragedy and pain I often felt woefully inadequate to do my job, but I did my best to serve and comfort.

I learned what every good funeral director knows: the first viewing is the most traumatic time for family members. It is, usually, the first time they see their loved one dead. This provokes myriad reactions, often heart-wrenching, sometimes humorous. The comments I heard were as varied as the speakers. Some people cried, some laughed, others screamed, fainted, pretended to faint, refused to enter the room or to look at the body. And people really did threaten to jump into graves along with their dead loved ones, although I never saw anyone actually do it. Reactions to grief were personal as well as cultural.

There were those who were profoundly comforted by seeing the deceased looking his or her best, especially after having seen that person suffering from an illness. Those comments, were of course, the easiest to hear. But the variety of responses ranged from the humorous to the grim.

"He looks so good!"

"He looks just like he's sleeping."

"She looks so young."

"She looks beautiful!"

"You made her beautiful!"

"He looks better than when he was alive."

"She never looked so good!"

"He looks so healthy!"

"Who's going to cook and clean now!?"

After viewing our hair and cosmetics work, one man told us, "My wife wasn't that pretty in life." I hoped she could not hear this in the hereafter.

Another man insisted we re-do his mother to look "plainer and older" because we had made her look "too good."

We attempt, as funeral directors, to make death pretty. We create an illusion, an illusion less startling than the reality.

Often the feet of a body in a full-open casket became a focal point. "His feet are crooked," someone would say.

Others, in a more disbelieving mode, would insist vehemently, "That's not my mother! She doesn't look like herself."

This comment usually elicited a snide, under the breath comment from the funeral home employees: "You've never seen her dead before."

Sometimes after seeing the made-up and newly coiffed deceased, a relative would scramble to check the toe tag or hospital ID bracelet, on the off chance the wrong body had been moved.

Many times bodies look markedly different after death and the embalming process. Features are sometimes swollen, retaining water, especially with the increased use of respirators and life support technology. These bloated bodies need special treatments. Packs of phenol, a caustic chemical which dries out tissue, is one such treatment, as is a stronger embalming fluid and letting the body lay on the embalming table longer than usual. This delays the viewing, however, to which many families will not agree. In spite of advice from the funeral director that a small delay yields better results, most families insist on visitation as soon as possible. In our practice, we tried to direct them, but in the end, it was their call.

Hair styles often had to be merely guessed at, without a photo or description from a family. "Old lady hairstyle number one or number two?" we'd ask each other.

Odd requests were not uncommon. Among the most frequent:

"Can someone stay with him overnight?"

"Will you cover her? I don't want her to be cold."

"Leave a light on overnight. She never liked the dark."

The most common complaint from families was about a swelling in the neck. Many times this was another consequence of fluid retention; at other times, it was the result of an unskilled or careless embalmer who embalmed with the pressure gauge turned way too high on the embalming machine.

The guys made me smile with their stories. "Did you hear that man today? 'She's not smiling. She doesn't look happy.' What could I say to that? *No, she doesn't look happy. She's dead.*"

"Or the one who seriously asked, 'Can you make her smile?' I wanted to say, *Let's tell her a joke.*"

"How about the one who kept saying, 'Why did God take her?' I wonder if he knew she was *only* ninety-two!"

The men went on and on, one feeding off the other's irreverent remarks.

"'The hospital killed him. We're going to sue.'"

"'Let him sleep for awhile, he'll be okay.' *Sleep?*"

"'What did you do to her? She was so beautiful!' *Beautiful? She's three hundred pounds!*"

In truth, though, I noticed some mourners seemed more interested in reading the flower cards than viewing the body. Almost everyone remarked that the bodies felt cold. That was just a perception—actually the bodies were room temperature, due to the absence of blood coursing through their veins.

I suspect what many were thinking as they approached the caskets, was *Better you than me*. For I began to see that no one truly accepts death. Most people, let alone doctors and hospital personnel, can not even bring themselves to say the word "dead."

Passing, sleeping and other comforting euphemisms are used in its place. "She passed...passed away...passed on...expired... (*no, warranties expire*)...he's away...on a journey...went away...only sleeping...exited this world...departed...with God...he's at rest."

Our own jargon bordered on the inappropriate, if not humorous, at times. It wasn't uncommon for a staff member to ask the funeral director who accompanied the family into the reposing room at the time of the first viewing, "Are they happy?" meaning *Are they pleased with our work?*

"No, they're not happy."

"They're not!? Why not?"

"They want their loved one to be alive."

And almost always, mourners spoke of regret and feeling guilty about things they didn't get to do. Thinking there would "be more time."

"I didn't think he was going to die," was an often heard comment.

Who ever knows?

I came to believe in the "When it's your time, it's your time" philosophy. It was the only thing that made sense. Who could account for the vagaries of life? Why did a healthy person die young? Why did freak accidents happen?

Nevertheless, the odd deaths were perplexing. One man was struck by lightning on a golf course. What killed him was the religious medal around his neck, which became a conduit for the electricity. A tooth abcess, a twenty-three-year-old thought she'd take care of upon return from her honeymoon, became a massive, lethal infection. A parked car left in gear ran over a pedestrian. A member of the "Polar Bear Club" jumped into the frigid, January waters off Coney Island and died instantly of heart failure.

I had become so morbid by the time I had little more than a month to go in my apprenticeship, I knew I badly needed a vacation. Checking with John, he said it was alright to go. The fact that he never quite got around to letting Rae know was an oversight I didn't find out about until my return.

Always torn between the responsibilities of my chosen career and the time commitment it demanded, I still yearned to enjoy being young and to do the things young people did.

The older generation of funeral directors had been indoctrinated into the concept of providing service seven days a week, twenty-four hours a day. This was something at which my generation balked. The older generation resented that their subordinates were not conducting their careers as they did.

"I had to sacrifice and so should you," was the prevailing attitude.

Believing I had permission from my boss, a friend and I left New York. With the help of some friendly long-haul truckers who communicated with us by CB radio and alerted us to speed traps, we drove into Clearwater, Florida the next night.

We spent a few blissful days in Disneyworld. Wanting to stay longer, but knowing I had to get back to work, we left and drove as far as the charming Georgia city of Savannah and checked into a motel. By the start of the Labor Day weekend, we were back in New York.

When I reported to work on Monday, Rae stood guard at the door, arms folded in front of her. She was gunning for bear. I was barely in the door when she unleashed a torrent of words.

"Who told you that you could take a vacation before you completed your apprenticeship?" She demanded.

"John."

"That's not what he told me!"

I glared at him in fury. He stood silent.

"Let's just see what the state of New York says about taking vacations when you're serving an apprenticeship! Next time you'll learn to play by the rules!"

Rae punished me with both a prolonged silence and a call to the Bureau of Funeral Directing in Albany. The outcome was that I had to make up the time and then some so my apprenticeship was extended several weeks.

Rae continued to make me jump over hurdles. "You'd think that since my work was so abominable, in her eyes, she would have been glad to let me finish early," I grumbled to Bart.

"She isn't going to let you finish till she's done teaching you," he said, "so just grin and bear it." I had no other choice so I sucked it up and continued learning—sometimes with mixed results.

John tipped everybody and usually they all accepted gladly. But a few weeks later his generous tipping policy got me into trouble. Or, if not in real trouble, certainly into an embarrassing situation.

Newly licensed, I moved a body from a New York City hospital for one of our trade accounts on the east end of Long Island. After I finished, I stopped at the New York City Department of Health to file the death certificate in exchange for the necessary transit permit to leave the city. I handed over my paperwork, along with a cash gratuity (as was our usual practice) to the person I thought was the clerk on duty, unaware that she was actually the person in charge at the time. She angrily threw the paperwork back at me along with the two dollar bills and shouted, "I don't take!"

The older, more experienced funeral directors who were in the office gathered around the window, looking on in amusement at my mortification. The clerk would not explain to me what I had done wrong. Instead, she continued to berate me in front of the seasoned group. From a pay phone I called John, not really able to explain adequately what had happened as I didn't understand it myself.

"Don't worry about it," he said. "I'll come down and take care of the problem myself."

Feeling a failure again so soon after my confrontation with Rae about my vacation, I bought an ice cream cone and sat on the steps of the building waiting for John. Soon I saw a familiar face, one of the funeral directors we cooperated with, Joey.

"Hi, Joey," I called out.

A hyper man on his calmest days, he grabbed me by the hand and pulled me up. "John sent me to straighten this out," he said.

"You want some ice cream?" I said, proffering my ice cream cone to him.

"No, I don't. I want to get this over with. I have work to do," he replied, clearly not happy to be there.

"Kids!" he muttered as he led me by the hand back into the office of the Department of Health. Together we went into the burial desk office and up to the counter. Joey called the clerk by her first name.

"She wants to apologize," he said, flicking a finger at me.

"No, I don't," I said, surprised but defiant. I had thought Joey was there to defend me.

"Say you're sorry," he hissed into my ear.

I refused and he strengthened his hold on my arm, twisting it ever so slightly behind my back. "No," I repeated, "I'm not sorry. I didn't do anything."

He turned to the clerk. "She's sorry."

"I want to hear it from her," the woman said frostily.

I stared silently at her as Joey grew increasingly annoyed and impatient. "You know how kids are," he said giving the clerk a wry smile.

Realizing this was a stand-off, the clerk chided me in her best schoolmarm voice. "If you ever try to bribe an official of this department again, you and the funeral home where you work will both be subject to losing your licenses. Do you understand that, young lady?"

I nodded, grateful to get this over with. I made a mental note to tell John he must be more careful in the future about these "gratuities."

I thanked Joey profusely once we were outside.

"It's alright, kid," Joey said with a laugh. "You owe me one."

I discovered just how hyper Joey could be one day soon afterward when he called the embalming room at the funeral home one day looking for John.

"What are you doing there?" he asked.

"Embalming your body," I responded, thinking he'd be pleased.

"Stop right now!" he yelled into the phone. "Where's John? Get John!"

I put my boss on the phone. Joey didn't like me practicing embalming on his bodies, he told John. Some of his funerals were mob-related. Since he wanted only John to embalm his bodies, I stopped for a time. But with the pressure of work, one night a few weeks later, John told me to embalm one of Joey's bodies.

After I had finished, the body was called back to the New York Medical Examiner's office for an autopsy. It seems homicide was suspected and the medical examiner was acting on an anonymous tip.

Joey was angry and protective of the family, as a funeral director should be. He wanted the funeral to proceed as scheduled. Instead of the authorities going through the time-consuming process of getting a court order and delaying the funeral, Joey agreed, with the family's permission, that we would escort the remains to the medical examiner's office after the evening visitation hours, whereupon the autopsy would be done. Joey would bring the remains back to the funeral home that night so the funeral could proceed the next morning. This would be the least traumatic to the family, he decided.

"Did you notice anything unusual when you embalmed the body?" John asked after he got off the telephone with Joey.

"No. Like what?"

"Like a puncture mark? A knife wound?"

"No. I think I would have noticed that." Then I realized the body was lying on its back and a wound there would not have been immediately visible.

John decided he would be the embalmer of record to spare me, an apprentice, the responsibility. It would also spare him Joey's wrath for not having embalmed the body himself. So just before ten that night, John, Bart and I set out for Joey's place to remove the body from the casket and take it to the New York City Medical Examiner's office for an autopsy. After visiting hours ended and the mourners had left, we removed the fully dressed and cosmetized woman from the casket and placed her on a stretcher. We carefully undressed her and transferred the stretcher to the back of the transport wagon. When we arrived at the M.E.'s office, we saw that a large contingent of police detectives, amplified by several F.B.I. agents, were there waiting for the body. While the autopsy was being performed, the four of us decided to take a break and go to a local pub for refreshments. Once we were seated at a table, Joey and Bart ordered drinks and Joey asked me what I'd like to have.

John answered for me. "A glass of milk."

"I think I'd rather have a Jack Daniels," I said.

He shook his head. "Wait a few years 'til you can handle the hard stuff," he said with a wink.

Back at the M.E.'s office, we learned that after all the late night commotion, it had been decided that nothing suspicious had happened and the death was ruled a "death by natural causes."

As we left the building followed by the swarm of police and FBI officers who had attended the autopsy, a passerby looked at me intently as we walked down the steps. I heard him say to his companion, "She must be an important person."

I smiled to myself. I thought I was important. I thought all funeral directors were.

CHAPTER 7

People Are Dying to Meet Me

My big day had finally arrived and I was officially licensed as a funeral director in the state of New York. It proved anticlimactic, though. It was just another gray, late autumn day spent, as I had many others, moving bodies out of dirty, unsanitary hospital morgues. In fact, it was the same work I'd been doing for the entire year of my apprenticeship. The only difference was that now I could make arrangements on my own. Coincidentally, the removal I made from Cabrini Hospital took me past my former embalming school.

Nobody gave me a party, sent me a card, congratulated me or even acknowledged this special event in my life. But it didn't matter, because I felt on top of the world! I'd accomplished what I believed to be an arduous challenge: becoming a female licensed funeral director without financial support or the benefit of family in the industry.

I knew, even if no one else did, that it was through great personal sacrifice and a myriad of emotional turmoil that I had arrived at this place. The naive girl of a year before was all but gone, replaced by a wiser, more ambitious young woman.

I didn't allow myself to think about the drawbacks: the low wages, the blatant sexual harassment, the mudslinging between colleagues, some people's lack of ethics and the missing solidarity within the industry. *When it's my turn, I will make it better*, I told myself. Without reservation, I pushed forward in my death immersion education.

I wanted to be one of those "respected members of the community" as funeral directors like to think of themselves. In fact, I was shocked when I learned we had a poor public image. My saving grace was that I didn't fit the stereotype; I was an oddity. But whatever image was presented, I came to realize that ours was the only job for which you had to apologize and make excuses. Nevertheless, I felt it was up to me to right this impression and I was determined to do it.

Riding with John to the health department to file a death certificate, I asked a question important to me.

"John, now that I have my license, does that mean I can bury people?"

"No, you can't," he answered.

"I can't?" I asked in surprise. "Why not?"

"You need to be registered as a business by the funeral directing bureau and also with the county clerk. On the back of the death certificate it asks for your license number and the registration number of the funeral home," he explained. "Here, look at it," he said, handing me the death certificate which had been wedged into the sun visor.

I shook my head slowly. "I didn't realize this. So you mean to tell me when a person becomes a funeral director he can't just bury someone, not even a family member, without a registration?" I asked incredulously.

"That's right."

"The right to bury someone should come with the license. I can't believe you can't even bury in your own family."

"Don't worry, if your mama dies or someone like that, a boss will sign it out through his registration. Or if someone calls you for a funeral, you could use somebody's registration number, maybe. They will usually work out a deal with you."

"Like what kind of deal?" I asked skeptically.

"Depends. Usually they will take half the call, at least."

"Half the call!? Just for letting you use their number? That's crazy. You get the call, do all the work and they take half."

"Sometimes they take more than that. They take the whole call and throw you a few hundred. And some bosses don't allow people who work for them to do their own calls. They have to give it to the firm."

"John, where do I get a registration?" I asked point blank. Silently, I vowed I would never hand over calls or share one bit of them with greedy undertakers who wanted to make money off others' backs. I had to have my own registration. "I haven't come all this way to spend the rest of my life working for someone else, John. I want to handle funerals personally." I also wanted the freedom to give discounts to close friends and family and to serve them as I would wish to be served.

"Someone has to let you use their funeral home as your business address. The state requires you have a telephone listing and the funeral home has to have an embalming room to qualify, even if it's never used," he explained.

"How much does it all cost?" I asked.

"The cost of your phone bill every month, two hundred dollars every two years for the registration fee and whatever deal you work out with the funeral home."

"What do you mean by 'deal'?" I asked cautiously.

"Some funeral homes charge you rent every month. Others just want the removal, embalming, dressing and casketing, when you get a call. There has to be something in it for them. And remember," he added, "when you hang your license, never go after business in that same neighborhood. Those calls belong to the funeral home you've registered out of."

Immediately, I could see that the second option John had mentioned was the better choice. That way you only paid when you were doing business.

"John, can I register out of your place?" I asked boldly.

"Let me speak to Rae," he said, which was his automatic answer for almost every important question.

"Okay. Please try to convince her. This is really important. I want to build up my own business."

Parking in front of the health department, a seedy building in an even seedier neighborhood, John handed me the death certificate.

"Scoot on in and file this, honey. I'll be right here waiting for you."

I dashed up the steps of the building, trying to avoid the junkies and winos loitering about.

As I made my way to the door I thought out a plan. Once John and Rae agreed to let me "hang my license"—the insider jargon for being the licensed manager of a registered firm in a building you owned, leased or just used as a home base—I would contact the appropriate authorities and pay the required fees. I filed the certificate, hurried back to John waiting in the car and we drove back to his funeral home.

Luckily, Rae, who now seemed more accepting of my skills, agreed to let me hang my license in their business and in a few days, after rejecting such business monikers as Metropolis and Gotham Funeral Home (these evoked images of Batman), and even toyed with Cosmopolitan Funeral Home (quintessential Cosmo girl aside, it just didn't sound right), I registered as ALEXANDRA K. MOSCA, Funeral Director. I was convinced that in no time at all, people would begin to call me, a conviction shared with other newly licensed funeral directors. We were all going to set the funeral world on fire and revolutionize the industry with our youthful effervescence and modern ways.

Full of big, bright dreams, I set about trying to promote my business. It proved to be no easy feat. I called upon priests and ministers and placed ads on church calendars and weekly bulletins; I ordered stationery, business cards, information sheets, arrangement forms and every other funeral-related form imaginable from the printer. I began to participate in civic and religious functions, anything to further publicize my services or as John would say "get my name out there." I took an advertisement in the local newspaper promoting my new business. I even went as far as running an extension telephone line to my apartment seven miles from the funeral home so as not to miss a single call.

Next, I approached my local newspaper, the *Bayside Times*, with an idea for a column: "Ask Alexandra." I proposed writing about the funeral industry in question-and-answer format, regarding matters of death, funerals, burials and cremations. The editor liked my idea and hired me as a freelancer. The letters were slow and sparse coming in, so I often resorted to answering my own or friends' letters. However, I made sure the information was useful for any and all readers who needed to know about the business of death.

To widen my contacts, I volunteered to work on preparing the bulletins for one of the largest Greek churches in the area and I attended meetings there for several months. I chose a Greek church as I felt there was a need for Greek funeral directors. There were more than enough Italian Roman Catholic funeral directors to go around in the area. Funeral homes, I knew, were very much divided along ethnic and religious lines. Families tried to choose a director of their own ethnicity or at least their own religion. The staff of the Greek church was polite and cordial, but they were older and dealt with the few established Greek funeral directors. Not speaking the language fluently—those five years of elementary school Modern Greek were not enough—was a detriment.

The funeral business, unlike any other business, is extraordinarily limiting in ways to get your name out and accepted. The simplest gesture, that of giving out business cards, is often rebuffed. The implied message, "keep this card in case someone dies," is not well received. Sometimes, as quickly as I handed out business cards, mumbling almost apologetically, "If you ever need my services...of course, I hope you never do," the card was handed back like a hot potato or discarded. Other people simply answered, "I hope I never need you," knocking on wood as they spoke. I soon learned that many people were more suspicious than they admitted.

In their relentless quest for business, I saw certain colleagues of mine behave in greedy, mendacious ways. Quick to rush to hospitals or send flower baskets left over from funerals, ostensibly out of concern for a seriously ill friend or neighbor, they were not above mentioning to the family, "If I can be of service in the event he doesn't make it, keep my number with you." Undertakers do not make welcome hospital visitors. I always felt terribly uncomfortable paying a hospital visit to any one, not wishing to offend with my presence. In a quandary, I debated whether to visit or not to visit. But, I'd always visited friends in my pre-funeral director days and decided I would continue to do so, out of caring—not looking for business.

Many friends said in jest, "You'll bury me one day." These words made me terribly uncomfortable and I usually responded with a joke or a reassuring word about their obvious, glowing health. Sadly, several times those prophetic words came to pass.

At that point in my career, my main problem was the age old dilemma: how to get business without appearing to be a vulture. People died every day, but how could I get them to call me was something I pondered. Why did people select a certain funeral director? What, I wondered, went through their minds at the time their loved one died? Did some people actually thumb through the yellow pages and call a particular firm, simply because it had an eye-catching advertisement?

One thing, I learned, was certainly a detriment. Unlike other businesses, most people called a funeral *home* and not a funeral *director*, an important distinction. For many things people will drive great distances for the best professional service, but not so when selecting their funeral services. Most opt for the funeral home that is in the neighborhood, no matter the particulars. In the days when not everyone drove a car or people knew all their neighbors, this made sense. In today's mobile society, it made none. I began to see that when making that urgent phone call to a funeral home to inform them of a death, the majority of people took pot luck. They had no idea whether the directors who were to handle their cases were experienced or just out of school; whether or not they performed embalming or had the bodies handled by outside firms; whether the directors pushed for expensive caskets because they were earning commissions, or if the funeral homes' staffs were small and personable or large and distant.

I found it was common practice in the larger, corporately owned funeral homes to deal with a number of funeral directors; one director took the first call information, another made the arrangements with you, a third director was there for the first visitation and finally yet another directed the funeral. A relationship with the family was never developed. In fact, the likelihood that a family member was only known to the director by information on a sheet of paper, was strong. Caskets in these big firms were often tagged with the deceaseds' names, so that they would be identifiable and the wrong bodies not placed in the wrong rooms; a not uncommon occurrence. The rule of thumb seemed to be, the larger the funeral home firm, the less personal the service.

I vowed that my service would be the opposite of cold and distant. My beeper, which was attached to me like an appendage, was my constant companion. I was always conscious of its sound. It became to me the sound of death calling.

Not surprisingly, that is how I was contacted for the first funeral I handled on my own, a funeral for a family member of a friend.

Within a month of being licensed, I was called to handle the funeral arrangements for the mother of Camille, a close friend. Nervous, wanting everything to go perfectly, I agonized over each and every detail of the funeral.

Although I'd been sitting in on planning arrangements as an apprentice and had made several arrangements myself since becoming licensed, making funeral arrangements with a dear friend was a totally different experience. I'd always had John and Rae to turn to for back-up when I was in doubt or didn't know the answer to a family's question. Now I was on my own; I keenly felt the total responsibility on me. Such awesome responsibility made me think deeply about what it meant to be a funeral director and just what was expected. I was asking myself many questions about the nature of my career. What were my responsibilities? Was it all these things? Service and support after a death, coordinating all the details of a funeral, celebration of lives that had been lived, paying homage to that life, helping people embrace the death process? How could you make the service meaningful for people who viewed funerals as terrible ordeals to be gotten over with as quickly as possible?

On the day she called, I gathered up my papers and my casket catalog and went to Camille's family's home instead of having them come to me. This was one of the most important tips I'd received from school and it had stuck with me. Making arrangements in your own living room was more comfortable and less intimidating than in a funeral home and seeing caskets in a catalog less jarring than seeing a room full of them.

In time, my client families would come from diverse locations and I would continue to accommodate them in this manner. I would see the relief on the faces of the people who were grateful not to have to go into the casket selection room. Of course, some opted to see the casket "in person," but many more saw that as a great source of anxiety.

I arrived at Camille's family's home, a home I'd been a guest in hundreds of times, but this time was different. I was now there in a professional capacity, albeit, also as a friend. And everyone was looking to me for guidance and comfort. As always, I took great care in dressing. And although black was the order of the day in the funeral home where I worked, I thought black attire was too formal for making arrangements with such close friends and best reserved for the day of the funeral. I wore gray.

I rang the bell with great trepidation.

"Alexandra's here!" I heard Camille's voice announce.

The family greeted me with hugs and kisses, as usual.

"Can I get you coffee?"

"How about a sandwich?"

I tried to converse informally while jotting down copious notes, wanting everything to go perfectly, agonizing over each and every detail. Yet, instructions from the family were few.

"We'll leave that up to you. We trust your judgement," was the answer to most of my questions.

I understood they believed in me and trusted my judgement even when I didn't, but I was worried that I would disappoint them. How to charge them became another problem. It seemed awkward and uncomfortable as they were friends. The finance part would always remain an uncomfortable subject for me. I could not help feeling as if we were exacerbating people's grief with our charges. I hated making my living off, essentially, the grief of others. Yet I knew funerals were an unavoidable necessity and dealing with someone dedicated to being sensitive and caring was far better than having to go to an unsympathetic stranger. But as to billing for my services, I still had a difficult time. The payment, in most cases, was due at the time of the service.

"Funeral directors are not bankers," was the new thinking.

In fact, one colleague had a placard on his desk with a wry sentiment: *Souls do not reach heaven without payment.*

For someone needing funeral services, it was highly preferable to call a person he or she knew. The funeral director down the street who was a stranger certainly wouldn't think of that individual's needs as anything but the proscribed funeral service. In what should be the most intimate of all services, there was little intimacy about this interaction.

Camille and her husband, John, trusted me explicitly. Since it was Camille's aged mother who had died, I wanted everything about this funeral to be perfect. I loved Camille and John; they were the parents I wished had been mine. I was so honored that they had placed such trust in me, the first people to do so.

I had met Camille's mother only once, when she was in a nursing home; so I had no personal feelings about the death, not unlike the other funerals I had assisted with at the funeral home. Bart and I had gone to the nursing home together to pick up the elderly woman. Bart embalmed her and together we dressed her. I did her hair and make-up. The next day I was at the funeral home (I had arranged with Fred Passarella to use his facilities) to greet the family. They seemed pleased with everything I had done so far and happy to have me in charge, just as I hoped they would.

I directed the funeral and everything went according to plan. Camille and her family were grateful, but I was never sure if it was my skill and competence or beginner's luck. The day of the funeral, I went to the deli, along with the pallbearers, for coffee and the kindly deli clerk remarked, "How cute, young lady, you're hanging out with the guys."

I wasn't able to say, "No, today actually I'm the boss," because I really didn't yet feel I was.

The men I worked with were courtly, old-fashioned types for the most part and they were very protective of me. Directing the burial in a rain-soaked cemetery, the hearse driver, a concerned look on his face, suggested I stay inside the car so I wouldn't get wet.

Camille and John's trust and confidence in me spilled over to other friends and neighbors in the North Shore community where I had grown up. As time went on these people turned to me to care for their deceased family members. Years later, I buried some of them as well, in funerals that were always sad and difficult for me.

Finally, though, after Camille's mother's funeral, I began to build my business. No easy feat. As Peter aptly exclaimed, "If some funeral directors we knew had to depend on their personalities to get business instead of inherited wealth, they wouldn't get any."

At the same time, certain terms to describe me began to be bandied about; terms to which I took great umbrage. The first being "career woman." Although it might have seemed to others that I was living the life of a modern woman, I never considered myself a "career woman." I preferred the terminology "woman with a career." What someone does and who a person is are two distinctly different things. Too many of my colleagues confused having a career with having a life. Although I wasn't having much of a personal life at the time, I knew I wanted both a career and a home life.

The other terms at which I bristled were "working out of one's hat" and "freelancer." These terms, used by other funeral directors, described a funeral director without a permanent facility of his or her own and seemed to suggest instability—my instability. All funeral directors had the option to rent chapels (and other facilities) to accommodate families closer to their homes. The families who sought me out came from diverse locations and to accommodate them I went to them instead of them coming to me and I utilized, for a fee, other mortuary facilities. After a period of time, I had a fixed base of operation and was, in fact, much more stable than most of my peers.

In an effort to gain new business, I gave out business cards to everyone I knew and with whom I came in contact, even enclosing them in my Christmas cards. Odd perhaps, to find a funeral director's card tucked between good wishes for the holiday season, but those of us in the business saw it differently.

The Christmas season, in fact, always seemed to be our busiest. One of the reasons was the suicide factor. Many studies documented the increase of suicides at this time of enforced gaiety and cheer. The sense that everyone else was happy, healthy and basking in the love of family and friends in front of a brightly lit, tinsel-tossed Christmas tree made many people despondent enough to take their own lives. However, suicides alone didn't account for the "Christmas rush" at funeral homes.

Just trying to get normal holiday shopping done was impossible at this time of the year. One evening, after a hospital removal, I begged Bart, "Just hide the hearse in a dark corner of the Bloomingdale's parking lot." Reluctantly, he agreed and sat in the darkened car, the corpse in the back, while I quickly ran into the store to pick up some gifts.

Of course, we did many helpful holiday activities, like delivering one hundred poinsettia plants to client families. And then there was the clothing drop for those less fortunate.

Understandably, families rarely wanted back the clothing which had been worn by the deceased when they died. I decided to collect and take the discarded clothing to a laundry, where the clothes would be washed and pressed. Then Bart and I would donate them to a charity. Once, when we had a large pile of coats and warm outerwear, we drove into Manhattan and down to the Bowery, where we handed out the laundered coats and jackets to the homeless street people who congregated there. The men, however, looked at us oddly as we wished them a Merry Christmas and proffered warm pieces of clothing.

"Why don't they seem happy to get these things?" I asked in frustration. "They must be freezing in this weather."

"Maybe it's because our car has the name of the funeral home emblazoned on both sides," Bart replied wryly.

Nevertheless, I felt we had done something good. But for those in our industry the general mood was bleak at this time of year. The air of urgency caused by a death sometimes brought out the worst in people, especially when the death occurred on or near a holiday. The grief already felt was exacerbated and I quickly decided that Christmastime was about the worst time there is to check out.

Then on Christmas Eve, Rosa, a woman I'd known most of my life, called to tell me that her mother had died that day. Her brother, Frank, a former detective who typified the suspicious, hard-nosed caricature of a police officer, seemed extremely bothered by the fact that their mother had displayed the bad form to die so near the holiday, when he had so much to do. As if the poor woman had a choice!

Rosa recommended me, telling Frank she had known me from the time we were small children, but that testimonial was not enough for her brother. He spent a good part of that day calling funeral homes for prices until finally, in early evening, convinced he wasn't going to get a better one, he called to tell me he was going to allow me to handle the funeral. The problem, of course, was that by now, all the places I needed to call: the church, the cemetery, etc. were closed. All we could do was retrieve the deceased and make a few arrangements.

I sat with Frank and his two sisters to make plans for the funeral. The ex-detective took control, arguing against every suggestion I made and using colorful language. Rosa and her sister looked mortified.

Finally, fed up, I put down my pen and looked him squarely in the face. "Frank, I've heard all those words before," I said in measured tones. "I've even said many of them, but your sisters are clearly embarrassed and out of respect for your mother, I would appreciate it if you would stop. I realize that the Christmas holiday is about the worst time anybody could die, but a person does not get to choose the day of his or her death. We must deal with it."

Frank was somewhat subdued after my words. Truthfully, I had startled myself with my restraint and composure. It seemed the patience I lacked in my personal life I now had in abundance in my professional one. Appearing calm, unruffled and understanding were important parts of my job and I strove to communicate these qualities.

Despite the difficulties, with the help of Bart and John, I was able to have the visitation take place the next day. That it was Christmas made no difference. The family made clear that they expected to view the deceased at two o'clock on Christmas afternoon.

"She better look good! I could have gone anywhere," Frank growled as I led the mourners into the reposing room. I was confident he'd have no complaints. I worked with two of the best embalmers in the city of New York.

As I've said, there's nothing as isolating, sad and lonely as spending Christmas Day in a funeral home among the grieving. In this case, the widower was an elderly man who had been born in Italy and spoke almost no English. It was difficult to comfort him with words. I hoped kind gestures and sympathetic facial expressions would convey what words could not. Frank, unfortunately, tortured me with words and demands for the next three days. I knew I had won him over, however, when he turned to me as we were leaving the cemetery on the day of the funeral and said, "You did all right!" That was high praise from Frank.

As the months rolled on, I learned that it made no difference what day, month or year it was in the funeral business. We worked around the clock, one death segueing into another.

One afternoon I received a call from Larry, the bookie for whom I had once done a favor. His father had died and he was calling to ask me to handle the funeral. Larry had kept up with my career and knew just where to find me. At the end of our lengthy conversation about the funeral arrangements, he told me in which funeral home he wanted the visitation to take place, then casually added, "Oh, just one more thing. Don't come to the funeral."

"Don't come to the funeral?" I was perplexed. "How can I not come to the funeral, Larry? I'm the funeral director."

He cleared his throat noisily. "I know, but don't come. Some of my customers will be there and they may remember you. It won't look good for either of us."

"Well, is it okay if I at least direct the funeral?" I asked in exasperation.

"Yeah, that's okay."

How weird is this? I thought to myself.

In fact, that was hardly the only weird thing that happened to me after Larry's father's funeral. Not long after we buried the man, I was at the Bayside Diner with my hearse driver and some of the pallbearers on the morning before a funeral, when in walked a man who looked vaguely familiar. As he passed our table, the man stopped and stared at me.

"I know you!" he said in a familiar gravelly voice.

Suddenly, I recognized him. He was the man who owned the bar where I had worked several years before. It was Benny, Larry's friend. I didn't want my funeral industry colleagues to know about that. I needed to keep their respect for me as a professional.

"I'm sure you're mistaken," I answered, turning back to my breakfast.

"No, I never forget a face. I don't remember your name, but I remember you."

"You must have me mixed up with someone else," I insisted, feeling increasingly uncomfortable.

"Now I remember. You were one of my barmaids!" he said triumphantly.

The guys heads all snapped up at the word "barmaid." He had gotten their attention.

I felt my face begin to flush. "Sorry, I've never worked in any bar. Now please excuse us."

"Yes, you did!" he insisted.

At this point, one of the men with me came to my rescue. "Hey pop, this girl is a funeral director and she went to college. She's not the kind of girl who would work in a bar. Now scram."

"Okay, okay. I'm going," the man said. "But I never forget a face."

"Imagine him thinking you served drinks to drunks in some dive," my hearse driver said.

"Yes, imagine that," I responded weakly.

I felt badly about the incident and would have acknowledged the man had I been alone. But my new identity as a funeral director was tenuous and I didn't want anything to detract from it. Years later, the incident would not have troubled me at all, for by then I had finally achieved the confidence and self-esteem that at the beginning of my career was still elusive.

Another incident that rocked me came up shortly after that when Peter held an art exhibit at a local catering facility. He invited many of my funeral industry colleagues who had also been his clients. Dave McGinness, the industry's state inspector, came up to me at the reception and told me that someone had reported me for the serious crime of inadvertently used the wrong terminology in one of my advertisements. Himself a guest, Dave said apologetically that he would have to come to the funeral home on Monday to write me up.

I nodded miserably. Dave, of whom I was fond, was strictly "by the book" and would not disclose who had reported me for it would have been unethical to do so. "Sorry, Alexandra. It's my job," he offered apologetically. We both wondered why anyone felt threatened by me or would take the time to notice and report anything as minor as using the wrong word in an advertisement. Fortunately, Bart stepped in and helped me resolve the problem.

Peter's art show was a success and he got several new commissions. When I contacted the *Bayside Times* about the show, they agreed to run a small piece about it in their next edition. "Funeral Director leaves her mark on canvas" was the caption under a photograph of me standing next to one of the portraits Peter had painted of me.

Later that summer I read a short piece in the newspaper about a woman who was newly licensed as a funeral director, one of the few in New York state. I showed it to Peter.

"Look at this story. It's interesting, but I think my story is more so. If they'd print this, maybe someone will print my story."

I sent a letter to a reporter at the *New York Daily News* and it turned out that he also wrote for *American Funeral Director*, the industry's premier trade magazine. Before I knew what had happened, I was on the cover of the magazine wearing white (so unfuneral-like!) and posing with my cat, Morticia. Inside was the story, titled "Model Mortician."

My friend Elly was the first to see the magazine and she called, gleefully exclaiming, "You're famous!"

Although *American Funeral Director* hardly rivaled *People* magazine, this bit of publicity proved to be the forerunner of things to come.

Another year passed swiftly and as the days wore on one seemed very much like the rest as I lived my life mostly among the dead. One cool April night when I was dog tired from the press of work, I was sent to embalm a posted body. I always want to see the death certificate before I embalm in order to know the cause of death. In this case, no death certificate was to be found. There was just the odiferous corpse of a young man lying on the table. The marks on his arm looked like tracks from mainlining heroin.

I should have paid more attention to what I was doing, but never had I been more exhausted. After I finished embalming the body, I began to sew up the lengthy incisions. Everyone always remarked about the perfect stitches I made: neat, symmetrical and close together. Confident that even in such a weary state, my stitches would be precise, I didn't at first feel the needle as it pierced through the flesh of my palm, essentially sewing my hand to the corpse. Horrified when I realized what I had done, I pulled the needle out. Tears of fright and anger sprung to my eyes as I realized I might have just contaminated myself with some contagious disease from the dead junkie. I flung the metal instruments with which I'd been working against the wall. I didn't want to kill myself like this, alone in the middle of the night in some dirty, stinking embalming room.

It was 2:00 A.M. and there was no one I could call. Although there were closer hospitals, I didn't trust them. I began driving back to Queens to St. John's Hospital. Not sure I would make it, thinking I might die en route, I drove with the interior car light on repeatedly checked my hand. It had bled inward and was turning a nasty shade of purple.

At the hospital I made it into the emergency room, registered and sat waiting for my name to be called. As time passed I grew more and more afraid. Although those on either side of me were called in to be seen by the triage nurse and then a doctor, my name wasn't called. After an hour of waiting, my fears escalating, I impatiently asked the tall, red-haired orderly on duty how much longer it would be.

"I could be dead by the time you get to me!" I told him.

"What makes you think that?" he asked with a small smile.

"I think I might have blood poisoning," I explained, trying to keep my voice level and calm. "Look at my hand." I held it up for him to see.

"What happened?" the orderly asked.

I told him about the incident in the embalming room, expecting him to be surprised, as everyone seemed to be, that I was a mortician.

Instead, he stared hard at me then smiled again. "Oh, you're her!" he said.

"Her who?" I asked in bewilderment. This wasn't the reaction I had expected.

"The lady funeral director—the one on the cover of that magazine." He laughed at my confusion. "I'm working my way through medical school as an orderly and also as a receptionist in a funeral home. I saw the article about you in *American Funeral Director*. So you actually embalm! I figured you just looked good in the reception rooms."

He promised to try to speed things along for me and I was soon seen by a doctor and given a tetanus shot and a prescription for antibiotics. Luckily, the tests run then and after showed nothing wrong.

I stayed home from work the next day, still afraid the doctor hadn't made the right diagnosis and I was seriously ill. Bart called to tell me he had finished up the stitching and the body looked good in spite of my mishap.

"I'm still worried about my hand," I told him.

"You'll be fine," he assured me.

And though I was fine, the incident with the needle was one I couldn't and didn't forget. Nevertheless, duty called and I was soon back at work.

CHAPTER 8

Dead Ends

On June 3 I moved a body out of Cabrini Hospital in Manhattan. Little did I know then that this would be my last removal for a long time. The next day, Rae began criticizing me and wouldn't stop. We ended up in a shouting match. In the last few weeks the atmosphere at the funeral home had grown tense and was growing tenser. It was not only my relationship with Rae, who still acted like she had to perfect my every skill. I had not imagined the ceaseless pressure of embalming. And my constant long hours had taken a huge toll on my personal life. In fact, I had none. My working life had gotten out of control. I worked like there was no tomorrow and my relentless schedule was wearing heavily on me. I was experiencing burnout; my temper rose frequently and I ran out of patience easily. I felt like I had to get out of there. I called and told John I was leaving, which also meant I had to remove my business registration as well.

"You'll be back," he said confidently.

If there's ever a time to quit a job, then it has to be summertime. The next few weeks were filled with the beach, Peter's photos, a day on a friend's boat in the Long Island Sound; typical summer fun. Then in July, a girlfriend, Diana, and I decided to act on a longtime desire to move to Florida.

On July 9 my friend and I set off for our new life in the perpetual vacation land of Florida. The first few weeks were heavenly. Of course, we did more swimming and eating then apartment or job hunting. My spirits turned buoyant as I took daily walks on the white, pristine sands of St. Petersburg Beach. After long, sunny days spent gathering new energy, I got stronger and stronger, emotionally and physically. Having cleared my mind of extraneous clutter and gained some perspective on my life, I decided that I wanted my professional life back and planned my return to the funeral industry.

But things took an awful turn the night of July 23. In a parking lot on the way to dinner, I fell and shattered my leg in three places. For the next three weeks my home was in a small Florida hospital. In a cast up to my thigh, I lay in traction, unable to sit up and eat the cute little meals they served. Embalming seven days a week at the funeral home didn't seem so bad to me compared to this. Not used to being helpless, I grew angry and depressed. Then I happened to see a television program about healing from injury and how one must fight to regain one's strength; giving in to depression was the worst thing one could do. With that in mind, one evening when an orderly had left my dinner tray too far away from me and I couldn't maneuver myself into a position in which I could eat, I grabbed the edge of the tray and flung it, with the uneaten meal, across the room. Hitting the wall, bits of food splattered everywhere. A nurse came running in and listened to my tale of frustration. After that, my tray was placed on the table next to me and a nurse always remembered to come into my room and help me sit up. Asserting myself was therapeutic and allowed my healing to begin.

My leg, I was told by the doctors, was going to take some time to mend. Once again a decision had been made for me. The dream of permanently living in Florida had to be scrapped and I had no choice, in my condition, but to go back to New York. Diana planned to return as well. I made arrangements to fly back on July 30. Luckily, I knew Delta Airline's New York manager, a part time photographer who had taken some photos of me in the past. He waived the fee for the other two seats I would need, as I was in a cast, could not bend my leg and it stuck straight out in front of me.

The next four months consisted of doctors, therapists and accumulating debts as I recuperated from my accident. Peter, Judith and another friend, Lois, were loyal visitors. Bart called faithfully to keep me informed on what was going on in the industry. But the helplessness, inactivity, especially at night, caused me to feel more and more lonely. I developed an interest in Monday night football, even penning a fan letter to Don Meredith on Halloween night, telling him his show had become the highlight of my week. He sent me a personal note and an autographed photo in return. In fact, letter writing became a pastime, sustaining me through the monotonous days. On September 9, I wrote a letter to a news anchor at NBC protesting the anti-funeral broadcast that had just run. I never received a response, but then I never really expected one.

Mid-September my orthopedist changed my cast to a slightly shorter version which allowed me a little more mobility. I was finally able to get around some and even out of the house, though slowly and with discomfort. And with money dwindling and no job, I began to worry a lot about the future. Times were uncertain, but death was still constant. Three weeks later, Lois's husband died in the aftermath of a robbery and she asked me to handle the funeral.

Frustrated that I could not drive, I had to depend on a friend getting me to Lois's home to make the funeral arrangements. I wanted to do as much as I could, but to my dismay, I had limits; limits I railed against.

When I hobbled into Lois's house and saw her grief-stricken face, words failed me. It was never easy to know what to say when someone close died. As funeral directors, even with strangers we were always searching for comforting words. I've always secretly thought that we should be able, because of our work with death, to say something not only comforting, but profound. Yet the words that came always seemed to me to be less than adequate, meaningless and trite no matter how sincerely felt. Lois's home was ladened with sorrow and shock. The pain of losing her forty-two-year-old husband and father of her two young daughters, coupled with the shock of his dying in such a sudden, violent way, created overwhelming, almost unbearable pain. As awful as a terminal illness is, family members have time to reconcile themselves to, if not accept, the inevitability of death. When death is sudden, from homicide, suicide, an accident, heart attack, stroke or aneurysm, it is much more difficult, if not initially impossible, to accept.

Sudden deaths preclude the opportunity to say and do all the things left unsaid and undone. For those left behind, the "what ifs" run rampant. What if he stayed home from work that day? What if she left five minutes later? What if he took a different highway? Torturous questions. All the more so, for the impossibility of knowing whether the outcome would have been different.

Lois was going through all of those questions and a myriad of emotions, as well as being faced with the horror of the situation. In addition, the state of New York mandates an autopsy be performed when a death results from what the state deems to be unnatural causes. Despite pleas to the Queens Medical Examiner, which I suspected would be futile, the autopsy was performed, yielding no more information that what was originally known.

The wake, a particularly sad one, was held at Fred's funeral home. Wakes differ in tone by the age of the deceased and circumstances of death. The older the person and the more natural the circumstances of death, the higher the volume of chatter in the room. Even laughter many times is acceptable. For younger people and tragic circumstances, the atmosphere usually is quieter, more subdued. In the case of the death of a child, the room, I have noticed, often remains totally silent.

Many people attended the wake for Lois's husband and I was glad for the support shown to her. The day of the funeral, October 3, I was still on crutches, but was able to do what needed to be done, along with help from Bart. Although I felt I was conveying less than the picture of strength a funeral director should, it felt good to be useful and needed again.

A few days after the funeral, I asked Bart if I could accompany him on his rounds, which included moving a body out of Elmhurst hospital and driving to the Board of Health. I just needed something to do. Since I couldn't be much help to him, I tried extra hard to be good company.

At last, on November 10 the plaster cast on my leg was removed; then the real trials began. I needed to find a job, but was afraid I was not yet physically capable of doing the work that would be required. I called several funeral homes and asked if they were hiring. Nobody was. It was very discouraging. I continued making cursory attempts at finding a job, but nothing turned up. I badly needed to earn some money and, once again, Peter came to my rescue. He employed me as his sample model and even taught me how to paint the decorative frames he used to highlight his works. He was painting a mural at another funeral home and asked me to give him a hand with the project.

I felt sort of odd being in a funeral home helping Peter with his painting instead of doing funeral work, but it saved the day while I searched for employment back in the funeral industry. The year ended with Peter coming by to present me with the most recent portrait he had painted of me.

By then I had depleted the rest of my meager savings and still had not found a job. I tried funeral home after funeral home and then, in desperation, put in an application for a firm handling temporary office work. I also took the New York State real estate agent test. Who was I kidding? I hadn't been through all this to end up in any of those places. But all my inquires within the funeral industry were met with a resounding "No, we don't need any help."

Finally, after being turned down for still another funeral home job at the end of January, a chance encounter with two trade embalmers in the funeral home parking lot as I was leaving, led to an offer.

"How'd you like to do some embalming for us?" asked one of the men.

"I haven't embalmed in over a year," I answered truthfully.

"It's like riding a bicycle," the other assured me. "And besides, it will only be part-time."

"Well, I need work very badly," I said, pushing to the back of my mind the rumors I'd heard of their questionable reputations. "I'll give it a try."

I'd gotten satisfaction from embalming work in the past and I certainly had to find a way to make some money. We agreed that I'd begin the very next day.

When I got home I immediately phoned Bart and asked him what he thought about my working for the two men. He wasn't convinced it was such a good idea. "Be careful of those two. Their reputation is unsavory at best," he admonished.

"How many reputations aren't? I can't worry about that now, Bart. I have to land a job soon or I'll be in trouble."

Well, my prayers were answered. The first day I embalmed four bodies entirely on my own. It had been more than a year, but I found what the old-time embalmers said was true: embalming was a lot like riding a bicycle—you don't forget.

These trade embalmers had the large account at Gillespie's funeral home, as well as lesser accounts with smaller funeral homes in various parts of the city. One funeral home was in the South Bronx. Over the next few weeks, I embalmed more homicides, which were all full posts, than I did when I worked in Queens.

I worked from eight in the morning until after eight at night. Each day, I walked into a large embalming room with four tables, bodies on each, covered with sheets, with a note on the detail desk as to which body to embalm first. One Tuesday morning, I removed the sheet to embalm the first body of the day and uncovered the corpse of a pleasant looking red-headed woman who appeared to be in her mid fifties. She had a sweet face with freckled skin and looked very familiar. Suddenly, the gold nameplate around her neck caught my eye and I sucked in my breath. It was Peggy, the waitress from the Northern Cross diner, who had waited on me years before, the same year I had met my first funeral director. Now I had to embalm her.

The two trade embalmers—they were brothers—I worked for seemed weird and one of them, Norton, had taken a shine to me, much to my discomfort. On Valentine's day, he gave me a gift-wrapped box. Dismayed, I hesitated before taking it from his hand.

"Open it!" he insisted.

"You mustn't give me gifts," I said and opened the box to discover a gold chain necklace inside.

Norton went on to make his feelings for me quite clear. He asked me out over and over. Always I made excuses. Never had I felt more uncomfortable. From then on we had a strained working relationship at best; at worst, I considered him a baboon. Worse still, with Norton pressuring me to have a relationship, I now felt I had to leave. Trade embalming wasn't by any means the work I wanted to do, but it paid the bills. Nevertheless, I decided I had no choice and told Norton I was quitting.

"You can't quit!" he screamed indignantly.

I did. And within days, I found all four tires of my car slashed. And when they were replaced, it happened again. My situation seemed to get worse and worse.

I kept in touch with my old friend, Elly, who was having her own employment problems. She too, could not find a job in the funeral field. Reluctantly, we spent an entire weekend calling on funeral homes, to see if there was even a slight opportunity to pick up some "lady attendant" work, something we'd sworn we'd never do. No matter, the attempt was futile. Every funeral home we approached already had someone and these women never retired from the job, they had to die first!

Fortunately, even though I was not actively courting business through my own funeral home registration, a few funerals did come my way to tide me over. But most days, I spent my time at the gym exercising and doing therapy. It was almost six months later and my leg was still not back to normal. To make some extra money and keep myself occupied, I also started writing articles about death and funeral issues I thought the general public needed to know about or would at least be interested in. After all, I reasoned, everyone will someday have to have dealings with funeral directors. All my articles were rejected. During this period, I also penned a letter to *Playboy* magazine about possibly writing an article for them. This was not the usual funeral consumer piece I was pitching, but rather an article about my portrait modeling for Peter incorporated with my work as a funeral director. Along with my query, I mailed them about a dozen photographs of Peter's portraits of me. The way my luck had been going, I never expected a reply so I was most surprised to receive a response from them saying that although they were not interested in the article I had proposed or running photographs of the paintings, would I be interested in sending nude photos of myself so they could evaluate my *Playmate* potential?

"Send them something!" Peter urged.

"Are you kidding!? I can't do that. I'm a funeral director."

But *Playboy's* response gave me the idea that maybe I could model—as long as I had clothes on. That spring, I read about some new modeling agencies which had sprung up in Manhattan. They were modeling agencies for petites, with a height requirement of 5' to 5'4". At 5'4", I just qualified. So, one afternoon I went to an open call at the agency. The line of young women was out the door and around the corridor and back into the stairwell, numbering in the hundreds. Seems every one of us had been told we were model material. After a grueling wait of several hours, I was seen. The selection process was swift and impersonal.

"How tall are you?"

"What do you weigh?"

"What size clothing do you wear? Dress, slacks, blouse? Shoes? Hat?"

We were instructed to turn in several directions, to show our body angles and our profile. Then we were told to wait again in another line. Much later, one of the modeling scouts returned, systematically going down the line, pointing and saying yes or no.

I had chatted with a few of the girls on line with me, one in particular, and felt badly for her when she was not selected. I saw the disappointment in her face and felt a twinge of guilt when the scout told me I had been chosen. A week later, photographs were taken and I was soon included on the roster of new faces. In the meantime I took a part-time job as a receptionist in a Jewish funeral home in Manhattan. I worked nights and was there, basically, only to answer the telephones. This funeral home seldom had visitations, but it was housed in a big, architecturally interesting old stone building and I enjoyed walking through the floors and looking at the handsome, artistic features. Even though I knew this job was a dead end, I wanted very much to be working in a funeral home again. The only perk in my work was that after being sent on "go sees" for the modeling agency during the day, I was already in Manhattan in plenty of time for work at the funeral home. That job, however, didn't last very long.

By the end of the year, I was again searching for employment. I heard there was a job opening at Kazan Memorial Chapel, a Jewish funeral home in Queens and went there for an interview. This was to be a full-time position, but once again it was a receptionist job. I took it in desperation and hoped that the receptionist position would only be temporary until a licensed position opened up. In the meantime, I looked forward to working in the Jewish end of the business, as it was called, because I wanted to learn all aspects and religious mores of the industry. What I didn't know at the time was that a licensed job there was never going to happen for me. They had no intention of hiring a woman. Instead, they used me in both a licensed capacity and as an errand girl, while paying me a receptionist's salary. The large staff, all men, were tough to deal with. After the novelty of working with a woman wore off and the "trying to get a date with her" maneuvers stopped, things were tense and unpleasant. Only the hearse and limousine drivers befriended me, as they understood what it was like to be treated like second class citizens.

At Kazan Memorial Chapel, two things struck me immediately: almost no one was Jewish, except for the owner who was not a licensed funeral director and so could not make arrangements with the client families, and two of the managers. Nevertheless, the entire dynamic, as well as the focus, was different than that at the Christian funeral homes I'd worked for earlier.

Here, services were more focused on the eulogy part of funerals rather than on religious rituals as was the case in Catholic funeral homes. There was little, if any, emphasis placed

A pensive Alexandra turned three, gets ready to blow out the candles on her birthday cake. Her wish for a happy family life goes unanswered.

Even on vacation in Miami Beach, Florida, Alexandra looks wistful.

Visiting Santa at a local department store was one of the happiest times in Alexandra's often sad childhood.

Already showing signs of beauty, at the age of five, Alexandra's portrait was taken for a child modeling agency.

As Alexandra got older, her adoptive parents increased pressure on her not only to engage in the "right" activities, like learning to play piano, but to do them perfectly.

While she was still attending American Academy - McCallister Institute of Funeral Service, Alexandra became friends with and began modeling for Peter, an accomplished painter.

Peter sets up his easel as he prepares to begin painting Alexandra's portrait.

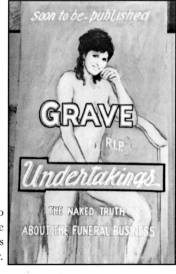

When Alexandra decided to write her story, supportive friend Peter painted this spoof of the book cover.

Chosen to model for *Playboy*,
Alexandra is nervous at the
start, but the professionalism of
editor Jeff Cohen, photographer
Pompeo Posar and the entire
magazine staff put Alexandra at
ease in the *Playboy* studios.

Cohen and Posar visit
Alexandra in New York
to take pictures of her at
the funeral parlor and in
a cemetery to accompany
her pictorial in *Playboy*.

Alexandra in a cemetery
holding the *Playboy* issue in
which her pictures appeared.

After posing in *Playboy*, Alexandra
is a featured guest on regional and
national television talk shows.
Here she poses with Regis Philbin,
then host of the *Regis Philbin Show*.

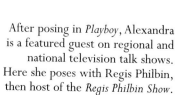

Alexandra and Matt Lauer, then host of *P.M. Magazine.*

After meeting and befriending Allison Bly, the "Dynamite Lady," Alexandra joins her for one of Allison's many performances at baseball games.

Alexandra and the two women who pretended to be her, backstage on the *To Tell the Truth* set.

Despite the excitement of posing in *Playboy* and appearing on national television shows, her career as a funeral director is the major focus of Alexandra's life.

on how the body looked, because no embalming was supposed to be done in accordance with Jewish religious law. Visitation was not the rule, although it did occur, mostly in cases of interfaith marriages or for a person who had been prominent in the business community. Sometimes a brief inspection for identification purposes was made, but more times than not, no family member even looked at the body. I wondered how they could be sure the deceased in the casket was even their loved one. Didn't they need "the tangible confirmation of death" that viewing their loved ones' bodies facilitated? This had been a concept thoroughly ingrained in us in school. Much to my surprise, embalming, even though contrary to Jewish religious law, was sometimes performed.

I also noticed that prices were appreciably higher than those at Christian funeral homes, to compensate for the sale of what are called "Orthodox" caskets, which are the least expensive option. The clientele rarely questioned these prices, as they seemed accustomed to paying them. Possibly they did not realize they could call a funeral director from any funeral home, especially if the funeral was to be held at grave side bypassing a funeral home altogether. This lack of knowledge registered years later, when a Jewish acquaintance told another I did funerals for "cheap" prices and his words filtered back to me. In truth, my prices were average, definitely in the ballpark, but certainly not cheap. I was momentarily stung until I realized this man only had dealings with a Jewish firm whose prices were double the average. No wonder my prices seemed "cheap" to him.

At this point, my take home pay was $134 per week, $25 of which went to the union for the privilege of working. Bert, one of the funeral directors from another firm who I ran into regularly had taken a shine to me. To try to win my favor, he promised me a job where he worked.

"It is hard to sell a woman," he told me, "but I think I can."

I promised to go out with him later, after I got the job, explaining that I was "too stressed now and have work problems."

"They could use a lady funeral director. The place needs some polishing up. Hustle yourself, do removals and work like the rest of the guys," Bert urged. "Being a woman, you're going to have to take a lot of potshots if you get the job. People may even say you're my girl."

"I don't care what anyone says as long as they pay me a decent salary as a licensed funeral director," I told him.

He also encouraged me to do the "lady work" (hair and makeup) as well as dropping his name at several funeral homes. Name dropping was something I thought tacky and would not consider. In the end, after all the flirtation and assurances that he "could probably sell his bosses on the idea of a woman," Bert told me his firm had "gone with a guy who had to put food on the table for his wife and children, as well as a roof over their heads." That firm was not the only funeral home to have such an idea. I wondered if they thought single women lived and ate for free.

Tara, a woman funeral director I knew slightly, was urging me to sue as she had done. But I did not want to end up blacklisted and as unpopular as she. I knew if I sued I would never get a job even if one came up down the line. So I made the best of things and focused on making myself helpful to our clientele.

It became my practice to make sure all the remains were presentable if the family desired a private viewing or to make an Identification. I closed the eyes and mouths of the deceased, shaved the men, styled the hair of the ladies and applied light cosmetics. I thought it would be easier for the mourners to see their loved ones looking peaceful. People were never prepared for what death looked like *au naturel*. The guys mocked me for this. They said the families had not paid for these extra services. I didn't care. For me, common decency overrode any and all corporate dictates. You could not run a funeral home by dictates. It was the most personal of services and had to take all the human variables into account. They may not have cared, but I did. I thought my colleagues should take the position of "Suppose it was your family member. Is that the way you'd want to see them?"

For the most part, the work was much easier, but there were some customs I had not been told about and several times I ended up feeling quite foolish, hoping I had not offended anyone. The guys I worked with just laughed.

One afternoon two well-dressed women approached the reception desk, asking where they could wash their hands. Naturally, I directed them to the ladies rest room.

"No, we'd like to wash our hands outside," they insisted.

"Outside? It's cold outside. You'd be a lot warmer and more comfortable washing up inside."

They refused and gave me a strange look. I was befuddled. I later learned it was a custom of certain religious Jews to wash their hands outside the funeral home.

Another time, an afternoon service was beginning. All the people had gone into the chapel except for one lone man who remained in the lobby.

"Sir, the service will be beginning shortly," I reminded him.

"I can't go in. I'm a Kohan."

An estranged family member, I thought.

"That's okay. At times like this, petty grievances are forgotten. I'm sure they'll be glad to see you."

"No. I can't go in!" he was adamant.

Thinking he was afraid, I even offered to go in with him. He gave me a disgusted look and walked outside.

The guys howled when I told them about Mr. Kohan.

Later I was informed by another laughing member of the staff that in certain religious sects, Kohans were considered royalty and were not to mix with others at funeral services.

Not long after this, I first learned about and began to do sign-ins. "Sign-in" is funeral speak for an outside funeral director who meets a funeral at the cemetery to essentially "sign-in" the funeral, as required by law. This is instead of the funeral home sending it's own director, thus it is cost-saving but impersonal.

Mindful of that, when hired to do a sign-in I did my best to make this most impersonal interaction somewhat more personal. I always arrived early, introduced myself to the immediate family members, chatted with them a bit and asked what they wanted to be done with the casket: should it be lowered or ground level. Did they want the grave filled in with dirt before they left the site? This was a Jewish custom to which some adhered at each funeral. I accompanied the mourners to the grave, listened to the rabbi's prayers and waited until the interment ended. Most directors "signed and ran."

That January, *New Woman*, a popular women's magazine, profiled me and my career (which pretty much was not happening at the moment) under the heading "Women to Watch." My coworkers read the article with derision and hung it up on the wall as a joke.

Elly, my only female friend in the funeral business, had given up on finding employment as funeral director in New York and gone off to take a job in Alaska. She wrote me long, detailed letters about the funerals there and about embalming unusual cases, such as one man who had been mauled to death by a bear.

I continued to pose for photographs and paintings by Peter, as well as being sent on "go sees" for the modeling agency, although working days pretty much hampered my availability for modeling jobs. And worst of all, I was temporarily unregistered as a business, so that even if a funeral came my way, by law I was not permitted to handle it.

I felt I had traveled a long, hard road for nothing, especially when a funeral director turned to me one morning and said, "It takes big person to admit they made a mistake." I wished people would stop saying I had made a mistake and that women in the funeral industry were a mistake. Those words, however, only made me more determined. The more obstacles thrown at me trying to prevent me from reaching my goal, the more my drive to reach it intensified.

One night some weeks later, as I drove home from the funeral home through a particularly seedy area after doing a double shift, another motorist pulled up next to me and kept pace with my car, all the while motioning frantically for me to pull over. Tired and eager to get home, I wondered if something was really wrong or he wanted to rob and kill me. I looked at him closely and decided he looked too concerned to be a killer. I took a chance and pulled over.

"Get out of the car, hurry! It's on fire!" he yelled.

I jumped out.

"Run!" he screamed.

I ran and when I got about fifty feet away I turned around to see flames shooting from under my car. Within seconds, the entire thing went up like a bonfire. I reflected on this upsetting and frightening event when I finally got home, tired and bedraggled. I decided it was an omen that my life *had* to change. *But how was I supposed to make that happen?* I asked myself.

That same month one of my bosses decided to send me on a personal errand of picking up the owner's mother and driving her to upstate New York. Although in family-owned funeral homes employees frequently had to do personal errands for the owners, the union in this funeral home said we should not. I was tired of being taken advantaged of and tried to contacted the union representative. I called his office, but the telephone was answered by someone who clearly had no time for me.

"The union's closed today. Do what you are told and complain Monday," he said and hung up.

I drove as far as a local diner and called a friend who knew all about cars. He told me how to make the car's battery appear to have died, by only removing a single wire. I followed his instructions, which worked like a charm. After calling the funeral home and reporting my problem, I sat in the air-conditioned diner in front of which I had managed to "break down." I ordered an ice-cream soda while I waited for help to arrive. The boss was sending the porters to help me. They knew less about cars than I did.

When they arrived and checked out the car they confirmed to my boss that the car's battery was indeed dead. After several attempts, getting nowhere with the jumper cables, I suggested the now sweaty workers join me in the air-conditioned diner for a cold drink. While they sipped their refreshments, I surreptitiously replaced the wire. The next time the engine would turn over, but it would be too late for that personal errand now.

"I don't know what you did, but I know you did something to that car!" the boss growled at me when I finally returned to the funeral home.

"Really, you give me too much credit. I don't know a thing about cars," was my response.

That Monday, I called the union and spoke to the representative. That was the first and only union job I ever held and I learned that there was some compensation for being a union member and paying those dues. The union had to at least make an attempt to advocate for you. The union delegate at the time was a nice man who knew that my bosses were taking advantage of my being licensed while designating me a receptionist and that they had been less than truthful with me when I was hired. In addition, he was well aware that I had been insulted, degraded, snapped at, ignored and generally treated badly.

He told me that the funeral home at which I was working had never hired a woman in a licensed funeral director capacity and thus, with discrimination suits being filed in many other industries, they were ripe for being sued. Tara, who'd been encouraging me to do as she'd done, now grew even more vocal. I still felt it was something I would never do, but the funeral home and union could not be sure of that.

At a breakfast meeting with the union representative, I told him I was considering a lawsuit. To stave off any potential problems, the union official spoke to my bosses, who agreed they would lay me off, which made me eligible for unemployment, if I agreed not to sue. I agreed, envisioning a summer at the beach. However, I only collected for two weeks before I began frantically searching for work again as well as a place to register my business, which was even more important to me. Soon I realized the only work available was a job I always said I wouldn't do—cosmetizing and hairstyling of the deceased. *At least,* I told myself, *maybe I can begin to make a decent living again.*

CHAPTER 9

Promise Them Anything

I swallowed my pride. Once again, I was considering the only job in the funeral industry reserved exclusively for women, the position of "Lady Attendant." I now found out more than I ever wanted to know about the job and the term. Lady attendant, an archaic term that stuck, originally denoted a woman who "attended" to the dead. In historical times, she would dress and style the hair of a deceased woman. Using a woman to care for deceased women retained a modicum of discretion and modesty. A lady attendant was often a licensed funeral director, but not necessarily. And if she was licensed, she most likely could not find work in other areas of funeral service, such as embalming and more visibly, making arrangements and directing funerals. Thus she was relegated to traditional "women's work." When a licensed woman could not be found, this job was usually thrust upon the wife or mother of a funeral director, who was neither a funeral director herself nor a cosmetician. Now I saw why Rae had wanted to hand this job off.

Worse, I quickly found out that on top of this work being scornful, the women who did it were casually referred to by some as whores. As funeral folklore had it, part of their function while working was to bend over the caskets and hike up their skirts for the pleasure of their employers. As if this wasn't bad enough, the work stigmatized a woman. If a woman did the hair styling on one body, she'd be labeled a hairdresser, but if a man carried a casket on a particular day, he was not reduced to pallbearer status for the rest of his life. It was believed by many in the business that if someone who did not have a funeral director's license were to do the same work usually done by licensed personnel, then we would appear less professional and lose credibility.

Although demeaning in its treatment of women, I was considering lady attendant work. I badly needed work and told myself I wanted to gain more experience in all the aspects of the funeral business so that I could someday have an establishment of my own. Theoretically, there were some parts of the lady attendant work which sounded good. Your time was basically your own; you were your own boss. You set your own hours, ran in, did the body, then left. You were an independent contractor.

In reality, the accounts for whom you were working set the time, with every account choosing the twelve noon to twelve-thirty time slot. No one seemed to care if you had other work to do. Every funeral director felt as if he was the only account you had to service. Like a self-absorbed baby, each believed he was the center of the universe. And even when you arrived, the funeral director was often not ready for you. It was hurry up and wait. None of them cared one whit about wasting your time, detaining you or making you late for another appointment, thus inconveniencing another undertaker. Work that should have taken an hour at most, often turned into several hours. Some accounts, of course, were more inconsiderate than others.

Well, given that I was in a bad financial way and still looking for work and a funeral home from which to set up and register my own business, my mind was open to this sort of work, distasteful as it was. It was on one of my job hunting excursions that a tradesman passed along the information that one of the older women who did lady attendant work was moving away. "Perhaps you'd be interested in taking over some of the accounts she had with funeral homes," he suggested.

It turned out she was looking to *sell* her accounts, not just have someone take them over. This was a ridiculous prospect and she got no takers. I also turned her down, as there would be no assurance the accounts would agree to keep me. In the end, she moved away and her accounts were divided between other, more established lady attendants. Although I called upon several of the funeral homes for which she had worked and offered my services, I was unsuccessful in all but one.

Gerard J. Neufeld Funeral Home in Elmhurst, Queens, hired me to do lady attendant work and turned out to be not just a busy funeral home account, but the place in which I finally was able to register my business. This time around I called it the Hellenic Funeral Home.

Ray and Joe Neufeld, both in their thirties, like so many others in the industry, had been born into funeral home families and now the brothers were running their late father's business. But they were quite unlike many of the funeral directors I had met. Fun-loving as they were, they clearly had managed to escape the snobbishness and sense of superiority seemingly inherent in many of the offspring of funeral industry families. In fact, the two men were a breath of fresh air.

We grew to be dear friends, spending long hours conversing about the business and life in general. Laughing, we called these long talks our "bonding sessions." They listened patiently as I filled them in on my lady attendant adventures. And in these tumultuous days of my career, they found themselves in the position of defending me to some of my colleagues who knew me by gossip only.

They did not make the impossible demands many other funeral directors made of me, nor did they indulge families in the silliness that some funeral directors did. There was never a time they asked me why a corpse was not smiling, nor did they ever ask me to make a body look happy, healthy or for that matter...alive.

Our working relationship was good, mutually respectful and fun. Yes fun, for these two brothers enjoyed playing practical jokes.

Over that year, little by little I picked up some additional lady attendant's work, which in addition to handling a few of my own funerals, got me by financially. Frequently, the situation was that a funeral home already had a lady attendant, but would call me if the funeral was out of their usual area and their "girl" was unwilling to work anywhere but locally.

Once in a while I still went out on "go sees" for the modeling agency, but I thought it impractical, as it took me away from my "real work." Peter continued to paint me when I had the time to pose.

A little bit of luck came my way when an old friend of my adoptive mother became the pastor at a local Greek church. He began to recommend me for funerals and I assumed the financial burden of the church calendars that year. His parish was small and I had high hopes that we would grow together. However, not speaking the language once again became a handicap.

I got involved in some civic functions at the church, going to meetings and volunteering on committees, only to learn most of the other committee members insisted on speaking Greek. Not speaking the language was an impediment in building up a clientele and, I discovered, sometimes the consequences were humorous.

At a meeting at the church one evening, I brought along my florist and friend, Demetrios, who was fluent in Greek. He translated the ongoing conversations, quietly intoning the English version in my ear. However, by the time he translated several of the jokes told throughout the evening, I found myself laughing too late, inappropriately so, as the conversation had gone on to other matters. The committee members looked at me strangely and some rolled their eyes. Not only was she a woman undertaker, they probably thought, but she might be a little crazy!

A few days later, I was set to drive into Brooklyn to meet with the owner of one of the casket companies with which I did business, to pick up a new casket catalog. I arrived too late for the lunch the man had planned. It was a thoughtful gesture, especially since I was certainly not one of the company's biggest customers. But then I had heard Henry was a real gentleman of the old school. Generous, magnanimous, thoughtful and upbeat. Not only did he prove to be all those things, but to me, at the time, he was also the most attractive man I'd ever met. Sort of like a dashing, romantic hero in a romance novel, if you can imagine a romance novel taking place within the funeral industry.

Arriving late and a bit disheveled because of the rainy weather, I waited in the lobby, trying to make myself presentable. I had no idea what Henry looked like. I knew him only by name. Soon, a man of about fifty with a full head of thick, wavy gray hair, dressed in a tastefully expensive yet understated gray suit and a stunning silk tie, came walking down the stairs to greet me.

"Hi, I'm Henry," he said in the most endearing Brooklyn accent I had ever heard. "And you missed the lunch I had planned for us," he added with a smile, extending his hand.

I made my apologies and after paging through the casket catalog with him, he showed me around the casket selection room. At one point, he leaned against a casket and said out of nowhere, "I guess you know my story. I'm in the process of getting a divorce."

I hadn't known much about him until that day, except that he had built the casket company up to the present successful enterprise it was today, from the small company his father had begun out of the basement of his Brooklyn brownstone. This was becoming too good to be true! Handsome, debonair, thoughtful, rich to boot and soon to be single.

Then he asked me if we could take a rain check on lunch.

"Of course, I'd like that," I said and he smiled back at me.

I was instantly smitten with the man who was a prime example of dark, sophisticated good looks. But for all his sophistication and sartorial splendor, there remained an endearing boyishness about him. To my mind, he was the quintessential Brooklyn Boy who had made good. Well-liked, fun to be with, Henry knew everyone and took me to some of New York's finest restaurants. Price was never an object. He ordered lavishly from menus, finding pleasure in people's enjoyment of their food, always picking up the checks for friends and business associates alike. I was not only in lust with him, I wanted to be as popular, fun, generous and helpful as he was.

"Do you need anything?" he constantly asked, not only of me, but his other friends and business associates, as well. It was common knowledge that he had helped many a flagging funeral home. And he made you understand that he really wanted to assist you whether it was with time, influence or money. His attitude about money, and he had earned much of it, was that it should be shared and used to aid others.

"It's only money!" he was quick to say. His kindness was reflective of his generous spirit. He showed his caring by lending a hand to solve others' problems.

"Life's too short to worry. There aren't many problems money can't take care of."

He was so perfect that he became my idol. Unfortunately, circumstances and our more than twenty-five year age difference prevented us from ever having a really serious relationship. But he left an indelible impression on me and for years afterward I compared all the men I met to Henry...and they always fell short.

That summer, my friend Marge, who had been diagnosed with pancreatic cancer several months earlier, entered the final stages of her illness. I visited her daily, watching sadly, as she became weaker and frailer at each visit. It saddened me even more when other friends stopped coming to see her. Except for her family, I became her only visitor. When I asked people why they had stopped, they said they "couldn't stand" seeing her like that.

They couldn't stand it? Marge was the one in pain and dying; she needed their support. How selfish and insensitive people could be!

Marge wanted to believe she would get better, but on some level, she knew she would not. She told me that she wanted me to handle her funeral, feeling comforted a bit, I think, by that thought. She knew it would be personal and loving. However, her husband called me late on the afternoon she died, to tell me, I thought, to fulfill her wishes and handle the funeral. Instead, he told me he was "calling a friend from their church and of their nationality" to handle it. I wondered to myself where this "friend" had been throughout Marge's illness. I felt so conflicted. On the one hand, I knew Marge wanted me to handle everything; on the other, I didn't have the heart to tell her grieving husband that he was going against her last wishes. I thought of Rae and once again wished I had her sense of confidence and decisiveness. She would have told him quite clearly that he was making a mistake.

To me, both personally and professionally, not honoring a loved one's last wishes is a grave breach of trust. I did not attend Marge's funeral, as is my practice when the next of kin doesn't follow the wishes that his or her deceased loved one has expressed to me. Funeral directors have debated the protocol. Should one go to a funeral when one has been slighted? Some funeral directors have admitted they do it to make the family of the deceased feel uncomfortable. My rationale has been that if I am not close enough to the family to be entrusted with the funeral arrangements, than I am not close enough to attend the funeral. There is no middle ground for me, except in the case where a person has a closer relationship with another funeral director, lives out of state or is a colleague. A mutual friend of ours did go to Marge's funeral and later commented to me, "She looked terrible! They should have closed the casket. It wouldn't have been that way if you had handled things. You would have made her look beautiful."

Maybe I should have been more direct with her husband? I'll always feel badly about not saying something to him. I felt sad and pondered the inexplicable reasons a person calls the wrong funeral director when the time comes. Shouldn't the most personal of services be done by a friend, if possible?

Back at the Neufeld Funeral Home, Ray and Joe did their best to cheer me up. We lunched together and talked about the age old hurtful subject of "When you are not called to serve." People did not understand the hurt we went through. It was not about the money, but rather about matters of trust, faith, loyalty and honor. I know it was about that for me.

As agreeable and easy as Ray and Joe were to work with, I was about to meet their polar opposites, people who would become my most troublesome and annoying account. Their funeral business showed me the worst aspects of the industry. They were a funeral family who believed others were born to serve them, who made impossible, unreasonable demands and who thought themselves above all others, including the law. Still, my acquaintance with them provided me with experience in diplomatically dealing with impossible demands as well as ways in which I could better serve families over the years.

The meeting took place while I was visiting Henry one Sunday at the casket company. In walked a tall, hulking, lumbering lummox with disproportionately large feet. He ambled over to us, his back hunched. Immediately, Henry jumped up and embraced the man, greeting him effusively, as if he hadn't seen him in the longest time.

"Alexandra, this is Sonny Calabrese, my good friend. Alexandra's a lady attendant. Maybe you want to call her sometime," he said.

Sonny smiled and shook my hand, as I cringed at being introduced in this way. "That's very possible. Write down your number," he said to me.

I scrawled my number on a piece of Henry's company pads and handed it to Sonny.

"Sonny and I got some things to talk about now honey; so you be on your way."

"Will you walk me to the car?" I asked, disappointed our time had been cut short.

"Sure."

Standing outside by the car, I asked Henry, "Do you think Sonny will really call?"

"If I ask him to he will," Henry assured me, as he quickly kissed me goodbye.

And within a week Sonny did call, asking me to meet him for coffee at a luncheonette near his funeral home. As it turned out, of all the funeral directors Henry had asked to call me, Sonny was the only one who ever did.

Several days later, I met Sonny for coffee. He exuded a smug sense of superiority and spoke in an affected manner; no matter what he said, it came out sounding like a prepared speech—condescending, patronizing and insincere. I had heard that Sonny wanted to be a politician and so surrounded himself with minor political figures. He also had a pathetic habit of name dropping which only made him look foolish in others' eyes. "He can't resist the urge to demonstrate what a busy, important person he is," one colleague told me. "He doesn't understand that money cannot bring class, breeding or education, all of which his family lacks."

At first I went by the supposition that the Calabreses were normal—eventually I realized they were nuts—but it was not too long after beginning work there that I understood that their family's funeral home was the ultimate in dysfunction. I was familiar with incompetence, but this was the supreme example—they gave new meaning to the word incompetence.

At our meeting in the luncheonette, Sonny told me that Vivian, the woman who had been doing his lady attendant work for thirty years, was now getting too old to continue and that her work no longer satisfied him. I knew her slightly and did not have the heart to take work away from an elderly woman in failing health.

"Does she know you are looking for someone to take her place?" I asked.

"Don't worry about that. I'll take care of explaining things to her. She'll understand," he reassured me.

"I hope so. I don't want to hurt anybody."

"Well, let me put it this way. I'm looking for someone new. So I'm hoping you are interested, but if not you, then I'll offer the position to someone else."

"Since you put it that way, I am interested. Just please let Vivian know."

"I will."

But he never did. Instead, I found out later that Vivian learned she'd been replaced, as people often did in our business, by reading the newspaper obituaries.

On the dark side of a narrow street, amid a row of brownstones, lay the Calabrese Funeral Home. It looked foreboding on the outside and even worse on the inside. Darkness predominated. I opened the door and walked into a shadowy foyer; not only was the decor dark, but the lights were out as well. My first impression was that I was in the Munsters' family house. Flocked, maroon wallpaper, dark, stained, well-worn carpeting. Neo-Dracula furnishings. Dark, dull colors predominated. This building screamed funeral home. The premises were outdated and badly worn down.

A piercingly shrill voice yelled down the steep staircase.

"Who's there? Who is it?" the voice demanded.

This turned out to be Sonny's sister, Sissy, who was in business with him, although she was not a funeral director.

Theirs was a weird brother/sister act, whose pet childhood nicknames, Sonny and Sissy, incongruously still stuck to the two aging proprietors. Complete opposites in temperament and personality, they looked uncannily alike—both had the same face—except that Sissy was under five feet to his six feet.

As I came to know him better, I observed that Sonny usually seemed disinterested in the workings of the funeral home and more interested in attending meetings and playing "Mr. Big Shot," except for the times when a deceased political figure was to be waked and the family had spent a great deal of money on the funeral. Then, puffing up like a blowfish, Sonny would play funeral director and admonish us to "do a good job." As if we usually didn't.

For all the families we served, I always did my best regardless of their status or financial standing. I felt a family's grief was never to be measured by what they could afford to spend. Ironically, Sonny's sentiment that people should spend freely on funerals did not extend to his own financial sensibilities. Notoriously known as a skinflint, one of the guys asked me after I'd had a rare lunch with Sonny whether or not he ordered anything or merely ate the bread. An almost apt description. Sonny had, in fact, only ordered a bowl of soup to accompany the bread. Yet, he had the nerve to deride his competitor down the street, who was free with a buck and regularly treated the neighborhood senior citizens to meals. We all got a laugh the time Sonny's jacket was inadvertently cut up the back and placed on a dead body. Sonny left with the deceased's jacket. We decided he had most assuredly gotten the better deal.

Sissy and Sonny made unrealistic and impossible demands on me and the embalmers, referring to us as "our girl" as in "our girl will do it" and "the boys." Each and every time my beeper read out their number, I knew I was in for it! As time went on their demands became increasingly preposterous.

Their lack of knowledge about the business they had inherited was staggering. They promised bereaved families anything, things that any competent funeral director knew were impossible.

On one occasion, I was summoned back after my work on a woman's body had been completed, as Sissy had assured the family that "my girl will cut the neckline on the dress, so she won't choke." This was clearly an absurd comment. I stared at her in disbelief, trying to get close enough to whisper that the autopsy incisions reached almost to her throat, but to no avail. As the family huddled sorrowfully around the casket, Sissy became more vocal in her demands.

"She's choking. Make her stop choking," Sissy insisted as she flitted around like a nervous butterfly.

Trying not to show my exasperation, I pulled a bit at the neckline of the dress. Eventually, Sissy was satisfied.

The Calabreses liked their bodies to smile. They took personal delight in the families remarking, "Oh, she's smiling," and the pseudo-comfort it offered, evoking images of the deceased being in a happier place. But when a mouth did not form naturally into an upturned expression, evoking the perception of a smile, Sonny or Sissy would order, "Make her smile! She's not smiling!" They would insist we somehow make the corpses look like they were enjoying their final showing. I was awaiting the day they commanded us to resurrect the dead. Some people thought we could!

Unrealistic at best, the Calabreses' demands were often impossible to satisfy, but they persisted in promising the families who came to them anything and everything. I never was sure if they made these promises because of their limited or non-existent knowledge of the business or simply because they were afraid of losing business.

For example, if the corpse had a leg amputated, they wouldn't try to guide the family into selecting a half-open casket. No, they would order us to make it look like there was a leg there by using stuffing in the trouser leg and dummying a shoe. No matter how inappropriate a dress—short sleeves on arms black and blue from hospital IVs, a low cut top on a body which had been autopsied, a short skirt on burned remains in a fully open casket—they would insist we make their ideas work. I sometimes felt more like a tailor than a funeral director.

On a typical day, I would arrive at the funeral home all set to work on a body. If the funeral director had bothered to ask the family for a photograph, it could be a big help…sometimes. More often than not, the photo was old, faded and outdated. Frequently, families supplied photographs of a twenty-year-old when we were working on their eighty-year-old grandmother! Sonny's or Sissy's instruction: "Make her look like the picture," bordered on the ludicrous.

Sometimes, as the result of illness, age or chemotherapy, a woman had little or no hair. Some families brought in wigs or turbans; some did not. When such was the situation, I would say to Sonny, who I knew had already seen the body, "There's no hair to work with."

"Get some," was his response.

He'd often say in front of the family members of the deceased, "Make her look like she used to."

"How? I don't know what she used to look like," I'd whisper to him.

"Well, she hasn't changed that much," he'd usually reply.

If we used a hairpiece, Sonny would sometimes complain, "It looks like a wig."

"It *is* a wig," I'd say, pointing out the obvious.

"Well, make it not look like one."

Sissy made every first viewing a problem by quickly asking the family before they had even made a comment, "Would you like to change something?" Of course, many people believed their loved ones had been beautiful or handsome and expected to see this in the casket, even though the deceased may have grown elderly or experienced a long illness. Weight was another problem. Embalming does not cause weight gain, but some families insisted their hefty relatives had not been so until we got hold of them.

Others thought the person looked younger and more attractive after we had done our work. "Hate to say it, but she looks better than when she was alive," was a comment I heard at many first viewings. Embalming filled out tissues and fine lines better than collagen ever could. It was often instant plastic surgery.

Of course, many people's last glimpse of their loved one was as he or she was dying in a hospital bed. Now they were dressed in long, flowing gowns or neat suits, coiffed and in full make-up. Who wouldn't look better?

After doing this work for a while, I became confident that I could make almost any body look good. In fact, I felt I could just about do it in my sleep. Unfortunately, I began to dream about the bodies and in one recurring dream, I was reaching into a casket and cosmetizing a body that was still alive.

Funeral directors like the Calabreses so frequently promised the impossible to families I half-expected to hear: *Can you bring him back to life, Mr. Funeral Director?* And the response: *Sure, we can. Just have a seat in the lobby, give us a few minutes and we'll have him breathing again.*

Although Sonny and I had identical professional credits except, as a colleague put it, "You weren't born with a silver spoon up your ass," Sonny treated me as an inept inferior. Working for these people was a nightmare and at all times I had to exercise supreme patience. They seemed totally inept about the simplest things. My beeper began to go off regularly, time after time, with no number. After awhile, I knew it was them; everybody else I knew was capable of inserting a number into the beeper. I'd call and they'd swear they had inserted their number.

They never seemed to be clear on the details of the funerals they'd scheduled such as when their visitations would begin.

"What do you tell people when they call?" I asked one day.

"I tell them I don't know," Sonny said with a shrug.

"I tell them, call back!" Sissy responded arrogantly.

Often they would change the visitation time and not bother to tell me or the "boys." Once they even forgot they had a funeral and didn't move the body out of the hospital. Luckily, I arrived early and alerted them.

In spite of the fact that I didn't much care for Sonny and Sissy, they seemed to like me, often inviting me to social affairs and trying to fix me up with dates. At times, I felt pressured to socialize with them. At that point, I could honestly say that not only had I met some of the worst men *in* my business, I also began to meet them *through* my business.

An ill-fated relationship with their friend Nino, a divorced lawyer, ensued. I should have known that anyone Sonny introduced me to would turn out to be similarly pompous and condescending. These qualities were made apparent when I related to him the story of a particularly gruesome crime that had been all over the news the previous day.

A wealthy Westchester couple had been axe-murdered by the man's daughter. Bart was handling the funeral arrangements for the female victim, a former Queens resident.

"Is she viewable?" I had asked Bart when he told me he was handling the funeral.

"Go take a look."

I did. The axe-murder victim was not a pretty sight.

That horrific image stayed with me through dinner with Nino that night. I could not help talking about the case and what I had seen.

"She murdered her father and stepmother with an axe. She should get the death penalty," I said emphatically.

"Alexandra, there is no death penalty where she comes from," my date reminded me in a sneering, condescending tone.

"Well, she should get it anyway."

"Don't be ridiculous. She's only nineteen and has a lot of money. With the right attorney, she'll get off, get the psychiatric help she needs and someday return to society." He looked off into the distance. "I wish I were handling her case," he said wistfully. "I could charge her a fortune."

I stared into his face with utter contempt.

"She didn't just have a bad day or lapse of judgment, she axe-murdered two people," I said in utter disgust. "Would you let her stay at your house? Baby-sit your daughter?"

"Well of course not, but that's not the point, silly girl," he laughed.

"Well here's one," I said. "Goodnight and goodbye." That was the end of our conversation and our relationship. I only wished that I could leave my place of employment as easily.

CHAPTER 10

Death Takes a Holiday

I felt increasingly depressed and restless. The work I was doing for Sonny and Sissy was going from bad to worse. The trade was slow in general, thus affecting all the accounts I had with other funeral homes. And as if that was disheartening enough, my personal funeral business was also on the quiet side. I seemed to be going nowhere. Once again, Peter suggested that I pose for *Playboy*.

A simple "no" was my response. Anyway, I thought it would not work. Nothing else seemed to.

Weeks turned into months as my unhappiness and boredom increased. One afternoon, while perusing a newspaper stand for a magazine to read, I spotted a new *Playboy* issue with Roxanne Pulitzer on the cover. I remembered feeling sympathy and understanding when reading in the newspaper about the "born on the wrong side of the tracks" woman who married a member of the wealthy Pulitzer family and then had gone through a messy divorce with him and court fight over custody of their children. I could also feel her anger, identifying with the victimization she was experiencing from narrow-minded peers. After all, I was living it, by being just a bit different. My hat was

off to her for fighting back with her *Playboy* pictorial and interview.

I showed Peter the feature. When he saw my keen interest,
he once again brought up my trying to get a *Playboy* appearance.

I laughed self-consciously. "It seems silly to be giving it so
much thought. They haven't asked me. I really don't have any
decision to make."

"This time will you let me write to them?" he asked quietly.

"Why not," I said and shrugged. What did I have to lose?
I was certain they wouldn't answer anyway.

But Peter was certain they would. *Playboy* magazine had
begun to feature women on their pages who were over the age of
twenty-one and involved in what they considered to be unusual
professions.

"What could be more unusual than your profession?"
asked Peter.

He had a point...

Peter wrote to them, got no response and wrote again.
There was no answer during the next six months.

"See, I told you they wouldn't be interested," I told him.

"These things take time," he assured me.

A week after my birthday in August, a young woman who
said she was from *Playboy* called.

As I'm sure many others did, I responded with disbelief.

"Is this a joke?" I asked the caller, who identified herself as
the photo editor's assistant.

"It's no joke," she assured me. "We'd like to bring you out
to Chicago for some test shots. Are you still interested?"

"I...I sure am!"

"Can you be here next week—the first week of September?"

"Sure."

The way I was feeling, I would have taken a plane that very afternoon and waited outside their offices. In a state of euphoria, I rushed to call Peter.

"I got a call from a woman at *Playboy*!" I said excitedly. "Can you believe it? You were right and I'm glad you were!"

Early the next morning and on every subsequent morning for the next two weeks, I went to the gym, intent on cramming in as much exercise as I could before leaving for Chicago. Caught up in the momentum of the treadmill, being beeped about a funeral became an intrusion, for the only body I was interested in at the time was alive and mine.

When my airplane ticket arrived, I carried it with me, sometimes fishing it from my purse at work, just to reassure myself that I was really going to Chicago to meet the crew at *Playboy*.

I decided to tell only my closest friends in case it didn't work out.

However, I also decided I'd better call our state licensing agency and inquire as to whether there were any statutes against my posing for the magazine.

"You want to know if it's against the rules for a funeral director to pose nude for *Playboy*?" Dave, the state inspector asked, bewilderment in his voice. "Hold on while I check. We've never come up against this sort of thing before," he said with a chuckle. Returning to the phone, he reluctantly assured me it was okay but "probably not a good idea."

Of course, I was not about to back out of this opportunity, but even so, before I left for Chicago I thoroughly discussed the matter of my posing with some of the funeral directors with whom I did business and was friendly. I received few negative reactions. Most encouraged and reassured me that it would make no difference in the industry, except to a few hypocrites and jealous colleagues, who wouldn't approve of anything I did. In fact, most of my peers said they were looking forward to the issue. And my friend Henry, the owner of the casket company, assured me that "Everyone's gonna wanna do business with you." I wasn't sure I shared those sentiments, especially after hearing from the vocal minority who predicted in dire tones that posing would destroy my career. Realizing one can never please everybody and that it was foolish to try, I decided not to allow my anxious thoughts to interfere with my opportunity.

Two weeks later I was off to Chicago. I savored every detail of the trip. I smiled at everyone I encountered, wanting to tell the other passengers that I was going to be tested to be a model for *Playboy* and that with a little luck on my part, they would one day see me in the magazine. But even if I'd been confident enough to tell these strangers, who'd believe such a story? So I kept my excitement to myself.

On arrival that night, I checked into the Knickerbocker Hotel in the heart of Chicago, where the assistant with whom I'd spoken had made my reservation. The desk clerk seemed especially gracious as I signed the register. I felt a bit self-conscious, but reminded myself that the hotel staff probably was accustomed to *Playboy* models checking in.

As soon as I got up to my room, I called the editor to let her know I had arrived. After some polite inquiries about my flight and accommodations, I was instructed where to report in the morning.

Too nervous to eat dinner, I took a walk down famed Michigan Avenue, Chicago's premier shopping district, full of curiosity and trying to tire myself out. I knew sleeping would be difficult.

At 6:00 A.M. the next morning I was wide awake. After a light breakfast from room service, I did some sit-ups, showered, dressed, applied my make-up with extra care and headed to the magazine site which was conveniently located nearby.

It was an unassuming office building, only recognizable by the *Playboy* sign. But as the elevator opened on my designated floor, I saw lavish reception areas, offices, photography sets, wardrobes and make-up rooms. As I made my way towards the reception desk, I passed walls adorned with poster-size photos of popular centerfolds and stars who had appeared in the magazine or on the cover.

I gave the receptionist my name. A few minutes later, Pompeo Posar, *Playboy's* senior staff photographer, came out to greet me. A distinguished photographer with an illustrious history, he charmed me immediately with his Italian accent and continental savoir faire.

Then I met Jeff Cohen and his secretary, two people I felt I already knew after our considerable telephone contact. They made me feel welcome, gave me an informative tour and reiterated their belief that the *Playboy* group thought of themselves as a family, a belief I came to share.

We were to begin the test shots that very afternoon, but first I was shown into a make-up room crammed with every conceivable product and color. I spent a glorious hour being fussed over.

Heated rollers were gently wound in my long hair and allowed to bake as Pat, the make-up artist, swirled cream on my face to remove the make-up I had painstakingly applied. Then she tried out various shades of lipstick, blush and eye-shadow on my face. We finally agreed on deep, rich colors to compliment my black hair and olive skin. Being professionally made up was relaxing and soothing. Glancing into the mirror, I could not help thinking I looked better and better as she continued her work. After the cosmetic makeover was finished, the curlers unwound and my hair brushed, combed and teased into a lush mane, I was ready for the camera. I loved the glamorous result, a definite transformation from my daily business look.

Next we walked around the block to a high-rise building and took the elevator to a penthouse apartment, which had been lent to *Playboy* by a local millionaire for the test shots. I was awed by the spectacular view of Lake Michigan and the Chicago skyline. "Is it alright if I snap a few photos with my camera?" I asked wanting to record as much as I could of this fantasy.

"Of course. Relax," Pompeo told me, "there is no pressure." He asked me questions about my work in New York. We chatted and got to know one another as he quietly began to take some photos of me, initially clothed. He was exceedingly patient as I slowly relaxed and loosened up. Little by little he instructed me to remove articles of clothing. After an initial nervousness, I began to feel more comfortable...it all seemed to happen so naturally...and my fascination with the technical details of a photo shoot superseded any residual hesitation I was feeling about his taking shots of me scantily clad or in the end, totally unclad.

It amazed me how much planning, effort and teamwork went into *Playboy's* photographs. More amazing to me, however, was that I was the one being photographed. I felt disbelief throughout the test session that this could actually be happening to me. Out of the thousands of hopeful young women who contacted *Playboy* each month, I had been chosen to be tested.

Realistically, I knew the chance of being selected to actually appear in the magazine was, given the logistics, very slim. Twelve issues of the monthly magazine included one centerfold, one special feature and occasionally a young woman who had a special story about her occupation. That still only added up to thirty-six women a year. Very small odds of being chosen, indeed.

I told myself that I would be satisfied with just being given this opportunity to test, even if I did not end up on the pages of the magazine. But I knew in my heart that was not true. I wanted very much to be chosen as a *Playboy* model.

By early evening, many rolls of film had been shot and my hair as well as make-up had been refreshed a number of times. Pompeo finally decided he had taken enough photographs to determine my potential.

The group walked me back to the hotel. I took the elevator to my room where I wearily ordered room service and called New York. I was concerned about my business and wanted to find out what I was missing and what work was scheduled for me when I returned. "Tomorrow I'll be on a flight home and I can go straight to the funeral home if need be," I told Ray Neufeld.

I left Chicago not knowing what the outcome of my photo session with *Playboy* would be. As the days wore on, I received no word from them and became convinced I hadn't made the grade. I even began to disclose to close friends that I did not make it. I was feeling terribly depressed at having come so close yet not seeing this dream materialize.

However, one week later, on Friday the 13th—always a lucky day for me—I got the call I was no longer expecting. Jeff Cohen called to tell me they were pleased with my test shots and it was full speed ahead. He expressed surprise that I had not called to find out the results and felt badly that I had spent the week needlessly worried. "We want you to return to Chicago on October twenty-first to shoot the actual layout that will appear in our magazine." He asked if that would give me enough time to prepare.

"Plenty of time!" I assured him, not wanting him to change his mind.

I was on cloud nine! I phoned several friends to tell them the good news; then Peter and I went out for a true celebration dinner.

For the next month I was on a high. Even my funeral work for my accounts, which had become rather mundane, enthused me. I smiled and laughed easily as I counted down the days until I would return to Chicago. I tried to keep my impending magazine spread a secret, knowing I might be criticized by my colleagues. I learned, however, that the news had leaked throughout the industry.

Arriving in Chicago, I once again checked into the Knickerbocker Hotel. It was too late to call Jeff at the magazine, so I settled in, ordered a light dinner and made some calls to New York to check on business. Then I laid down but was unable to fall to sleep. I got up again and wrote some postcards. After that I got back into bed. I was anxious to fall asleep. I wanted at least eight hours in order to look fresh in the morning for the photo-shoot.

At 9:00 A.M. the next morning, I checked in at *Playboy* enterprises. Jeff and Pompeo were waiting. "We're anxious to show you the set we've had created for you," Pompeo said. Excitedly, they whisked me into the huge studio to see their creation. I could not help laughing out loud. They had put together a set which evoked images of haunted mansions and eerie castles, to set the tone of my occupation. Antique furniture was draped by white sheets, as was the full length mirror. Stone lions, candelabrum, vases full of red roses and even a cemetery gate were used as decorations. Hidden from view, a dry ice machine released smoke, creating a misty effect.

"How do you like it?" Jeff asked eagerly.

"I love it!"

"Good! We wanted you to feel at home," he joked.

It was on to make-up and then into the wardrobe room, which looked like a Frederick's of Hollywood catalog come to life. I tried on many variations and combinations of garter belts, stockings, bras, panties, sheer blouses, negligees, and high heeled shoes, mostly in black. I modeled everything for Jeff and Pompeo who decided on a few changes, including a red see-through slip, red heels and red gloves for an alternate color scheme.

The photo session began late in the morning with plans to work throughout the day, except for a brief lunch break. Pompeo instructed me on basic poses and would often assume the pose he wanted for me, with comic results. Each new sequence of photos was initiated by a Polaroid snapshot to get an idea of the lighting and composition. Once satisfied, Pompeo switched cameras and for a time the click...click...click of the shutter could be heard.

"Give me that sexy look...c'mon, you can do it again...I know you are tired...just a few more pictures...that's it...you're getting it...good...good...very good..." coaxed Pompeo.

At 6:00 P.M. Pompeo was still shooting pictures and I was tired. We'd been at the photo session since late morning. The exhilaration I'd felt earlier in the day had given way to exhaustion. All my life I had enjoyed having my picture taken, never realizing what tiring work it could actually be, waiting for the light to be perfect or a camera angle to be just so. Trying to make sensual expressions while naked was turning out to be not as effortless as it appeared in all the photographs in the *Playboy* magazines I'd seen. I wanted to laugh out loud when I was trying to look sexy for the camera and thought my expressions must look silly instead.

Pompeo finally signaled that we were taking a break. "Shine...your face is shiny darling...It's time for some powder and a little touch up. Let's stop for a few minutes and finish for the day when you return."

I nodded, arose from the couch on which I was posing, wrapped a silk robe around my nude body and left the huge photo studio to have my make-up retouched.

As I walked down the corridor toward the make-up room, I caught my reflection in the mirrored wall and smiled. Shiny face and all, I felt happier than I had been in a long time. Posing for *Playboy* magazine was absolutely a fantasy come true.

It was also just the respite I needed from the business of death. It was a joy for me to be made-up, instead of making up dead bodies. Everybody here seemed to enjoy their work. It was so different from my environment. And each person I met treated me with the utmost respect and courtesy; a far cry from the way women were treated by the majority of the male funeral directors I had met.

"So it's time for a touch up," Pat, the cosmetologist said knowingly.

"Right."

I seated myself on a chair relaxing for the first time that day as she fussed over me.

"Looking forward to going back to the hotel and ordering some dinner?" Pat asked with a smile.

"I sure am! I'm starving. Frozen yogurt just doesn't do it. But I still have to watch what I eat so I don't gain any weight until this week is over. Then I'm going to eat anything I want."

Nevertheless I told myself that curbing my voracious appetite was a small concession for this opportunity. Hungry as I felt, I had even been able to find mild amusement in the lunch breaks at the *Playboy* studio, watching as the photographers and technicians ate huge hero sandwiches or deep dish pizza (a Chicago specialty), while the models munched on salads and yogurt and sipped diet sodas through a straw so as not to smudge their lipstick.

"Well, that's it. You're perfect again," Pat told me as she lightly dusted powder over my face for the last time that day.

"Thanks. See you tomorrow."

Back in the studio, Pompeo posed me once again on the couch we'd been using as a prop all that day. I tried to cooperate patiently with a number of quick changes until he was satisfied with my pose. Then he began to snap frame after frame with his very expensive, very intricate, Nikon camera.

"Great...beautiful...How are you going to feel when you see yourself in the magazine?"

"I can't imagine. I just can't wait!"

"You're going to shock the public darling. They've never seen such a beautiful funeral director—and without her clothes on. But what do you think the people in your business will say?"

I looked up at him and smiled pleasantly, but his question had jolted me back to reality.

Though I'd checked with a few of them, just what would the others say when they saw the magazine? That was a good question. They'd probably say a great deal! The whole funeral industry might blast me. But I didn't want to change anything. This was a once-in-a-lifetime experience. I was always going to be a funeral director and, God willing, one day I would own my own building. But I would probably not get another chance to be in a famous magazine. A magazine which, like it or not, was synonymous with beauty, desirability and sexuality in our culture.

I had given a lot of thought to what the bereaved families I served might think of my posing. I cared a great deal what they, more than the funeral directors, felt and in no way wished to offend them. I hoped the families would understand that I wanted to grasp this opportunity. When my stint with *Playboy* was concluded, it would be back to funeral homes, cemeteries and helping the bereaved.

As I reflected further, I was struck by the irony of both what I was doing for *Playboy* and what I did in my capacity as a funeral director. In a bizarre way, the two positions held a number of similarities. The funeral industry is for the most part, hushed up and quiet, as is posing nude; both have a somewhat taboo connotation. We, as funeral directors, prepare and cosmetize bodies for viewing and that was just what was being done to me by the magazine's make-up artist. *Playboy* wanted to present a perfectly turned out body to the public and that's exactly what funeral directors strove to do. It was the crux of our industry. In fact, both industries could claim aesthetics as the core of their foundations and the end result of each was very much "in your face." There was much hoopla and fussing over presenting the body at both a funeral and at *Playboy* and, in the final result, the body would soon be buried and before too long the magazine would be off the newsstands and in the recycling bin. It would be on to the next deceased body for the funeral director and for *Playboy*, on to the next model's body.

Ephemeral as it was, my association with *Playboy* was something I was doing purely for my own pleasure. It was also the respite I needed so I could return to my true career with renewed vigor. For me, posing was not a means to an end. The experience was finite. I was not thinking of continuing to pursue a modeling or acting career, as were most of the other models who appeared in the pages of the magazine. Nor did I see this as my ticket to fame and fortune. I already had a career to which I had committed myself. I knew it was important that I differentiate between what was transitory and what was permanent. And my career in the funeral industry—being a funeral director—was of paramount, lasting importance to me.

Sensing I had been a million miles away, Pompeo repeated his earlier question: "What will the people in your business say?"

"It will give them all something to talk about," I answered thoughtfully.

Finished with the day's shoot, we said goodnight. I left the studio, changed into street clothes and returned to my hotel room for another night of room-service, television and calls to New York to check on business. I smiled thinking my male friends who had enviously envisioned the wild happenings at *Playboy* would be sorely disappointed by the reality.

The magazine, while concerned with the models' comfort and happiness, did not encourage nightlife. This was business and they expected well-rested, bright-eyed models to report to work in the morning, not those who were bleary-eyed and hung over.

My remaining week there followed a similar pattern: rising early, reporting to make-up, sipping on a cup of coffee while being made-up, posing under very hot lights for hours, being touched-up on the set and experimenting with new poses, which often took some doing. One day, dangling horizontally down a small set of stairs, I surprised myself with my agility. Those gym sessions had really paid off.

When my expressions waned, Pompeo encouraged me to think sexy thoughts, and Jeff visited the set to voice encouragement.

Mornings, we went over the previous night's shoot. Jeff and Pompeo tactfully expressed their displeasure when dissatisfied.

"I'll do better," I assured them.

The night before I was scheduled to return to New York, Jeff, sporting his trademark bowtie, took me to dinner in a snazzy restaurant located in Chicago's Water Tower, a building Chicago natives like to boast is higher than New York's Empire State Building.

As we discussed the publicity efforts which would follow the magazine's publication, I refrained from ordering the cappuccino ice cream that he was having for dessert.

"Imagine all the publicity you'll get and then double it. Your life will never be the same again," Jeff cheerfully forecasted.

I was in high spirits my last day in Chicago, enjoying the black cats brought in for some photos. Unfortunately, the cats would not cooperate with Pompeo and my allergies got the best of me. But we laughed a lot, trying to get them to pose with me and watching them explore the set.

Finally it was time to stop and I went back to the hotel. As I began to pack I realized that I was in no hurry to leave Chicago. I wished it were possible to stay there indefinitely—I fantasized for a few minutes about living a different life—perhaps even working for *Playboy* enterprises. This, my second photo shoot, had proven to be even more enjoyable and interesting than the first. Knowing they had really chosen me to appear in *Playboy* made me less anxious. I was caught up in the glamour, excitement and gaiety of a lifestyle so diametrically opposed to mine that for the first time I was not looking forward to getting back to business of death.

Sad to leave, I was cheered as I recalled Pompeo's and Jeff's assurances that we would be together in two weeks. They were coming to New York to shoot pictures of me in the funeral home and cemetery. Clothed, this time.

An early evening flight from Chicago brought me into New York just in time for a good night's sleep before the next day's funeral, full of dreams about all I'd encountered during my modeling session with *Playboy*.

Just after dawn, the jarring sound of my beeper awakened me. Temporarily disoriented, I anticipated room service and make-up, and then reality set in. I was back home in my apartment, where there was no room service and the only make-up on my face would be that which I applied myself.

No, I was not going off to be photographed at *Playboy* this morning. Instead, I was on my way to bury somebody. My real life was about to begin again. The short dream-like interlude was over.

Several weeks later, Jeff and Pompeo arrived in New York to take the cemetery photographs of me which would accompany the layout. Unable to get permission to shoot in any local cemeteries, we were forced to take some pictures surreptitiously in a picturesque graveyard. The weather cooperated in an ironic way. The damp, cold day was an eerie mix of clouds, overcast sky and intermittent rain. Just right for our purposes. In spite of the depressing weather, the day turned hilarious as our entourage, Jeff, Pompeo, Peter, the lighting men and I scouted out optimum photographic settings in the cemetery while being dogged by the cemetery security patrol. Hiding behind large tombstones, waiting for the security car to pass, Pompeo and Jeff looked decidedly uncomfortable.

"This is a new first in picture taking for *Playboy* magazine," Jeff announced, carefully stepping around the graves in his path rather than on them.

With the cemetery security patrol close on our heels, we had no time to waste. Quickly, we located a semi-hidden spot, set up the equipment, took the shot and then just as hurriedly moved on. I began to feel slightly anxious, imagining all of us getting arrested for "defiling the sanctity of a cemetery." But as I was somberly and conservatively dressed in my funeral director's garb, I figured the cemetery personnel couldn't find what we were doing too offensive.

Within an hour Jeff and Pompeo decided that we had taken all the photos we would need. It was on to our last stop, the funeral home, to take some photos of me doing my work. Together we mulled over several possible shots, all agreeing that embalming room shots were off limits and decided upon one of me cosmetizing a simulated body (one of the lighting people) in a casket and another in the casket selection room with Peter posing as a client. Apparently, we simulated the body very well for when the issue came out people swore that we had photographed a real corpse.

"We've got everything we need!" Jeff announced jubilantly after the last shot.

Sadly, I thought that these would be the last photos *Playboy* would ever take of me. I didn't have long to dwell on it, because Jeff surprised me by asking me if I could fly to Chicago in two weeks to be featured on a live radio show to be broadcast from the *Playboy* studio. Delighted as I was to be planning on going back to Chicago and *Playboy*, Jeff and Pompeo seemed equally pleased to have concluded their New York cemetery/funeral home excursion. As they left for the airport, Pompeo, looking a little green around the gills, exclaimed, "In one day I have experienced more about funerals than I ever thought I would while still alive."

A month later, I took Jeff up on his offer and traveled back to Chicago to tape the live radio show. My appearance was written up in the next day's *Chicago Tribune*.

More months would pass before the magazine appeared on the newsstands and so I refocused on my funeral work. Then, at the beginning of the year, I received a call from an advertising agency based in Baltimore, Maryland about doing a television commercial for *Playboy* magazine. It was a new advertising concept in its experimental stage. My commercial turned out to be just one of two which aired.

The agency sent me a script and I practiced my lines over and over.

Unfortunately, the first week of February I came down with a bad cold on the night before I was to leave for Maryland. Too late to reschedule, I sneezed and coughed my way to Baltimore aboard a train where my seatmate was kind enough to make repeated trips to the beverage car to bring back hot tea for me. By the next morning, my cold was worse and my voice sounded awful. I had spent so much time memorizing my lines, but it was all for nothing. They scrapped my voice and used the voiceover of another actor instead. I did get to say one line though, although my voice was weak:"It's a tough job, but somebody has to do it!"

The technical crew kept repeating that line all day and smiling at me. When I left, they all autographed a group photo in which they appeared to be wearing nothing at all.

In New York, the commercial ran on several television stations, but I actually never caught it as it aired, just on the tape which had been sent to me from the agency. But my friends saw it and all said how beautiful I looked. I was pleased as well—the hair, the make-up, the photography were all so professionally done. Much to my chagrin, however, my voice sounded like that of a small child! Meanwhile I began counting down the days until the magazine would be on the newsstands.

At the end of February, I received an advance copy of the *Playboy* edition for which I had posed. My fingers shook as I hurriedly peeled open the adhesive wrapping. Quickly turning the pages, I found my photos. Although I had seen many Polaroids and proofs in the previous months, it was rather a shock to see the finished product. Two things struck me immediately: I looked thinner than I had ever seen myself and—gulp—the photos were more explicit than I had expected. And soon the whole world would see them!

Well, there was nothing I could do about that now. I had a publicity tour to prepare for. Several days later, I spent the day shopping with a girlfriend for new clothes to wear on the tour; a tour that would be kicked off by my appearance on the Regis Philbin show.

On the first Monday in March I took the Long Island Railroad into the city where I met Elizabeth Norris, *Playboy's* director of publicity, and Sheri Blair, a member of Mensa, whose photo had appeared in February's *Playboy*. We dined that evening at Lutece, a five-star French restaurant and talked about the next day's television appearance.

The next morning I was whisked by limousine to ABC Studios, ushered into hair and make-up, then left in the "Green Room" for an angst-provoking wait.

Hearing my name called, I made my entrance onto the set in front of the live audience. Nervous as I could be, I heard a small and squeaky voice come out of my mouth. Stunned by the lights and the proximity of the audience, something not apparent when watching the show on television, I stumbled over my words, not sure of just exactly what I was saying in response to the questions posed by Regis and Kathie Lee. Hearing the countdown to commercial was a welcome relief, but short-lived. Off the air, Kathie Lee perused the photos, scrunching up her nose, her disdain apparent.

"They're a lot more explicit than I thought they would be," I said apologetically.

The next evening, I left for Philadelphia to begin a two-week publicity tour of several East Coast states. In Philadelphia, I was a guest on *AM Philadelphia*, hosted by Wally Kennedy, the Philly equivalent to Regis Philbin. I found that I felt more at ease on this show than I had in New York, perhaps because I didn't live nearby. Wally was a nice, low-key sort of host and he would invite me back as a guest more than half a dozen times over the next several years. In fact, a year later, I inadvertently became his sole guest for an entire hour when another guest didn't show up and that remains one of my favorite interviews of all time. When I viewed the tape of my appearance, I saw a more confident, informed woman who no longer answered questions in a nervous squeak but in a mature voice.

After Philadelphia, it was on to more cities and more morning (and sometimes evening) shows. All the while, I was chaperoned by one of the press agents from *Playboy*. The various agents served as confidantes, den mothers and cheerleaders. Warm and supportive, they were especially good at building up one's self-confidence. "Did you always know you were beautiful?" one asked sweetly.

I wanted to answer that I didn't know it until then. I was always afraid of being judged. After all, beauty is a subjective thing and I feared people would see my photos, look at me or see me on television and wonder what I was doing in that magazine. I was afraid they would think that I was not pretty enough or that my figure wasn't good enough.

The press agents and I ate our meals together, traveled to shows together and worked together as I signed photos for those who asked for autographs. I must admit, the autograph signing seemed surreal, because I did not in any way consider myself a celebrity. But people, mostly men, seemed eager to get one.

While on the tour, I called New York several times a day to keep up with what was happening on the work front and on the home front. Peter told me daily how much he missed me and that he was doing artwork for yet another funeral home. My girl-friends were getting on with their normal lives and one night when we spoke they were all headed for a fashion show I had suggested, but now couldn't attend. "We miss you," they said.

"I miss you, too," I said. There was truth to the statement, I was finding out, that life on the road could be very lonely.

I had never been afraid to fly, but on the next part of the trip the small plane chartered for us from Buffalo to Baltimore hit an extended patch of turbulence and made for a very rocky ride. I made the sign of the cross when we landed and tried to act composed when I met the reporter from the *Baltimore Sun* who had come to interview me. His review was kind. He said of me, "The brunette is far more attractive in person than the typical *Playboy* pastry that she portrayed in the magazine."

When I arrived back in New York after the publicity tour, I received a call from the producers of *PM Magazine*, a popular magazine format show, hosted by a good-looking young man named Matt Lauer, now the co-host of the *Today Show*. Within days we filmed my episode. Matt substituted for the corpse as I straightened his tie and smoothed his suit jacket for the camera, simulating what I did for the deceased.

Then the producers of Regis Philbin's cable show called and said they wanted to book me on the show. Regis, along with his wife Joy, pretended to make his funeral arrangements with me. The segment was meant to be illustrative, to show how pre-arrangements are done, and of course, Regis being Regis, it was also fun.

Next, I was interviewed by a writer for *People* magazine, but the article never ran. I was learning that some things didn't materialize and others I never got to see. People would call me and tell me of things they had read about me, things that I never could track down, from Associated Press wire stories to articles in college newspapers. In fact, several students called wanting to write college papers about me.

Late in May, Elizabeth Norris called to tell me I had been booked on the *Phil Donahue Show*, along with four other *Playboy* models, one being Kathy Shower, the thirty-three-year-old Play-mate of The Year. Meeting Phil Donahue after years of watching his show was something I looked forward to. Hurriedly, I shopped for a new dressed for the event.

After checking into the Drake Hotel in Manhattan, I met up with Elizabeth and the other women, Kathy, Sheri Donovan, a radio disc jockey from Detroit, and Toni Westbrook, an Alaskan forest ranger. We dressed to the nines and went out to dinner, much to the delight of the restaurant management. Then we went back to one of the hotel rooms, where we sipped champagne, talked and laughed late into the night.

The day of the show, I found myself seated next to Vikki LaMotta, wife of the great heavyweight boxer Jake LaMotta. Not only was Vikki a true beauty, she had a wonderful sense of humor to boot.

"Sure, at my age they seat me next to the undertaker!" she quipped to the audience.

Phil passed around the various magazines we had appeared in to the audience members. One of the audience members mistook the other dark haired girl for me and Phil said, "Sure, you've seen one you've seen them all." Everyone laughed. Mostly the audience was kind, but a few middle-aged women did stand up and declare in strident tones, "I would never pose naked no matter how much I was paid! It's just not right!"

I was tempted to add, "I don't think you'll be asked," but I didn't.

When the show aired, Peter and some other friends kept asking me why I didn't speak up more. As there were five distinctive panelists, getting a word in hadn't been easy. "Check out who was around me," I replied. "And I'm not big on interrupting especially when I want to hear what others have to say."

Kathy and the others asked if I could stay in Manhattan and spend the next day sightseeing. As much as I would have enjoyed that, I had been beeped about a funeral assignment and had to go back to work. It certainly was a strange trip, I was thinking, to go from a national television studio to an embalming room.

CHAPTER 11

"Do You Embalm in the Nude?"

"**D**o you embalm in the nude?" a fellow undertaker asked me wryly late one afternoon. Almost six months after my appearance in *Playboy*, I was still receiving criticism from some, praise from others and attention from many. Certain colleagues who hadn't spoken two words to me in the past now barraged me with questions about what it was like to model for *Playboy*. Others resented my semi-celebrity status or chose to ignore it all together. I was no longer fazed by it all. I had returned to my old workaholic patterns, once again causing my romantic relationship to suffer. And again, I was not only repeating negative work habits, but allowing my work to intrude on every aspect of my life.

Having spent my share of time in the spotlight, I was anxious to show my colleagues my serious focus on our industry, but I soon realized that some of my colleagues expected me to move on. They seemed both surprised and resentful that I continued to do funeral work. This was reflected in the questions they asked.

"Didn't anything come of the *Playboy* layout?" became a common question.

In the beginning, I was bewildered by this query. Though I enjoyed the experience, *Playboy* had never been a means to an end—it was a one-time experience. I had no plans to leave the funeral business and attempt to forge a career in the entertainment industry. I did not think of using the industry as a springboard to vault into a new persona. Odd as it might have seemed to others, I was still stubbornly intent on becoming successful in the funeral industry.

As time went on, I was learning that my appearance in *Playboy* magazine was not endearing me to some of my colleagues. Instead, the ensuing publicity and semi-celebrity status alienated me further. I was invited on countless talk shows across the country and quoted time and time again in journalistic mediums from television to tabloids. The press seemed never to tire of the paradox of what I did for a living and what I represented. Plus, there was so much to be clever with. Headlines including, "The Merry Mortician," "Lady in Black," and "A Body To Die For," introduced me to readers.

Some in my industry were quite vocal in their denouncement of me. In their opinion I had "stooped" to exploiting the industry in the media. And often I did find myself unintentionally representing the industry—defending them actually, though I only wanted to speak for myself. My celebrity took on a life of its own and fan mail poured in from across the country, most praising me for lightening up and bringing some fun to such a dark business. Many seemed to believe that the spotlight I threw on the industry was good. Finally, I decided I would continue to defend the industry and shed some positive light on our mission.

In truth, many of my colleagues could hardly contain their envy and the little voices in their heads which must have repeatedly asked, *Why her and not me?* Understandably so. Everyone desires to be singled out for their special qualities.

A lot of people wanted to know what it felt like to pose nude and how it felt to have so many people you knew—and many you didn't—look at the pictures. I told them that on one level, it was strange, but the fact that the photographers were professionals made it much more impersonal, almost as if it was not really me.

"What did they pay you?"was another popular question.

This was a question I did not feel comfortable answering, so I said, "It was not about the money for me." Others asked what talk shows paid their guests. When I explained that talk shows usually did not pay guests, they emphatically shook their heads and declared, "I'd never go on television if they didn't pay me!" I seriously doubted that.

Then there were the people in my own industry who commented that they were offended at nudity. Peter found that amusing. "If these funeral directors find nudity so offensive, they'd better start embalming people with their clothes on."

Still others deliberately ignored the whole thing or, at least, showed no reaction when in my presence. Through it all, I remained unfazed. Admittedly, the layout proved to be more revealing and provocative than I'd expected, but I refused to be defined by what other people thought.

I didn't want to spend the rest of my life justifying myself and what I had done. In my opinion, immorality is not about taking your clothes off. It's about your standards and not betraying them.

At cemeteries, some of my colleagues pointed to me and stared, while others asked, sometimes surreptitiously, me for my autograph. And I also found myself ostracized by others, with certain funeral homes closed to me, so that I could not service clients in them. I was very surprised and hurt that one funeral director who I thought was a friend had stopped renting his facility to me. I had thought him to be so open-minded and modern; it didn't make sense. I heard secondhand that although he wished me well, he thought I should make a choice between being a funeral director or being in the public eye in an entertainment venue. In his opinion, I could not do both and expect to be taken seriously.

Another funeral director who had once written me a note thanking me for my friendship and for attending his mother's funeral, was said to be circulating a petition that demanded I be stripped of my funeral director's license.

Still others said I was a disgrace to the industry. A disgrace? Why? Because I had had some fun? Made some easy money? To me, this was the height of hypocrisy. After all, the funeral business is just that, a business. Well, gossip about me had flown around in the past and I'd survived. I'd surely survive this.

Surprisingly, most families reacted more favorably than did many colleagues. They liked the idea of having their family members' funerals handled by me. Just before the magazine hit the stands I handled the funeral of a man who had two daughters around my age. The funeral went well. The widow and her daughters, with whom I had hit it off, were quite pleased with my work and promised to keep in touch. However, when I received a message a few weeks later from my answering service to call Barbara and Liz about "the magazine," I was worried to hear their reactions. To my surprise and relief, when I called them back, they told me they thought it was great. They laughingly described how they used to play jokes on their fun-loving dad and, as Liz said, "He would have loved this!" Sharing their sense of humor, it's little wonder we became good friends.

After awhile, very few people who came in to make funeral arrangements recognized me. Time had passed. I had gained back the weight I'd lost for the photo shoot and without the professional make-up and artfully arranged hair I looked businesslike rather than glamorous. Of course, there was another major difference—I was dressed. Perhaps most of our families were not *Playboy* readers. But once in a while someone sheepishly said, "You're somebody, I know you are. I just can't put my finger on it."

I always gave the same response. "You're right, I am somebody. I'm the funeral director."

I continued to be asked to appear on television talk shows, meeting intriguing people along the way. In doing them I learned that there is a whole subculture of people who are not actually famous in the way society interprets fame, but well-known in certain circles. I got to spend time with some of these people and thus was afforded entry into walks of life I might not have been privy to otherwise. One such person of note that I met was Joe DiMona, a talented and well-respected writer with a substantial body of work to his credit. We met when I appeared on a New York talk show, *Midday Live*, hosted by Bill Boggs, a former newsman. The theme of the show on which we appeared was death and funerals. The show's panel consisted of me, a cemetery monument manufacturer and Dr. Thomas Noguchi, the famed Los Angeles coroner. Joe had co-authored Dr. Noguchi's book, *Coroner*, and had come to watch as Dr. Noguchi was being interviewed and praised for a job well done. I had already read the book and felt Joe and I had an interest in common—death. After the show, we immediately struck up a conversation. Joe gave me his number and address. "Keep in touch," he said.

The following week, he invited me to dinner at Elaine's, the venerable writers' hangout in New York City. Besides being a popular writer, he was also a lawyer and member of the Washington D.C. Bar. Best of all, he told great political anecdotes. At Elaine's he regaled me with stories and pointed out the famous in the crowded restaurant, visibly enjoying the kick I was getting from being there.

Joe took me to several parties, introducing me to many sophisticated Manhattan types. One party was hosted by a major modeling agency. Joe tried his best to get them to take test shots of me. But after looking over my 5'4" body, they bluntly told him that I was "not the type we use in our agency."

Joe and I kept in touch for a time until he began work on yet another book. He moved to Los Angeles. After one of my articles was published in *Newsday*, I thought of Joe and wondered where I could reach him. I knew he would be happy for me. I called his literary agent only to find, sadly, that he had died a year before and was buried in Westwood Cemetery, the same California cemetery where Marilyn Monroe had been laid to rest.

The rest of my time was pretty much business as usual. The dire predictions of some who thought my association with *Playboy* would finish me as a funeral director did not come true. Work continued to be steady. The same clergymen who had recommended me before my *Playboy* appearance, continued to do so. But I became uncomfortable on one occasion when I took a priest to lunch after a funeral service and he told me that several funeral directors had called to tell him about my *Playboy* photos. Graciously, he remarked, "I thought it mean-spirited of them." I'd always served his parishioners well, he said, and that was all that mattered in his eyes.

My life seemed to have taken an upward turn. Then one night, I was mugged. I was on a date with an official of the Long Shoreman's Union in Brooklyn. He often carried a gun, but perhaps it was for the best he didn't have it on him that night. We had returned to his car after dinner at a lovely restaurant in Astoria to see that his car window had been broken. When we got back to my Bayside apartment, I went upstairs to get a utensil so he could scoop the broken glass out of the car. Suddenly, just a few feet away from the car, a young man came up to me brandishing a knife. I was too stunned to scream. He held the knife perilously close to me as he quickly sliced the handle of my purse and grabbed it. Then he ran. I shouted to my boyfriend, who gave chase, but slipped on the ice and injured his shoulder. We spent the night in a local emergency room.

A few days later we took a trip to Atlantic City. After almost a week of daily massages, whirlpool baths and good food, we returned to New York, just in time for a major snowstorm and for me another funeral. The deceased was a man who had died during the same day the storm hit.

The funeral was scheduled to be held in Manhattan and I made arrangements to use a funeral home and facilities there. The body lay in the Bellevue morgue as the snow fell in thick blankets. The removal man could not make his way into the city because of the storm. We had to postpone the funeral for several days until the weather permitted driving and he could get his van on the road. On the first day of visitation, I cautiously made my way into the city. The body, I discovered, was not yet at the funeral home. The removal man soon called with excuses and I realized, to my dismay, that he hadn't removed the body from Bellevue as he had told me he would once the snow stopped. I felt terrible as I knew some family members were coming from long distances. Once he called back and told me he had finally gotten the body to the embalmer, I frantically kept calling the man at the embalming facility, who kept assuring me the body was finished and on its way to the funeral home. It wasn't. Like the removal man, the embalmer broke his promise and left me to face an understandably very angry family. I knew they were right when they said that since they were able to get to the funeral home, my tradesman should have been able to get the body there. At last the body arrived in time for the evening visitation, but by then the angry and upset family members had left. I knew I might be faced with a lawsuit, but was more troubled about the anguish the incident had caused them than any legal reprisal.

Although the family generously forgave me, I could not forgive myself for causing them additional pain.

Much to my surprise, the interest of the press in me continued and I was still being sought for talk show appearances. In fact, I learned I had become a *Jeopardy* question as well! Several excited friends who had seen the show called to tell me. The answer was: "The occupation of Alexandra Mosca who appeared in the April 1986 edition of *Playboy* Magazine." None of the contestants knew the question, but I was surely flattered.

In the spring, I was invited to appear on Detroit's morning show, along with two other women. The theme was "Women In Unusual Occupations." Upon reading the other women's press releases, I learned one worked as a master plumber and inspector for the city of Detroit and would not be staying at the hotel. The other was Allison Bly, a stunt woman from Florida. She was billed professionally as "Dynamite Lady," so named for her stunt, which used dynamite to blow up the box she was huddled in.

After arriving in Detroit late one afternoon, I left word at the reception desk in the hotel lobby for Allison, the Dynamite Lady, to join me in the hotel's atrium restaurant for dinner after she checked in.

In the restaurant I ordered an appetizer and a martini, which I sipped slowly while I waited. Before too long, a pretty young woman about my height and weight appeared before me, dressed in form-fitting, casual clothing which showed off a body in top shape.

"Hi, I'm Allison Bly!" she cheerily announced in a charming Southern accent. "I read about you. You're really weird touching all those dead people," she ribbed me good-naturedly.

"You blow yourself up in a box rigged with dynamite and you think *I'm* weird?"

We both laughed.

"Do you drink martinis with vodka or gin?" she demanded.

"Vodka."

"Me, too."

"Well, let's order you one, so you can catch up."

We couldn't stop talking as we discovered we had so much in common. An instant camaraderie enveloped us and we both experienced an intense sense of bonding. Charmingly unaffected, her sense of fun and mischief was infectious, something at this time in my life, I was sorely lacking. Allison had a bubbling enthusiasm and great appetite for life. *At last, a kindred spirit!* I thought. A woman with whom I could identify who had a uniqueness all her own, without any trace of ego.

I found myself telling her things I'd never told anyone before and she did likewise. The questions flew back and forth. "What was it like to be an average young woman, suddenly getting so much attention?" "What were good things to talk about on television?" "The right things to wear?" "Why were so many other women so jealous and mean spirited?" "Why couldn't they see it was all in fun?" At 5:00 A.M., we fell into our rooms and beds.

Two hours later the wake-up call came.

We met in the lobby and slugged down coffee, barely able to keep our eyes open. A limousine whisked us to the studio, where we met the third talk show participant and began our appearance on Detroit's morning talk show.

We were told to introduce ourselves with catchy, albeit silly, little teasers. Audience members then took a guess as to what we did for a living.

Allison's line was, "My job's a blast!"

Mine was, "I'm the last person you want to meet!"

After the show ended we were driven to the airport together, where we had lunch while waiting for our flights.

Allison left me with an autographed copy of her interview in a recent issue of *Woman's World* magazine and a promise to write. She did and asked if I would be a celebrity guest in her act whenever I could get time off. I agreed and she sent me a costume, first a little tank top with "Dynamite Lady" emblazoned on the front, which was worn with short shorts. Later, Allison had a sequined costume made for me to compliment hers.

We met in locations along the eastern seaboard. Some were bigger cities, like Myrtle Beach, South Carolina, Charlotte, North Carolina, and Virginia Beach, Virginia. Others were smaller towns; Gastonia, North Carolina, Watertown, New York, Scranton and Reading, Pennsylvania, Hagerstown, Bowie, Frederick and Aberdeen, Maryland and Great Gorge, New Jersey. Sometimes we stayed in luxury hotels; for instance in Great Gorge, we spent five days at the old Playboy Resort. Other times, the motels were no more than road stops. That was part of the fun. We ate in local restaurants, our favorites being the authentic Maryland Crab Houses. Together, we mulled over our press clippings, griped about less-than-stellar talk show appearances and traded funeral and media anecdotes. Quickly, we became best girlfriends.

Most of the time, Allison performed at minor league ball parks, sometimes before the game, other times at the seventh inning stretch or after the game. It was a good thing we both liked baseball.

Several hours before the game started, Allison began to build her box out of Styrofoam, paint it with the Dynamite Lady Insignia in red, white and blue and get the explosives ready. Sometimes, she would be interviewed by the press while she worked. On a few occasions, I was included in her interview, as the reporter found the idea of a Funeral Director assisting the Dynamite Lady made good copy.

"In my line of work, it's good to travel with your undertaker," Allison quipped. We made the front page of the *Reading Times* and later appeared together in a *Sports Illustrated* article.

I helped her get into her costume, escorted her onto the field, took her cape, handed her her helmet and gave her a hug for good luck. The announcer's voice blared over the loudspeaker, "Assisting the Dynamite Lady tonight is Alexandra Mosca, a mortician from New York City." Then I waited on the sidelines, holding my ears, knowing the explosion would be a lot louder than anyone expected. I always worried that Allison would get injured.

After the explosion, Allison was propelled for several feet and fell to the ground in a dazed state. Then I joined the ambulance volunteers (an ambulance was always kept at the ready) rushing on the field to see if she was all right.

Afterward, Allison rose, dusted herself off, waved to the crowd and left the field as her theme song, "Dynamite Lady," played and the audience cheered. For about an hour, I'd hand her the baseballs and photos her fans, patiently waiting in line, had brought for her to autograph. Then, depending on the time, we had dinner with the team owner or, if it was late, went back to the hotel to unwind. I was always sad when we parted. Being with Allison was an adventure in itself. She drove fast, played hard, had an infectious sense of fun and mischief and always made me laugh.

In my spare time in the fall of that year, I decided to act upon a long-held interest. After reading about auditions for a community theater in the *Bayside Times*, and knowing I seriously needed a diversion from the business of death, I went to the open audition of the aptly named Way Off Broadway Theater Company. I thought, How hard could this be? It's not Broadway after all. I soon learned, I couldn't have been more wrong. I watched person after talented person take the stage, read the lines, and then be dismissed by the impassive director. When my turn came, I felt totally unprepared. Afterwards, I knew my reading was poor and was not surprised to hear the director's stock dismissal phrase, "We'll let you know."

A few days later I learned I had not been chosen. I was disappointed but not surprised. Shortly thereafter, however, I learned the show had changed directors when the new director called me saying they needed a pretty girl for a non-speaking part. I jumped at the opportunity, not caring if I was just the "pretty girl," so long as I could participate.

I was required to come to all rehearsals even thought my part was so small, but I was glad I did. For it was at those rehearsals that I developed friendships with a wonderful group of people so different than my funeral industry colleagues. These talented actors were warm, generous and accepting. When they learned about my *Playboy* appearance and my work as a portrait model, they thought me a celebrity. Before long, I began spending time outside of rehearsal with the actors reading lines together, auditioning for plays and taking acting workshops.

At the end of October, I was profiled in *Newsday*. In addition to my work in the funeral business, the article mentioned my involvement in the theater group. My fellow actors all bought copies of the newspaper and made a fuss over it, one person even hanging a clipping up on the theater's bulletin board.

Although I greatly enjoyed my time with the group, I could never forget for a moment that I was funeral director, as more grave undertakings on the funeral home front beckoned to me.

CHAPTER 12

Buried in My Work

"**W**ill he rest better in the bronze casket?" a man asked me one evening as he perused the caskets in the selection room for one in which to place his father for his "eternal slumber." I looked at him uncertainly, not sure if he was serious. He was. I figured there were only a few like him, but then I met another man a few days later with the same fanciful grasp of reality. He ran his hand appreciatively over our most expensive (over ten thousand dollars!) bronze casket. "If it had a steering wheel," he said with a small smile, "I'd buy it!"

I was living, breathing and sleeping the funeral industry again, now that most of the excitement of being a *Playboy* model had receded. Nevertheless, I still was getting a few interviews as I remained some sort of curiosity. But the majority of my days were spent grappling with life and death issues and pondering my own mortality, as I examined just what it meant to die.

Are we all fated to fulfill a predetermined destiny? I wondered.

Time and again in my work as a funeral director I saw that people, just as I did, needed explanations. Unanswered questions haunted us. We were forever trying to make sense out of the senseless, looking for meaning where maybe there wasn't any. This is especially true when contemplating death. Why does someone die in a car accident? What if he had gotten behind the wheel of the car a minute earlier or later? Why did one person survive a plane crash, when others did not? Is it too simple to say, "It wasn't her time?"

I became convinced that one's date of death is written, metaphorically speaking, in some big book in the sky. Perhaps it was easier to believe this. The philosophy took away the guilt and the *what ifs* and *if onlys* people felt after someone close has died.

If you are a fatalist, you believe that each person is predestined to live a certain amount of years and die in a certain way. There is no escaping your fate. It simply is out of your control. As one of my colleagues put it, "If you're meant to get shot, you'll never be hung." Belief in fatalism also means we never will know the answers here on earth in our mortal lives. These matters are left to a higher power.

On a more earthly level, I thought about how my colleagues and I, as funeral directors, help others deal with accepting their loved ones' lives ending. What were we doing for these people? Was it enough? Could we do more? We were merely human beings. Some thought of us as vultures, preying on others' grief. Sometimes we were described in the newer literature, which favored the term, "death care industry," as caretakers of the dead. Was that all we were? Surely we were more than that. In some cultures, people who work with the dead are considered the lowest of the low. Yet, many families consider funeral directors to be people of honor and esteem. Although I couldn't get an exact fix on our role, I felt it was lodged somewhere between disposers of the dead and grief therapists. I knew one thing for certain: We couldn't do what every bereaved family wanted most, which was to bring their loved one back to life. What we could do was more basic: coordinate a meaningful funeral, lend a shoulder on which to lean, provide an ear to be a sounding board and offer a way to make the funeral process more bearable.

I tried always to find a kind word, to get the family involved with the funeral process so that no matter how small the detail seemed, it made them feel they had helped. For in this way, I knew they would feel closer to their loved ones.

"Who selected this dress?" I would ask family members when they brought clothing in for the deceased, knowing it was one of them.

"Oh, cousin Sophie did," someone would answer.

"It's lovely. Such a perfect color. Your mother will look beautiful."

I saw all of them beam with the satisfaction of having contributed to an important part of the funeral process. They felt a connection.

Funeral directors frequently say that all funerals are essentially the same and yet, at the same time, very different. Circumstances, personalities and expressions of grief are the elements which vary. And some people seemed to be dealt more misfortune than anyone should have to bear. Lucille, one of my clients, was one of those people.

I first met her when a relative of hers suggested she call me. Her fifty-five-year-old husband, Donald, was terminally ill with cancer and in the last stages. I met with her in their Bensonhurst apartment and liked her immediately.

A delicate-featured woman in her late forties, she was warm and kind. In the midst of talking about funeral plans for the impending death of her husband, she was concerned about me: "Have you had lunch? You need to eat, too. Let me fix you something." Lucille, a phenomenal cook, always wanted to feed people. Italian sausage, braciole, pork chops, succulent meatballs and tomato sauce good enough to bottle and sell were among the foods she regularly prepared. Though she was of modest means financially, she bought quality food. In this way, she showed her caring for others, fussing over them in a motherly way. When I left her home that day, not only had we gotten the difficult arrangements taken care of so she could concentrate on their last days together, but I knew I had made a friend, as well.

Not long afterwards on a blustery cold day in January, Lucille's husband died. We were to hold the wake at a nearby funeral home. That morning, I stopped by the trade embalmer to see how the deceased looked. I was dissatisfied. His mouth was just not right. *John Cox was right*, I thought, remembering a colleague who provided much valuable advice when I started out and once told me the mouth was the most important feature on a body. If the mouth doesn't look right, no other facial feature will either. A bad mouth throws everything out of alignment. Knowing I couldn't allow the family see their loved one in that state, I immediately called Bob, an associate I respected, who graciously offered to come over right away and work on the problem.

Bob fussed with Donald's mouth, eventually transforming it into a more natural and pleasing shape. In the meantime, I set up the flower pieces that had arrived. Bob finished his work within fifteen minutes of Lucille's arrival. With a sigh of relief, I escorted Lucille, her daughters and her large extended family into the chapel to view Donald. It struck me once again that the first viewing was one of the four most traumatic events of a death. The news of the death is, of course, the first, especially if that death is sudden and unexpected. The second event is the first viewing; the third comes the morning of the funeral at the time of the last goodbye, before the casket is closed forever; lastly, the final disposition of the body.

How can people possibly bear this? I wondered, knowing that the first viewing of the deceased confirms the reality of death. This was what we had been taught in school and was repeated in all of the funeral literature. It facilitated the acceptance and healing process, as well. So what of the people who choose not to view the body, even briefly? Did they never get to the next stage of the grieving process? Did they not accept the "reality" of death?

For some reason, I became even more affected when I watched the reaction of an elderly person to the first viewing, confronted with the reality of having to say goodbye to his or her long-time spouse. Sad as it was to see a younger couple separated by death, there was something so poignant about the person left behind after forty, fifty or sixty years of marriage. I felt it must be truly like losing a part of yourself, losing your other half. In the case of a younger couple, there was the probability of new love, certainly there was more life to come. There were rarely such possibilities for older people. How did he or she go on? Did they wish they too had gone? Did they ever get over it? I often overheard older people at funerals talk about how awful it was to be the one left behind.

At the last viewing, when family members and friends go up to the casket for final goodbyes, some people just look, some touch, some kiss and others cling to the body, weeping hysterically as they are led away. I felt sure that if it were me in that position, I would be one of the latter.

The day of Donald's viewing, after the afternoon visitation hours ended, Lucille invited me to join her family, which included her two daughters, Roseann and Dolores, for dinner. I always felt uncomfortable being invited to eat meals with the grieving families. What if they wanted to talk about things I shouldn't hear? What if I had disappointed them in any way? In this case, however, I could see Lucille sincerely wanted me to come along and I did.

The morning of the funeral dawned sunny and cold. I arrived at the funeral home an hour before the family was scheduled to be picked up by the limousine. I had paperwork to do and people to pay. I first checked the body, as was my habit, then was introduced to Sal, who would be driving the hearse for me. He had worked for the funeral home, where his sister manned the front desk, as a hearse driver for twenty years and took his job very seriously. He was just as friendly and helpful as he was quiet and unobtrusive.

As I led the prayers, Sal began the responses so the mourners could easily follow along. He coordinated the men, then loaded the flowers into the hearse, all with split second timing, while the mourners were saying their last good-byes.

Despite my sadness for Lucille that day, as the funeral director I was growing concerned. People were lingering a little too long with their final farewells at the casket. I glanced at my watch, knowing we were close to being late for church. I gently coaxed people out of the chapel and to their cars. I gave some of them tissues or a cup of water; sometimes I walked to their car with them. Relatives or friends lead others away from the casket into the car. I knew Lucille didn't care about being late for church that day and that she would gladly forego the Mass entirely, if she would instead be allowed another forty-five minutes with her loved one. But we had to go to the church and I gently told Lucille it was time to leave and guided her out to the limousine.

I knew that was best because religion is a great comfort for true believers. And Lucille, a devout Catholic, certainly was a believer. After a beautiful Mass in St. Dominic's in Bensonhurst, we headed to Hidden Hills Cemetery, where we endured almost an hour's wait for our turn.

I was quite upset about the long wait, not for myself, but for Lucille and her family. Meanwhile, Sal and I talked. He tried to calm me about the wait.

"It's not your fault," he soothed.

"That doesn't matter. The family and especially Lucille are going to be upset by this. It's the last thing they need."

When it was finally our turn to go to the grave, there were further problems.

To my horror, the row of graves was open trench style. The caskets of the previous burials were clearly visible. As a funeral director, I was horrified. *What must the family be going through?* I asked myself. Lucille sat rigidly in the car, too sickened to get any closer and see casket after casket visible under the ground. I was heartsick, blaming myself for this. I didn't know, but thought I should have. And I had suggested this cemetery when Lucille told me she wanted a cemetery in Brooklyn. My first instinct had been to suggest another, but thought the higher cost would present a financial hardship for her.

On the ride back from the cemetery, I was visibly upset about the way the cemetery had handled the burial. Sal continued to tell me it wasn't my fault. Then he told me something that surprised and made me feel a bit better about the day.

"You've made quite an impression on everyone these past few days, the way you handle yourself as a funeral director, the way you care about the people who are grieving. Your sincerity is so touching. When we heard you were renting here, we all wondered what you'd be like...given what we'd heard...well, you know what I mean," he said shyly. "Now that I know who you are, I hope to work with you again soon."

"I hope the same."

Not long after that the owner of the funeral home began to call me to do their lady attendant work. It was a big account and I began to spend more and more time in Bensonhurst, where I often visited Lucille and her family after work.

One night about a year and a half later, I received a page from my answering service; a woman named Dolores had died at

Maimonides Hospital. It passed through my mind that Lucille's daughter was named Dolores and so was her sister. I brushed this dark thought away, telling myself that there were probably a lot of women named Dolores living in the area. Still, I couldn't let it go. "What is the full name of this woman?" I could not help asking the admitting nurse, afraid of the answer. When she told me, I knew the worst. It was Lucille's daughter. With a heavy heart, I set out for Lucille's apartment, trying to summon up strength I hoped I had left in reserve.

Lucille's sister Toni answered the door with red-rimmed eyes. After embracing me, she led me into the bedroom where Lucille, eyes swollen from crying, sat on the bed. There were no words. Later, making the arrangements, I couldn't fight the emotions that overwhelmed me. As I read the words Lucille and Toni chose for the prayer cards, my eyes filled with tears.

> *Do not stand at my grave and weep*
> *I am not there, I do not sleep*
> *I am a thousand winds that blow*
> *I am the diamond glints on snow*
> *I am the sunlight on ripened grain*
> *I am the gentle autumn's rain*
> *When you awaken in the morning's hush*
> *I am the swift uplifting rush*
> *Of quiet birds in circled flights*
> *I am the soft star that shines at night*
> *Do not stand at my grave and cry*
> *I am not there*
> *I did not die*

The poem, sometimes cited as written by "Anonymous" and sometimes cited as written by Mary Frye in 1932, was a comfort to

Lucille and her family. But still, this was one of the saddest funerals I've ever had to arrange. As she had done just a little over a year before, at the wake of her husband, Lucille once again conducted herself with immense dignity. I was touched by the depth of her nobility and courage. Although she had neither material wealth nor position, being in her company was like being in the presence of some form of regal grace. Certainly, the love and support of a large, affectionate family helped. I couldn't help but think about how alone I would be in her situation. But Lucille was enveloped, and deserved to be, in the love and promises of people who would truly be there for her and never desert her. No, that wouldn't bring her daughter back, but this sad moment would be utterly unendurable without her family around her.

Lucille told me that after her father's funeral, Dolores had shared with her a fright of being buried; so Lucille, too proud to ask for money from her family, secured a loan to buy two crypts in Brooklyn's Greenwood Cemetery.

"I can take the bus and visit," she told me.

The morning of the funeral, after the prayers and before friends filed by the casket to say goodbye, I said these words:

"Before we continue our funeral service I want to say what I'm sure everyone here is feeling. Dolores was a special young woman who was very much loved and who will be sorely missed by all her family and many friends. We were all so very fortunate to have known her." I thought I sounded trite, but I meant every word from my heart.

Lucille wanted her husband disinterred from Hidden Hills Cemetery and entombed with their daughter in Greenwood. I thought this would be simple enough, but soon found that the cemetery was unyielding, unsympathetic and unmoved by the plight of a working-class widow who had endured repeated tragedies. "I promise you," I told her, "somehow I'll get this done."

I wrote letters and made telephone calls to any agency I thought could intervene, including the cemetery board. I either received no response or negative ones. Then, with almost all avenues exhausted, providence took a hand.

Marco Polo Ristorante, an upscale, continental restaurant with a most eclectic clientele, was an eatery I frequented when working in Brooklyn. On any given night one would see Court Street lawyers, local politicians, judges, business owners and the neighborhood "wiseguys" there.

One night, several months after Lucille's daughter's funeral, I was having dinner at the restaurant with friends. Glancing around, I spotted Howard Golden, then the Brooklyn Borough President and his wife, dining at a nearby table amid the legal eagles from the nearby courthouses and the town thugs. How fortuitous. Not normally so bold, but fortified by some fine merlot and a fierce conviction to help Lucille, I trailed Mrs. Golden when she got up to go to the ladies room. As we both adjusted our make up in the large mirror, I struck up a casual conversation and we traded names. Then I got to the point. "I need to speak to your husband about an important matter," I said and explained what it was. "And while I realize he must get many such requests, he is my last hope," I quickly added, knowing she wanted to get back to her table.

"Alexandra, call his office. I'll give him your name," she said over her shoulder as she walked out. So I did, first thing Monday morning. I followed my plea with an impassioned letter and was truly grateful when the Borough President's office interceded. Hidden Hills Cemetery was ordered to buy the grave back from Lucille. Now her husband's remains could be moved!

The cemetery owners, however, were very angry with me. I didn't care. I felt as if we had won a great victory. By now Lucille had become to me a figure of poignancy and dignity, who bore her grief with astonishing courage and grace. On December 30, Lucille signed the disinterment order.

Sal accompanied me the day of the disinterment. When we arrived at Hidden Hills, he offered to take the papers into the office for me.

"No," I said. "I did what I felt was right and I want to see it through."

"Well, are you scared?"

"Scared? No, I'm not scared." It was the truth. "What's the worst they can do, force me to be buried here myself?" I asked wryly as I stepped out of the hearse.

Lucille's husband was disinterred from Hidden Hills Cemetery and entombed in Greenwood Cemetery, side by side with his daughter, later that day. It took many hours, but was so satisfying. I hoped Lucille could now find some measure of peace.

On the way back that night, Sal and I stopped for dinner at a Brooklyn trattoria.

At the table, Sal raised his wine glass gesturing to me.

"I've got to hand it to you, Alex," he said smiling. "You said you'd get it done and you have. Truthfully, I didn't think it was going to happen, but you were so determined."

"I promised her. My efforts seem like a small thing contrasted with what Lucille has had to bear. I hope she can overcome her grief and go on with her faith intact despite the repeated tragedies in her life."

He nodded. "You're a good funeral director, Alexandra. I told you what we heard about you before you came here. It sounded like you were some sort of princess. You're not. I've seen you do things for people that would surprise those directors who criticize you."

"Thank you, Sal. I really appreciate you telling me that."

"Well, you've come a long way."

I smiled as his glass touched mine and we sipped a very fine wine.

I had, in fact, come a long way. It was then I realized that not only had circumstances changed, I had too. I had grown up. Of course, it hadn't happened all at once. But suddenly I knew with a stunning clarity that not in spite of, but *because* I had chosen to live my life amid death, I felt fulfilled.

CHAPTER 13

Only the Dead Know Brooklyn

The click...click...click of my high heeled shoes on the Italian marble floor reverberated throughout the quiet church as I somberly made my way down the aisle behind the gleaming bronze casket, bereaved family in tow. As always, the pallbearers waited at attention for me at the altar while I seated the family. I then joined the men in front of the altar and we genuflected in unison.

Afterwards, solemnly, with hands clasped, the pallbearers followed me down the side aisles and out the massive, gilded front doors of the church. Once the doors closed behind us, we were free to shake our solemn personas and speak. We had been working since before dawn and needed coffee to stay awake for what promised to be a long day. Five of the men piled into the back of the gleaming black limousine, while the driver held the front passenger's door open for me. Our limo cruised along the crowded Brooklyn streets, weaving around numerous double-parked cars. It always surprised me how much attention we garnered. People looked startled seeing a female face in the hearse. Spotting an Italian bakery up ahead, the driver pulled over to the curb and we got out. Opening the door of the bakery, the fragrance of coffee and freshly baked pastries wafted out into the early morning air.

Once inside, we ordered coffee along with assorted rolls and pastries. Perched on delicate, black bentwood chairs, we sipped the hot brew and enjoyed the delectable baked goods.

After ten or fifteen minutes I stood up. "Let's get back to the church, okay guys?" I said, "I'm nervous the Mass will soon end and we'll be late."

"Sure Al. Whatever you say," was the response as the men gathered up the paper cups and napkins, tossed them into the trash can and filed out the door.

In the year since Lucille's daughter's funeral, I was covering the Benson Funeral Home, making funeral arrangements, directing funerals and preparing the deceased women for visitation. Gaspare and Ursula Benson had been impressed with my work when I had twice rented their facilities. To get me on board as an employee, they promised more than they could or intended to deliver. And working for another family who lived above the funeral home, as they did, brought with it the same problems I had encountered in the past. There was too much familiarity. Once again, I was privy to private family feuds and personal idiosyncrasies.

Yet, for the most part, I liked the work. Our clientele was friendly and polite and I was working with a good group of employees. We were always in sync and this staff, unlike some I'd worked with in the past, seemed to respect me and not resent the authority of a woman. Maybe it was because they were relieved to learn their pall bearing assignment was with me and not Mrs. Benson, the owner of the establishment.

I, too, had problems with Mrs. Benson. She gave me a new appreciation of Rae, my first female boss, who may have been tough on me, but was not cruel. While it was initially disconcerting to me that Rae cursed like a longshoreman and barked orders at me, I could deal with what I came to call her earthiness. Her tough street persona may have disguised to others the sincerity and compassion that lay underneath, but not to me. I learned she had a big heart.

By comparison, Ursula Benson, a tall, impeccably dressed woman who favored tailored, almost masculine suits, not only looked glacial and intimidating, she *was* cold, calculating and snobbish. For all her airs, however, in truth she was no more than an aging harridan who no one took seriously. Mean and vindictive, showing utter contempt for the families she served, she surely was in the wrong field. She seemed unmoved by others' pain, never gave compliments and relentlessly blasted her employees' work. Behind her back we referred to her as Cruella Deville. There was never a moment in her presence when I felt I could drop my guard. She had a chip on her shoulder, an axe to grind with life and even the clergy kept their distance. Once I commented to a priest, "Ursula doesn't look old."

His response was, "She doesn't look real!"

Her husband, Gaspare Benson, who had been in the business all his life, was now nothing more than an old codger, regularly imploring the pallbearers and drivers to "feel my muscles."

Gaspare and Ursula liked to think they had trained the world in the art of embalming and cosmetology. While working for them I received many compliments on my work, for which they took the credit, leaving me to wonder how I had managed all those years before I met them. In fact, they took credit for a lot of things. The tall tales they spun were outlandish. Not only did Gaspare tell people he had been summoned to Rome to embalm one of our Popes, Ursula, as the story went, claimed her ancestors had founded the Bensonhurst section of Brooklyn and as an homage, encouraged her husband to legally change their ethnic surname to Benson.

Gaspare made a big show of cosmetizing a body, forcing us to watch as he poured on the dramatics, finishing by smacking the deceased's face with a huge powder puff, bits of powder flying in every direction.

Mercifully, this dysfunctional couple spent little time in New York, preferring their California residence instead. As long as they stayed away, things ran smoothly. Left in the care of their son, Gaspare, Jr., a man my age with a nervous habit of shaking his leg, the business did well. Gaspare, Jr., in spite of his tortured family relations, tried to relate to others and was a big improvement compared to his parents.

They did things big in Brooklyn. Sal often referred to some of the grand funerals at the Benson Funeral Home as "Broadway Productions." Before long, the neighborhood people and even the Benson Funeral Home became very dear to me. The families I served in Brooklyn were among the warmest, most appreciative people I've been privileged to know. In spite of their grief when a death occurred, they cared very much about doing what they considered the "right thing." I knew their efforts were sincere and not for reasons of "showiness," but I had trouble understanding why modest, working class families shared the odd goal of saving money for "the best funeral money could buy." I felt downright uncomfortable when making arrangements with a bereaved family of modest means who insisted on "the best." There were often so many floral pieces sent to the funeral home before a wake, the viewing rooms evoked images of lush botanical gardens. However, somehow they never thought they had spent enough, especially when it came to flowers.

"Where did they get the perception that they had to spend their last nickel?" I muttered. I tried to tell the clients that a funeral should be a tribute to a life lived, but not a financial hardship for those left behind. Though they seemed grateful that I was trying to save them money, they still insisted on spending lavishly. In addition to the massive funeral floral pieces, caskets were usually top of the line, rows of limousines were not uncommon and there was a formality, a solemn, sacred ritual to funerals that seemed to be exclusive to the "borough of Churches," as Brooklyn was sometimes called. After much agonizing, I decided that the final choice was theirs and tried to keep my mind on making the best, most efficient funeral arrangements I could. Breezing down the main roads in a hearse after a burial, strains of a Frank Sinatra tune playing softly, we often stopped for a couple of hot dogs at the world famous Nathan's of Coney Island. The grandeur gone, Coney Island was now run-down and often the site of violent confrontations and criminal activities. However, we felt safe as we double parked the hearse to order lunch. In an unsafe environment, we were protected by that universal symbol of death. Dangerous-looking people kept their distance from the undertakers.

As the months passed, I made some dear friends and I fell in love with Brooklyn. In love enough to move there for a time. To be closer to work, I told myself. Some of my friends were amused. "People move out of Brooklyn, not into it." But in my eyes, it was a mythological place that loomed larger than life.

In fact, I encountered requests for some of my most unusual funeral arrangements there. AIDS deaths had become more common and we were beginning to get our share at the funeral home. I fought back tears over one young man, wasted by the AIDS's virus, who valiantly came to see me to make arrangements for his funeral service in order to spare his mother the heartache.

With tears in his eyes, he told me of the recent death of his lover and beseeched me that when his turn came, "You must cover the red marks," (the result of carposi sarcoma) which had scarred his lover and left a horrible, lasting impression on him. He was twenty-six years old. Way too young to be dying. Just thinking about his plight made my stomach knot.

"They're doing a lot of research. People are living longer," I offered lamely, trying to voice some words of encouragement.

"It won't be soon enough for me," he said with sad resignation.

"Don't say that. Don't give up hope. Do you take vitamins? Are you eating right...?"

"Thank you for caring, but it's too late for me."

"It's never too late. Where there's life there's hope." Unfortunately, he was right and I was wrong. Six months later I handled his funeral.

Another AIDS death I encountered found a wife making the funeral arrangements accompanied by her late husband's male lover.

"Please keep this confidential," she implored me.

I promised, admiring her understanding and compassion.

Then there was Greenwood Cemetery, with which I fell in love on my first visit. As Sal skillfully maneuvered the hearse through the meandering cemetery roads, he delighted in pointing out the monuments of note, filling me in on the history behind those that had become legendary.

"There's the bride!" he announced jubilantly one Saturday, after locating an ornately detailed monument. He parked the hearse in front of a life-sized statue of a young girl dressed in full, marble-hard bridal regalia.

"She died on her wedding day," Sal explained knowingly. "Next time, I'll take you to see the guy who died in his bathtub."

Sal's sister, Flo, who handled the desk at the Benson Funeral Home, was quite a character. An attractive, no nonsense woman, she never hesitated to speak her mind. "What barn you out of?" she'd ask the new livery drivers, speaking out of the corner of her mouth. "Barn" was an old slang term for garage and proved just how long Flo had been in the business. They both liked me and Sal and Flo were quick to tell me that "Every family says how nice you are." Flo also told me the other Brooklyn undertakers were curious about me, asking, "How is she as an undertaker? What's she like as a person?" I remained an object of curiosity to many of my peers.

That summer, I flew out to Los Angeles with a friend to tape an appearance on the revival of the famous game show, *To Tell The Truth*, in which two impersonators and the real person tried to confuse the audience. It was Allison who had told the producers about me. She was taping the show as well, a month after me.

The show went all out for the guests, putting us up in a luxurious hotel, allotting plenty of spending money and a rented car to get us around. We had to drive ourselves to the studio in Burbank, the same studio where the Johnny Carson show was taped. The morning I drove into the crowded lot and tried to park the car, I found myself beeping the horn with impatience at the person in front of me.

She opened the car window and shouted, "You must be from New York!" It turned out she was the foremost women's billiard champ and was taping the show as well. Later, we sat together and laughed about the way we met.

One entire day was a dress rehearsal. I met the other two women who would be "impersonating" me. They had read my press kit and impressed me with how much they knew about the funeral industry. They were well prepared for the questions.

Several shows were taped the same day and I met a score of interesting people. In addition to the billiard champ, I became acquainted with a "little person" who had played in *The Wizard of Oz* and teenaged quintuplets who appeared in commercials and were scheduled to be guests on the Carson show.

On the day of the show, which was live, a friend who had accompanied me to Los Angeles drove us to the studio.

"Don't be so nervous," he admonished. "It's just television."

Then I said the oddest thing. "But it's what I do."

"No," he corrected, "you're a funeral director. That's what you do."

The show went well. My impersonators' answers were so good, no one on the panel voted for me. We won three thousand dollars, to be split among the three of us. At the end of the show, when we chatted with the panel they praised me for pretending so well that I was clueless about the funeral industry. I wanted to laugh. It wasn't good acting that made my answers fool them. I was so nervous I could hardly speak. I still got stage fright when I had to talk on camera.

When the show aired about a month later, I was told the entire staff of the casket company with whom I usually worked huddled around a television set someone had brought in. There was something so amusing and endearing about these men watching *To Tell The Truth* to see me.

The trip to Los Angeles had been fun, but it was quickly back to business. Months after, on a dismal November morning, the clapping of thunder echoed its strident tones across the vast expanse of an awakening city. Huge storm clouds were forming into a solid mass of darkened sky that hovered over the city like a dense black curtain. I shivered thinking it was some diabolical design of nature. A cold wind swept over the roof tops whistling through the courtyards and back alleys of a thousand tenement houses, spilling trash cans and sending their covers rattling into the streets.

It was the worst kind of day to direct a funeral.

"I feel so depressed," I told the hearse driver.

"Well, naturally. What could be more depressing than going to a funeral, especially on a miserable day like this?"

"No, it's not that. Conducting a funeral whatever the weather is my job. No, this morning something is wrong. I feel it in my gut."

The first evidence that showed I was right came when I saw the look on the monsignor's face as we entered the church. We had no crucifix. The family had not opted for one. The priest stopped the funeral and from the altar demanded one of us go back to the funeral home and get a crucifix. "I'll wait," he said in a frosty, authoritarian voice we dared not disobey.

Of all the religious services I attended in my role of funeral director, I found the Catholic burial rite to be the most beautiful. Part of the ending, "May the Angels come to welcome you. May the Martyrs lead you into the new and eternal city, Jerusalem,"always made my heart lift.

Later that day at another funeral, it took us much longer than we anticipated to return from our coffee break due to a heavy downpour that stopped traffic. I felt a sinking feeling in the pit of my stomach as I saw the priest, with the mourners, in the vestibule of the church. The Mass had already ended. Embarrassed beyond words, the pallbearers and I dashed up the stairs and they went into the church and took hold of the casket. I wondered if the family realized we had messed up.

Most of the time my duties went smoothly, but often screw-ups came in cycles. A few nights later, well after ten o'clock which was our official closing hour, I saw three people approaching the office. I knew it was a "walk-in" by the solemn expressions on their faces and the clothing the young woman carried. Physically and mentally tired, wanting to go home and get some sleep, I wished they had called and made an appointment for the next morning. After all, there was nothing I could do for them at this late hour. Nevertheless, I asked them to explain their needs. The body, they told me, had to be picked up at the hospital.

Then they thrust a worn housedress at me. I eyed it disdainfully and asked, incredulous, "You want her to wear *that?*" Quickly catching myself as I realized how I sounded, I added, "Then that's what she'll wear."

All the way home, I berated myself for my lack of sensitivity.

On still another morning, well before eight o'clock, I saw a balding man coming my way. "Can't a person even drink a cup of coffee?" I murmured, irritated. Then I looked closer at him. I could always tell when someone was there to make funeral arrangements; it was imprinted on his or her face. I pushed my irritation away and went out to usher the man into the office.

"Who passed away?" I asked, my pen poised to take the pertinent information. No response. The tall, thin man hesitated. I looked up. In whispered words that were barely audible, he said, "My son, he hung himself this morning."

"Where is he now?" I asked more gently. How petty and guilty I felt over being annoyed at having missed a cup of coffee.

And although he sat across from me, woodenly, stoically answering my questions, the pain in his eyes spoke volumes. Over the years I prided myself on becoming quite adept at deciphering between genuine grief and that which was put on for effect. This man's grief was so raw it was palpable.

Not long after the sorrowful funeral for the boy who had hung himself, Sal began to talk about retiring and moving to

Florida. I was happy for him, but sad for me. He was my favorite person with whom to work and if he left, I knew I wouldn't last much longer myself. He had made himself the buffer between me, Gaspare and Ursula.

After Sal left, the funeral home became more and more lonely. The Benson family, who had no loyalty to anyone, fired their embalmers. These were men I had enjoyed working with for a long time. Now, I had no allies in my camp. My own business had really peaked in those years, however, and I had less and less time available for that funeral business. Yet I couldn't seem to bring myself to just up and leave. I needed the decision to leave to be made for me. I knew well that people often stayed in unsatisfactory situations because they were comfortable and the job was predictable and offered a measure of security. That's what was occurring for me. *Funeral work is so tough to get*, I thought. *What if I give this up and can't find enough extra work to sustain me elsewhere? What if I make a mistake by leaving? There will be no going back.* Of course, if the decision was taken out of my hands and I was let go, I believed it would be part of fate's plan and I would have to move on.

That same year, a funeral magazine based in Florida contacted me about doing an interview. They wanted to know how I had fared during the four years after appearing in *Playboy*. The article was entitled "Life After *Playboy*" and was an interview in question and answer form.

Among the questions: "Would you say that your decision to pose has had a negative impact on your career?" "Has time smoothed over the problems you encountered with your peers?" "Has this experience affected your feelings about your career?"

I was also asked how I avoided taking the pressure of the job home with me. Their last question was, "How do you handle death all the time without losing your appetite for life?"

My answer was, "Ideally, I think the funeral business can teach you how to live better, that life is something to be enjoyed, not endured, which is part of the reason I did *Playboy*—to experience as much of life as I could." My response, I thought, was very telling.

After the article appeared, I took several weeks off and went to Florida with Peter to see my friend Allison and to get some rest. We stayed on Florida's West Coast, in St. Petersburg's Beach at the Don Cesar, my favorite hotel. Dubbed the Pink Palace by its guests, the hotel has an interesting legacy and was purported to be a favorite haunt of F. Scott and Zelda Fitzgerald. While there, I stocked up on the distinctive perfume they sold through their own label. Unable to be gotten anywhere else, the distinctive scent wafted through every part of the hotel, as almost all the guests took to wearing it.

Allison and I spent many hours on the beach, swimming, lying in the sun, parasailing, jet skiing and playing volleyball. Allison always seemed to bring out the athleticism I didn't know I had. We also posed for Peter, who shot over a dozen rolls of film. Some of the best pictures he took of us, frolicking on the beach like two teenaged girls without a care in the world, appeared in a popular swimsuit magazine.

One night, the writer from the funeral magazine who had done the recent piece on me came to the hotel with her husband to join us for dinner. During the evening, she told me how even Florida funeral directors were interested in my career.

After a while, feeling totally relaxed and renewed, I realized that I truly didn't want to leave and go back to the Benson Funeral Home. I prayed Gaspare and Ursula would let me go when I returned to New York. In my mind, I already had moved on. I wanted the thought to become reality. I wanted to get on with my dreams.

The flight back to New York was rocky, really rocky and at one point, when the airplane dropped hundreds of feet in a fit of turbulence, I had a vision of the beautiful young woman killed in the Avianca Airlines crash upon whom I had worked before I left for Florida. A vision of her made-up face lying on the satin pillow in the casket kept flashing through my mind as the airplane rumbled and pitched. A plane crash was, to my mind, one of the worst ways to go and I silently wished I hadn't worked on that corpse before my trip.

Fortunately, we landed safely and the rest of the year was so active and flew by so fast that it didn't leave me much time to dwell on my discontent with my place of employment. I did several more talk shows, Dr. Ruth's included. I liked Ruth Westheimer, who was as sweet and kind as she appeared on television and very concerned about the comfort of her guests. After a day spent being treated with interest and respect, I was whisked back home in a big, black limousine.

I was in my apartment only minutes when my beeper sounded. That really brought me back to earth. I was not a semi-celebrity of any kind, but a funeral director at the service of families and colleagues, alike.

However, a week later the lovely note I received from the producers of Dr. Ruth's show, thanking me for being a part of the telecast, made me feel appreciated. It read in part, "The show really worked beautifully and you brought style and charm to the program that everyone around here is talking about."

Supermarket tabloids, too, often printed amusing little stories about me. Stories about Allison were also in the tabloids and we'd pick up one another's and read them over the phone, laughing. Busy as I was, I found time to join Allison on the road that summer. Time passed and I continued working hard as autumn came and went.

Finally, my prayers were answered. At the beginning of the New Year, the Benson's cleaned house and I was let go. For too long I had been plagued by inertia and the fear of not getting new work, thus finding it impossible to quit of my own volition. Now I was relieved and happy to be out of that place.

I had bigger aspirations.

CHAPTER 14

It's a Dying Business

After my relationship with the Bensons was severed, I found myself in a contemplative mode. I was thinking about what the future held and whether or not I'd ever see some of my dreams realized. Meanwhile, life was going on around me and in some cases, sadly ending.

My friend, Camille, the first person to entrust me with a funeral and a lifelong smoker, had been diagnosed with advanced lung cancer. Her son called to tell me she had already been hospitalized. The next day I went to visit her.

Pale, devoid of make-up and dressed in a drab hospital-issue nightgown, this was not the glamorous, upbeat woman I had known all my life. She was scared and so was I. I didn't want to lose her and did not believe it would happen, in spite of evidence to the contrary. I was just like many of my clients, who thought that no one they loved ever would die.

Camille and I held hands and talked about mundane matters. Her loving husband, John, was there, supportive as always. They had one of the most loving, affectionate marriages I had ever seen.

"I'm scared," she said suddenly. "I'm afraid I'm going to die."

"Don't think that," I said, holding her hand tightly.

"You think I'm going to be alright?"

"Yes, I think so." I said, hoping against hope.

"I look terrible. I have no makeup on. I haven't been able to get my hair done."

"You could never look terrible," I tried to assure her. "When you come home, I'll come over and we'll put makeup on."

"Yes, that will be fun."

As I left, she asked me to apply some blush to her cheeks. I did and then pressed the compact into her palm.

"Keep this while you're in the hospital. And remember, when you come home, we'll do the rest."

She never did go home. She died a month later, on a snowy winter February night. I got a call in the middle of the night from her son, telling me the very sad news.

The next day, as I fixed Camille's dress and applied her cosmetics, the cosmetics I had promised to apply when she came home, tears streamed down my face. She was the closest person to me who had ever died.

A number of years before, Camille, John and I had gone to a local Catholic cemetery, where the couple selected graves for themselves. But when Camille died, John told me he wanted her cremated. I was extremely surprised by this, given that they had purchased the graves. John told me she had said once in conversation that she wished to be cremated rather than buried when the time came. This conversation, he said, took place before she had gotten ill.

I was troubled by his words, as people sometimes say things regarding their funeral plans, that they do not really mean. Yet, I didn't feel I had the right to try and talk him out of it. I just hoped he was certain cremation was Camille's wish. And while I believe that the reasons for choosing burial, cremation or entombment are all, to a major degree, except when following religious dictates, a perception or a feeling one has about one's mortal body, I am a believer in the comfort offered by cemeteries.

Cemeteries, to me, are an oasis of calm, serenity and comfort offering a place for continued communion with deceased loved ones. It is a real place to go and visit, to feel the presence of those no longer alive, even to engage in conversation with them.

However, I followed John's instructions. Camille was cremated. Several weeks after her funeral, I brought her cremains (ashes) to her son's Staten Island home, where John had been staying since his wife's death.

It was a somber beginning to the day, but as the hours passed, we talked on and on about Camille, looking at old photos and remembering so many good times. It was a comfort to all of us. In the midst of sharing these memories, my beeper sounded. I saw the telephone number. It was Sonny Calabrese. His timing was always the worst.

"I have a visitation beginning tomorrow afternoon," he told me. It was one of the rare times I had a day's notice when he needed my services. I explained to him, "I will need to be at your funeral home early, as I have to travel to Suffolk County out on Long Island later in the day to work on a difficult case."

A tragically ironic, as well as difficult case it was, too. The aunt of Frankie, a colleague of mine, had been killed when the car she and her husband were traveling in had been struck, as they pulled to the side of the road to fix a flat tire. They had driven down and back to Florida for vacation because they feared the dangers air travel could sometimes pose.

"Please make her viewable," Frankie said. "If anyone can, you can."

The way Frankie had described the situation, I knew several hours of difficult reconstructive work lay ahead for me the next day. I was worried about making both my earlier commitment plus this one.

"Please have everything ready when I arrive tomorrow morning," I said to Sonny. "I'll be very tight for time."

"No problem," Sonny assured me.

Still, I felt concerned.

The following day dawned sunny and cold. I woke early, ready to make my way to the Calabrese Funeral Home. I dressed quickly and, at the last moment, put on my new diamond bracelet. "This will lift my spirits," I murmured to myself. To put my mind at ease that the funeral home staff was ready for me, I first called the casket company to see if the casket had been delivered.

"They didn't order any casket," I was told by one of the workers.

"They didn't?" I was getting a bad feeling.

"Maybe they are using one out of their showroom."

"Maybe," I hoped. Just in case, I called the funeral home and Sissy assured me, "Yes, don't worry. Everything is ready for you."

Relief flooded through me. Maybe this hectic day would work out with a minimum of stress.

After being held up by having to drive through heavy traffic, I arrived at the funeral home and dashed into the chapel to do my work. The room was empty. No casket. No body. In a panic, I called the trade embalmers the funeral home used.

"What body? What are you talking about?" they asked in confusion.

And then the truth came out. Not only were Sonny and Sissy not ready, they had forgotten even to let the tradesmen know they had a body in the hospital that needed to be removed and embalmed for that afternoon's visitation.

"What a screw up," I said, biting my lip so I wouldn't say something worse.

As I looked around, I saw everyone was in a panic. I was angry, having wasted much time when I had to head out to Long island.

"You can't leave!" Sonny said sternly.

"I have to go. I have a long drive through Long Island to my next job."

"You need to wait!"

"I can't, I'm telling you! I have another commitment."

"Let them wait."

His gall was hard to believe. He was suggesting I wait hours for a body to be moved from a hospital, embalmed and then brought to the funeral home. Sonny didn't have any concern for the other family I had to take care of.

"You must be kidding!" I railed.

"Who's going to do the body if you leave, Alexandra?" he demanded to know.

"That's your problem. How could you forget to have the body picked up?" I asked exasperatedly.

"I don't have to explain to you!" he huffed.

"And I don't have to stay. I've about had it here."

"Are you saying your not going to work for me anymore?" he asked, his eyebrows arching in surprise.

I took a deep breath. "I can't deal with this anymore. I suppose I am saying that. Don't call me anymore for jobs, Sonny. Good bye."

I made a mad dash for my car and headed toward the highway. Traffic was heavy getting out of Brooklyn, as usual. Passing the Nassau County border, the traffic finally thinned out, but I was running really late by then. I reached for my car phone to call Frankie at the Long Island funeral home and assure him I was on my way. It was then that I noticed my diamond bracelet was missing from my wrist.

"Damn." I knew I had been wearing it when I arrived at the funeral home. The Calabrese funeral home was becoming synonymous in my mind with trouble.

Irate, upset and running late, I pressed my foot on the accelerator. Within seconds, I heard police sirens. *Damn! Can this day get any worse?* I thought, pulling over.

"Why do you think I stopped you?" asked the police officer.

"Look, I know why," I said tears springing to my eyes.

"You were doing eighty mile per hour, do you know that?"

"The truth is I was going faster than that! Now, please just hurry up and write the ticket, I'm in a terrible rush."

Surprised I was not trying to talk my way out of a ticket, he calmly asked me, "Just where are you going?"

"Look officer, I'm a funeral director. I just drove through some of the most God forsaken neighborhoods in Brooklyn to get to a funeral home, where it turns out, there was no body. Traffic is bumper to bumper getting out of Brooklyn. Now, I'm late getting to a funeral home in Suffolk County to repair the face of my friend's poor mother whose car was hit as she was coming home from vacation. On top of it, I just realized I lost my new diamond bracelet; then you pull me over when I'm trying to make up for lost time. Can this day get worse? So, either give me a ticket or lock me up. Spending the night in a jail cell is sounding pretty good to me right now. It might be easier than the day I'm having."

He looked at me as if I had taken leave of my senses. Then, thinking I was spinning some bizarre tale, he said, "Let me see your funeral director's license."

I handed it to him.

He looked at the license, then looked at me, shaking his head.

"You know what, Miss? I think you *are* having a really bad day. I'm not going to give you a ticket, because I think it might send you over the edge and make you more of a danger to other drivers. In fact, I'm going to try to forget I ever stopped you."

Surprised, I thanked him.

"Just don't speed!" he shouted to me as I drove off.

At last, I got to the funeral home and began my reconstructive work on Frankie's aunt. She was not in as bad a condition as I had suspected, mercifully. But since I had to rush, I felt extremely anxious. All of a sudden I began to hyperventilate. My head pounding, I felt a tightness in my chest that made me gasp. I was afraid I'd end up in a casket myself. Sonny and Sissy had that effect on people. I decided for sure, never to do more work for them.

Back at home later that afternoon, I lay down on my bed to get some much needed rest. The pounding in my head had not subsided. I wished I could turn my telephone off as other people did, but a funeral director, like a physician on call, could not. A funeral director must always be reachable.

The telephone rang. Still wishing I didn't have to answer, I picked up. It was the secretary from the Calabrese Funeral Home, telling me that Sissy's husband had died suddenly and that Sissy very much hoped I'd attend the funeral.

Oh my God! I thought. *What choice do I have!? I can't not attend. If I do, I'll appear uncaring.*

I learned that Father Louis DeGaetano was going to officiate at the funeral. We had met several years before when he had come to do the wake service (prayers for the deceased and the mourners gathered at the wake) at the Calabrese Funeral Home.

Afterward, we had sat outside on a bench for an hour talking about the vagaries of life, death, religion and spirituality. In time, we became close friends and he became the clergyman to whom I turned when I had questions with seemingly no answers or when I experienced a temporary crisis of faith.

The beautiful Brooklyn church was packed the day of the funeral. Father Lou was just one of the dozen priests on the altar. Funeral directors' families liked to have a plenitude of clergy at their funerals. Along with the relatives and neighborhood people, I saw many colleagues who I knew couldn't stand Sonny and Sissy and regularly ridiculed them. It offended me that some individuals went to other people's funerals out of duty and to "show face." Because many of us either did work for Sonny and Sissy or owed them something, we were all expected to be here to pay our respects to the family. I was appalled at the insincerity, the phoniness of it all.

A week later, it was an unusually cold St. Patrick's Day, with frozen snow on the ground from a storm which had hit the area a few days before. I was handling the funeral of an elderly little Irish lady, whose husband came to the visitation wearing a green tie and a shamrock pin.

"We always celebrated St. Patrick's day together," he sadly told me.

I wanted to cry.

I remained very busy throughout the spring, but Peter and I managed to spend Memorial Day weekend in Williamsburg, Virginia. One morning, we sipped coffee on a lovely outdoor patio and talked about the future.

I confided that I felt as if something important was missing from my life. Of course, I was a funeral director but there seemed so many jokes and misconceptions about my profession. I wanted others to know we were real people with dreams of love, families and fulfilling futures. And that we laughed and cried just as other people did.

By this time, Peter had taken thousands of photos of me. That June and throughout the summer we both were in playful moods and we tried the backdrop Playboy once had: cemeteries. It was not meant in any disrespectful way. To my mind, cemeteries are among the most beautiful, picturesque places in the world. And when I walk through them I think of the rich lives filled with sadness and joy of the many who reside there. Focusing on the connection many people make between love and death, Peter and I came up with the idea of producing a calendar of me in sexy poses in different cemeteries.

He began to take the pictures in various cemeteries around New York and soon, one appeared in a supermarket tabloid.

"Spirit of Dead Mom Appears in Model's Cemetery Photo," blazed the headline.

"A beautiful funeral director got the thrill of her life when she posed for a calendar featuring sexy shots of her in a cemetery," read the lead.

Silly as it was, I wrote up a short article about the subject to be included in a magazine's "Visit From Beyond" page, for which I was paid one hundred dollars. Bizarre subject matter perhaps, but sometimes I just had to express my sense of humor.

More tabloid stories appeared, some recycled from years previous, others new. The next thing I knew I received a call from the producers of Joan Rivers' talk show. I thought it would be a thrill trading quips with the famous comedienne. She was my favorite. On the program she introduced me as "The sexiest funeral director in the world." I made my entrance with the theme from the Addams Family playing in the background. Joan held up some of the tabloid newspapers I had appeared in, sharing the creative headlines with the audience.

We chatted about the stories, the cemetery calendar I was working on and how I began as a funeral director. Then she surprised me by asking, "Have you ever made love with the bodies around?"

"No! Never with any bodies around, but there was that one time in the bronze casket."

Hoots and hollers from the audience ensued.

I had just admitted, on national television, that I had sex in a casket. Not any casket mind you, but a top-of-the-line bronze one. It had happened with an old boyfriend, whom I'd never named. Though some may think the event crass, I must confess it seemed no different to me than, for example, a car dealer who has sex in a car or an office worker who uses his desk for a little hanky-panky. Such unusual settings provide that extra little bit of titillation.

The show was taped before a live audience several days before it was to air. The next day, as I was driving to a casket exhibit, I was caught off guard when a promo for the show came on the radio proclaiming:

"The sexiest funeral director in the world on tomorrow's Joan River's show."

Just about everyone in my business was already at the exhibit, so I breathed a sigh of relief that none of my colleagues had heard the promo. I was wrong.

When I arrived at the exhibit, a group of people came over to me.

"Welcome to the sexiest funeral director in the world," were the words with which one grinning colleague greeted me. I could tell by the glances and whispers that others didn't find it quite as amusing.

The calendar story plus my appearance soon got more press and I was invited to Philadelphia's morning television show where I was a guest along with a California police officer, turned call girl. The show was subtitled "Bad Girls of the Tabloids."

I had brought with me a mock-up of the calendar Peter and I created. It was a call-in show and one of the women who telephoned was very upset by the calendar, having just buried a loved one and believing cemeteries to be sacred ground.

"The cemetery is no place for cheesecake!" she told me in no uncertain terms.

Peter and I had already advertised the calendar for sale in an industry newspaper and received orders, but I began to rethink the project. Chastened by that caller and the fear that I'd truly offend, albeit unintentionally, I asked friends, as well as Father Lou, for feedback. Finally, I scrapped the project. Oddly enough, there is now a calendar of sexy models posing with caskets offered for sale on the Internet. I suppose Peter and I were ahead of our time.

Even though I didn't go ahead with the calendar, the tabloids continued to enjoy doing stories about me and my occupation. In September I was invited to be one of the guests on the *Geraldo* show. Another guest and I had a lot in common. She was a New York City police officer who had recently posed for *Playboy* and lost her job. She had been paid, as rumor had it, ten times more than I had. The theme of the show was "The repercussions of posing nude." Taking photographs after the show, Geraldo was friendly and gracious. During this period, the funeral business—and death—seemed to be hot topics. Two sitcoms, short lived though they were, dealt with funeral directors as main characters. And there was a bizarre new book out—a suicide manual, essentially—which explained how one could, in a number of pharmaceutical ways, end one's life. It had been published by a major publisher, who was scheduled to give a seminar at New York's *Learning Annex.* I registered for his class, for the opportunity to meet him and tell him of my articles and ask about the possibility of turning them into a book. His company seemed to be very open-minded, to say the least, about death. At the end of the seminar, I asked if I could send him some of my material. He agreed and I did. I received a brief note back saying that although he wished me the best, he did not think the topic of death would sell. That seemed ironic coming from him. What did he think happened to people after they committed suicide? They needed funeral directors, of course.

About the same time, I heard through the industry grapevine that Rae, my first boss, was ill. No one said how ill and so I didn't give the rumor that much thought at first. But then I heard about Rae's illness from more people and it began to sound like it wasn't just a minor problem. I couldn't imagine Rae sick. She had been the strongest woman I had ever known. I called John and inquired about her. He told me she was still in the hospital, but that she was doing alright. He never let on that Rae was dying. But there was something about his tone of voice that disturbed me. So that afternoon I went to the Queens hospital he'd said she was in to pay Rae a surprise visit. I was shocked to see her lying in the hospital bed attached to all sorts of medical apparatus. She was comatose. John stood nearby.

"Oh my God!" I gasped. "I had no idea. You didn't say how serious it was." John nodded but didn't comment. It was then I realized he also could not accept that a woman of Rae's strength could have become so ill.

We embraced as I left.

"Please call if you need me or if you just want to talk."

"Thank you. And please say a prayer for her."

"I surely will," I said.

I kept Rae in my daily prayers, but she was beyond all our prayers in this life. The woman I thought to be invincible died a few weeks later. I went to her wake. I kept expecting her to walk into the lobby to correct me, scold me, even yell at me, anything but lie there in the casket. Her life ended at a relatively young age. Her funeral was on a rainy Monday and I very much wanted to attend, but as it turned out, I had a funeral to direct and could not be there.

That same month, NBC News announced a new show that would feature people who had strange dual careers. I thought I was a natural for the show and wrote to them. They invited me to appear in an episode in late June. The very good-looking anchorman, Jim Watkins, interviewed me, opening the segment by saying that "We have been featuring people who juggle dual careers. Here is a very rare combination. Alexandra Mosca is a model/mortician." Then he asked the usual questions everyone asks about how I got started.

I explained how I tried to humanize my profession and how women seemed to be a little more sensitive, having an easier time at this job in some ways as they are emotionally more in tune with others.

"Are there more women entering the field?" he asked.

"Yes, and I hope I helped to pave the way."

"How does one of your careers play off the other?"

"Being a funeral director has influenced me very much to try other things. My career has taught me how to live better, to try anything, do anything, really live life and not be consumed by death. In other words, life is short, enjoy it while you can."

"That's a good lesson for everyone. Life is a finite thing and if you want to do something, do it now," Watkins responded.

The following Halloween, I baked a large cake and frosted it with brown and orange icing, atop which were all sorts of edible candies in the shape of pumpkins, skeletons, black cats, ghosts and coffins. I brought the cake to the casket company with which

I did business, along with an article I'd written about what consumers should know about arranging funerals. Luckily, the staff liked both—my cake and my article—and that felt good. Things were changing for me and, it looked like they were changing for the funeral industry as well.

A few months later, I discovered a book on the funeral industry written by the editor of *American Funeral Director* magazine. I was pleased to see a book on the subject and wondering how the author fared, I wrote him a letter and sent it to the magazine. About a week later, I learned the editor was no longer there when I received a phone call in response to my letter from the magazine's new editor, Ed Defort. As coincidence would have it, *American Funeral Director* was in the midst of putting together a special issue highlighting women in funeral service.

"Would you be interested in writing a piece for us about your experience in funeral service?" he asked.

Would I!? I excitedly said yes and was soon writing. I wrote and wrote, then wrote some more. The words just seemed to pour out onto the pages; an overflow of pent up thoughts.

Ed called about a month later to tell me the magazine wanted some photos to accompany the story and one to put on the cover. I was thrilled to hear it.

Two months later, when the magazine came out, Ed overnighted to me a copy of the issue, which was, at the same time, being mailed to funeral directors around the country. My story was published in its entirety, barely a word having been changed. For the second time in my career, I was pictured on the cover of *American Funeral Director*, but not only was I the story, this time I had written it as well. I was both proud and delighted. I called Ed and thanked him profusely. A low-key, modest man, I wondered if he realized just how life changing this experience really was for me.

CHAPTER 15

Days of Joy, Days of Grief

Three weeks after my photograph was on the cover of *American Funeral Director* magazine and my bylined article was featured in the issue, I picked up one of my closest friends and drove to a Long Island country club for the annual Metropolitan Funeral Directors Dinner.

Almost everyone had seen the magazine issue, since it was the most popular of our trade magazines, and they were talking about it. Many people made it a point to come over to congratulate me. I was tremendously gratified by the positive feedback and recognition from my colleagues. I hadn't known know how the article would be received. Would they say "There she goes talking about herself again?" Or, worse still, "Who cares what she has to say?" But from the reaction, I could sense I was no longer just a curiosity to them or a thorn in their collective sides.

That article was a turning point. I had proven myself. One successful well-wisher that evening told me that in spite of all his success, he'd never been asked to write his thoughts about the business for a magazine.

"Most of us old fogeys just aren't as interesting as you. And we don't look as good either," he added with a wink.

I seemed to be on a roll in my writing life, but things were not quite so rosy in my funeral career. Business was slow.

Why not get away? I thought. That might bring me some funeral work. It was an odd fact of life as a funeral director, but it seemed if you planned something, tried to go on vacation or actually got as far as leaving, new work would appear. The least likely thing to happen was the one that usually did. "What's the chance of that?" became an expression I used often in an ironic way.

I made plans to join Allison again. Her effervescence always buoyed my own spirits. And it was time for our annual Maryland blue crab dinner. Since this time no new work came my way, I decided to make my plans a reality. On a warm June day, I drove to the beautiful coastal town of Annapolis, Maryland. We dined at an outdoor restaurant on a canal. Boats were docked all around us. The night was lovely and we dug into our crabs, laughing and snapping photos of one another. Our waiter looked at the two of us in surprise when we ordered our third dozen crabs.

"You tiny little girls ate all that?"

We laughed some more. The next night I assisted in Allison's act and she had a surprise for me: a new sequined costume.

A month later, with the kernel of an idea for a magazine article urging me on I took a funeral director friend with me to Ferncliff Cemetery for the tour the cemetery had so graciously arranged. It was my friend's birthday and as I jokingly told him, "What better place for a funeral director to spend his birthday than a cemetery!"

It was a warm, sunny summer day and the cemetery looked magnificent. As I walked around I realized there were more famous people buried there than I had thought. Judy Garland, Ed Sullivan, Joan Crawford, Malcolm X, Tom Carvel, the ice cream scion, Basil Rathbone, the original Sherlock Holmes and Ona Munson, who played Belle Watling in *Gone With The Wind*, my favorite movie—all were there. This was going to make for a very interesting article, I decided, and set to work on it that night.

By December, funeral directing work came in abundance. December was always a busy month in my industry. On or around Christmas Day I always seemed to be conducting a funeral. True to form, a day after Christmas, I received a "death call."

The deceased was a young man in his forties who had died of cancer. I went to his mother's home to make the arrangements. She was surrounded by a large, supportive family. Sweet and polite as the mother was, her brother, who had taken over the arrangements, was difficult and argumentative. It was immediately obvious that he was looking for a way to nickel and dime me on every little thing.

These people were friends of friends, so as a courtesy, I gave them some financial consideration, which the brother made clear was not enough. I knew my prices to be very fair and found the quibbling over prices to be unsettling. It made him look cheap and crass. Even worse, it was apparent that this was not a family with financial hardships.

Although I'd be the first to agree that funerals are costly, I never did understand why people were not more concerned about good service and professional work, especially in the case of open casket funerals, which accounted for most of my business. The most important thing should have been how the deceased looked, not what the funeral cost. Over the years, more and more people have become "shoppers," calling and visiting funeral homes and comparing prices, while a loved one's body lay in a hospital morgue freezer. To me, this is just as unconscionable as the funeral director who overcharges, convinces families to buy unnecessary items and takes advantage of those in distress.

When this family came into the funeral home the next day to view the body, I could see relief wash over their faces. I felt satisfied, for that was what I always strove for: to make things go smoothly and be a little easier to bear for the loved ones of the deceased.

"I never saw a body look so good. He looks alive!" they exclaimed almost in unison.

Apparently though, it was not good enough to call me when another family member died several months later. I knew it was about money. Some people just aren't happy unless they feel they are getting something for less. For them, quality is not paramount, price is.

I spent Easter with my lifelong friend John, Camille's widower, at his son's home on Staten Island. John was now ill with cancer, but doing well.

My Ferncliff Cemetery article was published in September. The editor, Ed Defort, sent me many copies, which I gave out to friends. I was already researching my next article for *American Funeral Director* about the deaths and funerals of some of the country's most infamous mobsters, an expansion of an idea I'd had many years before.

The research was interesting, and made even more so when one of the burial spots of one of a mobster could not be verified. Who doesn't love a mystery?

In early December, I was preparing with great difficulty a female corpse for a visitation. Her clothing was just not appropriate. I mused on how often that happened and why funeral directors didn't intercede and "direct" the families to better choices. Someone needed to give them advice, guide them.

As these thoughts were spinning in my head on the drive home, an article was forming in my mind. I went home and began to write *Fashion To Die For!* I wrote it somewhat tongue-in-cheek, so that people wouldn't be turned off. The article imparted, however, important information for open casket funerals and the selection of proper clothing for a female deceased. When I was satisfied,

I called up a reporter I knew at the *Daily News* who was kind enough to pass it on to her editor. The editor telephoned me a few weeks later saying they were interested in the article and would get back to me.

I'm going to be published in a major newspaper! I thought ecstatically. My high spirits soon turned to sorrow, however, when, on Christmas Eve, my dear friend John died. It was his late wife Camille's birthday, which those close to him saw as some sort of sign.

We held the visitation the day after Christmas. Although we hung up photos of happier days and people talked of the many good times we'd all had with John and Camille over the years, how much he'd missed his late wife and how they were together again and at peace, I was extremely sad. Sad about John's death and sad, as I looked around the room, to realize that so many older friends and neighbors were gone; the generation before mine, the people I'd known all my life then buried, were now no more. I felt my youth to be gone as well. It was the first time I really felt, not just thought about, my own mortality.

The next morning, before I closed John's casket, trying not to cry, I kissed him good-bye. At that moment, I wanted what all my client families wanted, for him to be alive again.

In church, the feelings became overwhelming and I cried along with many others. Later, I wondered if people who didn't know that John had been my dear friend thought it odd that the funeral director had been crying. In fact, some months later, someone did relate a remark she'd overheard. It was so guileless and bittersweet that it brought a smile to my face.

"John was such a good man," the woman said, "when he died, even the funeral director cried at his funeral."

Less than a week after the funeral, the century was coming to an end and the new millennium loomed ahead. It would be the biggest New Year's Eve of my lifetime, but I didn't feel much like celebrating. Then, John's son and I spoke and decided to spend the evening together. The last day of the century, New Year's Eve, 1999, I spent with John's and Camille's son at a black tie party in a Staten Island mansion. I knew that John and Camille, if they could see us, would be pleased. They had always hoped we would marry.

In spite of the sad end to 1999, I had a powerful feeling that 2000 was going to be a pivotal time for me. It began with a modeling shot of me in *More* magazine. A number of friends and acquaintances saw the photograph and called me. Once again, the oddity of my career and youthful, feminine appearance brought me to the attention of others.

At the end of January, the *Daily News* sent a photographer to take a photo of me which would accompany the burial clothing article. It was slated to run that week. But when I picked up the newspaper on the appointed day and excitedly turned to the page it was supposed to be on, it wasn't there. I called the editor. He told me it had been rescheduled for the following week. They kept shuffling the date into March and then a new editor at the *Daily News* decided the article was not something their readers would be interested in reading. It was not going to run. I was crushed.

Maybe this year wasn't going to be so good, after all.

I sent the article out again and again, to no avail. I continued to think it contained important advice and information but no one else seemed to agree. In the middle of February, I finished my mobster funeral article, which turned out to be a lot longer than I had originally anticipated. I sent it to Ed at *American Funeral Director* magazine. He liked the piece and said he'd wait for the first opportunity, as far as space was concerned, to print it in its entirety, rather than split the article between two issues.

"Sounds good," I said. "I have another idea I'd like to run by you."

I pitched the idea of my writing an article on the death and funeral of Evita Peron, about whom I had once written a college term paper. Evita Peron was a most intriguing woman and her funeral was as grand as they come. Even the way in which she was embalmed was extraordinary. That part, I thought, would be of great interest to my colleagues who read the trade journal.

I began to reread the biographies of Evita that I had read years before and researched her life. In the next year, I would also write about the deaths and funerals of Marilyn Monroe and Vivien Leigh. Beautiful, complex, troubled women seemed to intrigue me.

The spring of 2000 was the beginning of a period of great aggravation in my funeral career. Months before, after sending a query letter to *Modern Maturity* magazine about doing a consumer piece for them regarding funerals, I received a call from one of their editors. An article on the subject of funerals was already in the works and being written by their staff, but he asked if they could quote from the information I had sent them.

"Sure," I agreed quickly.

The important part was that the information got out even if my article didn't. Strangely, although I had not written the piece they published, which was somewhat negative in tone, I got credit for it nonetheless. However, complaining calls came to Joe and Ray demanding to know how they could allow me to run my business out of their building, while I was writing negative articles about the industry.

"She didn't write the article," they patiently explained again and again.

Another result of that article was the calls I received from "shoppers." One was from a man pricing a simple grave-side funeral for his mother. I told him the costs involved and he said they sounded very reasonable. The next day he came into the funeral home to make the arrangements and at that time we agreed on the terms of payment. With his permission, I had his mother remains removed from her place of death, planning to meet him the next day at the cemetery. I was stunned when the next call that came to the funeral home was from a funeral director I did not know, screaming and cursing at me for insisting the expenses be paid at the time of the funeral. Not only was that my policy and the policy of almost every funeral director I knew, but who was this man and why was he involving himself in my business? He demanded that I change my policy for this man or else he was coming to take the body from me.

"Who in the world are you?" I asked in disbelief, trying to remain calm and contain my outraged response.

He told me his name and the name of his firm. It was one of the corporately owned funeral homes.

"In the future, take care of your own business!" I said before I hung up on him.

I called the man with whom I had made arrangements. Turned out, he had been less than truthful with me. Now he claimed he didn't have a dime to his name. He had called another funeral home, hoping they'd wait for payment since they were a big corporation.

In spite of his dishonesty, I felt sorry for him. I agreed to submit my bill to the nursing home, where there was a small burial fund. Then I called the corporately owned funeral home that employed the man who had yelled at me on the telephone and demanded an apology from him, a written one, which I got in the mail a week later.

The day of the funeral, Joe drove the hearse. We had arranged to meet the son of the deceased at the beautiful Gates of Heaven cemetery. When we got to the grave site, we couldn't quite believe our eyes. The middle-aged man was holding balloons and posing for photos along with his mother's casket, while a portable CD played the beautiful tune, "Con Te Partiro," sung by Andrea

Bocelli. The cemetery workers, Joe and I tried not to laugh. However, it took a long while before I could hear that song again without seeing the strange scene at the cemetery in my mind.

Before we left, I snapped a photograph of the grave of Dutch Schultz, one of the mobsters I was writing about in my article. Then Joe, a big baseball fan, and I drove by Babe Ruth's memorial, which I had never seen. Gate of Heaven Cemetery was beautiful and full of history and legends. That afternoon, I filed this thought away for a future cemetery profile.

Toward the end of April, my old friend Lois called to say her mother was dying and that she wanted me to handle the funeral. Although we hadn't been in close touch over the years, I was honored that she would call me. Such trust and loyalty meant a great deal to me. A positive offshoot was that our friendship was rekindled. More and more, I found that relationships with people one knew for many years held special meaning.

The next month, a funeral home on Long Island called concerning a woman who had prearranged a funeral with me, several years before, for her house-bound father. Her father now had died and she was in their funeral home making arrangements. At my request, the funeral director gave the telephone to the woman so I could speak with her. Believing her to be confused, as bereaved clients sometimes are about making arrangements, I asked if she understood that she and I had already made all the arrangements in the past and that there was no need to go to another funeral home; I would happily accommodate her needs wherever she lived in New York.

She spat out some nasty words and hung up the telephone on me. I was entirely perplexed. Later in the day, the funeral director who was now handling the arrangements called to ask me when I would be forwarding the money from the pre-arrangement account. I explained that I would be out of town, but certainly would send the money along as soon as I returned the following week. What I didn't know at the time, nor did any of my colleagues seem to know, was that we, as funeral directors handling pre-arrangement accounts, had only ten days in which to turn over the money on demand to another funeral home. We all believed the time frame to be thirty days.

"Ignorance of the law" mattered little when I returned to a barrage of letters from the state inspector. In addition to those letters, the director of a pre-arrangement group with the misleading and generic name of "preplan," wrote, trying to cow me as to the trouble I could be in for infringing on their copyright. Indeed, I had committed the unpardonable sin of writing on the wrong form. As "pre-plan" is such a generic term, I honestly didn't know it could be copyrighted. But this wasn't the worst problem. It seemed the Suffolk County funeral home had influenced the woman to write to the Department of Health stating that my call had "upset her." I bet! If anyone was upset by the tone of that call, it was me.

I was dismayed at the nonsense the State Funeral Directing Board spent their time on, while turning a blind eye to real infractions and intentional flouting of laws. Withdrawing the money from the pre-arrangement account, I mailed a check, hoping to have heard the end of the matter. Unfortunately, that was not to be. Soon, I received another call from the state inspector demanding to know why I had not sent the check.

"I sent it."

"They never received it."

Did I now control the mail?

"Did you send it return receipt?" she implored.

"No. Is that another law I didn't know about?" I was starting to get really angry. This behavior, on the part of the Long Island funeral home, seemed laced with malice.

This matter dragged on for months, with letters flying back and forth, along with threats of legal action. It was finally revealed that the address on the funeral home's correspondence was not their legal or mailing address. Didn't that bother the state? I had apparently sent the check to a nonexistent address, through no fault of my own. And it had been, not surprisingly, lost somewhere along the way.

The state inspector was satisfied with this explanation and ordered me to have my bank file the original check as lost and issue a replacement check. The fee for the replacement check was fifteen dollars, which, on principle, I had no intention of paying. The Long Island funeral home refused to pay the charge, as well, though they stood to gain in excess of $8,500. I thought they had caused enough trouble, by their own hand, and were being petty and cheap. We were at a standoff. Months elapsed before they, in the end, sent the fifteen dollars. If they had given me the right address to begin with, the whole matter would not have dragged on so long.

I thought seriously about asking Ed if I could write an editorial for the funeral magazine about professional relationships between colleagues and the lack thereof. This was a larger issue than what had happened to me. After all, if we were backstabbing each other, how could we help but have a poor image with the public? I filed the idea away in the back of my mind and decided to wait until after some of my other articles were published.

My article on mob funerals appeared in *American Funeral Director* in July. I had taken all the photos myself and was very pleased with this effort.

"A most interesting read," Ed praised.

Apparently, it was interesting enough to reprint in September's *American Cemetery* magazine.

The week the article appeared, Joe and I were on our way to a funeral in Pinelawn Memorial Park, in Pinelawn, New York. As the hearse wound its way down Pinelawn Road, we passed the headquarters of *Newsday*. I had been chattering on, and suddenly fell silent.

"Is anything wrong?" Joe asked after a minute, surprised by the extended quiet in the car.

"No. I was just having this fantasy as we passed *Newsday*, that I was a nationally renowned journalist, pulling into my designated parking space, to write my syndicated column about death," I explained.

"Well, get a grip! The reality is you're a funeral director riding in a hearse on the way to a cemetery to bury someone."

The parallel was so funny to me, I broke into laughter. Then I turned serious.

"I will write something for them someday. I just know it!"

One afternoon, in an impulsive mood, I called the Queens editor of *Newsday* and left a message on his voice mail about the article I had sent in on burial clothing. What was the worst that could happen? He would think me unprofessional and not respond.

Instead, much to my surprise, he did what most editors rarely do: he called me back. He explained that *Newsday* did not use "first person pieces," but that the subject matter was different and interesting. "I'd like to assign a reporter to write a story, for which we'll use some of your information and quote you, if this is okay," he added.

I readily agree, wanting to see this information and advice in print and read by the public.

The young reporter assigned to the task called me and asked if I could have some of my colleagues get in touch with her so she could interview them. I said I would and cajoled some other funeral directors into speaking with her. As they were all male, "burial clothing" for women was not a scintillating topic for them.

The piece never did run. In the middle of her reporting, the editor brought to the young woman's attention that he thought I was the real story. She called and asked me if I'd be interested in being the subject of an article. Indeed I was interested, amazed that there was, after all this time, curiosity about the funeral director who had posed for *Playboy*.

I stopped by the *Newsday* offices in Queens carrying some personal photos with me. This was such a thrill for me, just being there amid the excitement of breaking news. I had an appointment with the photo editor. He had to select pictures of me to go with the article, in addition to the one *Newsday* had taken of me in the casket showroom at the funeral home. I had been busy at work and didn't have time to wade through my photo collection, so I just scooped some up. The editor chose a photo of me with Regis Philbin, taken when I had been on his show.

Besides bringing photos, I brought several of my published articles, including my article on Mob funerals from the month before.

You never know, I thought. Maybe, just maybe, someone would look at them.

Much to my surprise, Tony, another editor made a point of coming over and introducing himself to me. He asked if he could look through the photographs, press clippings and articles I had brought with me. Of course he could!

One of the articles he scanned, my Mob piece, caught his attention.

"Who took these photos?" Tony asked.

"I did."

He asked some more questions about the article and I could tell he was genuinely interested, not merely being polite. As it turned out, we shared an interest in organized crime figures. He had written extensively on the subject over the years. This was my only article about them. However, I knew a number of them on a more personal level. As the editor and I continued to chat, he asked if I wanted to write something for the paper about funerals, perhaps ethnic trends, as Queens was so culturally diverse. I wanted to jump up and hug and kiss him for the opportunity he had just given me. He could not have known at that time just how much it meant to me.

After I left *Newsday*, I called the funeral home to tell Joe and Ray.

"You'll never guess what just happened. One of the *Newsday* editors asked me to write an article for them on ethnic trends of funerals in Queens. I told you I was going to write for *Newsday*. Remember that day, Joe?"

"So you did and now you will. Congratulations."

On Sunday, September 10, the article about me, entitled "Heavenly Angel" was to appear as the cover story for the *Queens Life* section. A friend called the night before, having gotten the early Sunday edition in Queens.

"How does it look?" I asked.

"Big," was his first word. "You can't miss it. The writer treated you very kindly. You're going to like it."

And I did, very much.

I worked on my article for *Newsday* for a long time, longer than I ever worked on anything. I wanted it to be perfect. But there was another reason it took so long. In the fall of 2000, I found myself enveloped in an all consuming clinical depression. The flip side of the anxiety disorder I had secretly suffered with for many years was that it grew worse as time passed and the weather grew colder and the days shorter.

"An overload of anxiety easily turns to depression," said a doctor I consulted. He prescribed anti-depressants, which he said would take up to a month to alleviate the debilitating and incapacitating symptoms.

In the midst of my despair, my friend's mother passed away and I had another funeral to attend. Trying to pull myself together, I put on my best black Ralph Lauren suit and drove to Brooklyn on a frigid winter day. The wind howled as we stood outside the church waiting for the funeral procession to begin. I bumped into some colleagues I hadn't seen in a long time and they greeted me warmly, telling me how good I looked. Good!? It astounded me to hear them say that when I felt so badly.

My condition was so overwhelming, that even the smallest activity seemed monumental. Trying to work on the newspaper article made me feel more like I was trying to write a doctoral dissertation on a subject, like astrophysics perhaps, of which I had no comprehension. Merely writing two lines tired me out mentally and physically. I dreaded hearing from Tony, the *Newsday* editor, who checked in from time to time to see how I was progressing. I was afraid he'd say, "Let's forget it."

"I'm working on it," I tried to reassure him when he called.

I wondered why I was feeling this way, when I had, at last, been given such a golden opportunity. Why couldn't I savor the experience?

At work, two weeks before Christmas, we handled the funeral of a woman who had committed suicide. She was not much older than I was. Working on her hit home in a big way. I had never truly understood how a person could feel so badly that suicide became the only option. Now I did.

Had anyone tried to help her? Why couldn't she be saved? I wondered desolately.

Although popular thinking views suicide as the coward's way out, I have always thought it takes a certain kind of courage to take one's own life, an act of desperation though it may be. However dark things were for me, I was not thinking of taking my own life.

When I got home that night, I lay in bed, feeling despondent and incapacitated. Allison called and when she heard my voice, she said, "I'm coming to get you and bring you home to Florida with me."

In the midst of my despair, one of the last lines from *Gone With The Wind* kept echoing in my head: "She thought of Tara and it was as if a gentle, cool hand were stealing over her heart." Florida was my Tara.

And Florida was so much less Christmasy. The Christmastime sense of enforced cheerfulness and merriment only made me feel more miserable. Yet, I did not have the strength to buy a ticket, pack a suitcase and get myself to the airport. Getting out of bed, showering and getting dressed had become Herculean tasks. Inwardly, I blessed Allison for being my true friend and promising to come get me.

Little more than a week before Christmas, I mustered up all my strength to interview a colleague for my newspaper article. It was a cold, wintry night, the wind howled and I sat sobbing in my car, willing myself to go into the funeral home to interview the director. My eyes rimmed in red, the little make-up I had applied, mascara and blush, now streaky, I knew I was a sorry sight, but I didn't care how I looked. I told myself I had to do this. I always followed through on things. *I am not going to let my illness destroy this opportunity,* I thought. I did that interview, difficult as it was, then drove home in tears.

The next morning I called Tony, the *Newsday* editor. I was relieved that he did not answer. I left a message on his voice mail, trying to sound cheery, saying I was going away for the Christmas holidays and that I would get in touch with him when I returned.

Allison was with me, having kept her promise to come to New York and get me. She had come in by plane the night before. I had not even packed, the task was too daunting for me to handle.

With her help, I simply opened drawers and closets, tossing into my suitcase whatever seemed appropriate. Not my neat, orderly way of doing things at all. Before I knew it, we were in a cab and heading to the airport.

One afternoon, several weeks later, Allison and I sat by the pool at her home, enjoying the Florida sun. I felt well enough to begin reading the first of five biographies of Marilyn Monroe I had collected. Her death and funeral were to be the subjects of my next profile for *American Funeral Director* magazine.

As I thumbed through the photos included in the book, the caption below one photo, in which Monroe and Joe DiMaggio were perched on lounge chairs much like we were, caught my attention. After Monroe had been released from a hospital, suffering from emotional problems, Joe DiMaggio stepped in to help. "Joe DiMaggio had been Marilyn's most loyal friend in these desperate months. Joe took her to Florida to regain her health," read the copy.

The irony wasn't lost on me, as I showed the page to Allison, who sat reading next to me.

"This reminds me of us. I feel like Marilyn Monroe all of a sudden. That makes you Joe DiMaggio."

Allison, her curvaceous body clad in a coral-colored bikini, jumped up and looked at me in mock horror. "Do I look like Joe DiMaggio to you!?"

We both laughed. It was the first time I had laughed in months.

In Florida I grew stronger and soon was able, if not eager, to return to New York. Once I was home, I got back into the rhythm of work at the funeral home and set about finishing the article for *Newsday*. I wrote draft after draft. I felt frustrated, but soon realized it was no longer my depression, but my relative inexperience which prolonged finishing the article. Finally, the piece was as good as I could make it and I sent it off to Tony.

On January 30, I received an E-mail from Tony, who said it was a "much better job this time" from my previous drafts. I printed out that E-mail and took it to work with me, so I could read his words over and over. I even read it to my co-workers, joking with them, that of course, they did not receive important E-mails from newspaper editors.

On Wednesday, March 14, 2001, the *Newsday* article, entitled "The Language of Grief," was published. It was truly a banner day for me. Before long, there were more articles for *Newsday* to follow.

This was a personal victory, as well as a professional one. I resisted the impulse to tell the clerk at the newsstand I frequented that I had an article in the paper, when she asked me why I was buying so many copies.

Later that day, I sent an E-mail of thanks to Tony whose patience, help and support I very much appreciated. I wanted him to know that, because of the bout of clinical depression I had just gone through, having my article published symbolized to me much more than just seeing my words in print. It may have been unprofessional to be so candid, but I sensed it would be well received, if unexpected. And I've always believed one should seize the moment and tell others how they have affected your life. For me, the publication of the *Newsday* article signified victory over a pervasive and frightening illness. I was grateful and thankful from the bottom of my heart for the opportunity. He e-mailed back telling me it was just the beginning.

CHAPTER 16

Flight 587

The months of 2001 passed, filled for me with mostly mundane funeral assignments, but few catastrophic deaths until, like most other Americans, I witnessed the tragedies of September 11. Then on Monday, November 12, which started out as an ordinary day, Father Lou, called me on his cell phone around 9:10 A.M. as he strolled through the St. Francis of Assisi School's gymnasium. The school was closed for the day in order to observe Veterans Day and he was making a check of the facilities. Father Lou reminded me, "I'm expecting a 9:45 funeral Mass."

In the midst of our conversation, a loud rumble sounded. Father Lou fell silent.

Finally, in a faltering tone, he said, "The building just shook! I'm walking over to the window—a gray object has seemingly dropped from the sky."

Then I heard through the phone the cacaphony of a loud explosion.

"I'm going outside to see what's happened!" His voice suddenly sounded filled with alarm.

Apparently, the cell phone was still in his hand as he left

the building. A few seconds later I heard a voice telling him there was a plane down on 129th or 130th Street. Then I heard a babble of raised voices yelling and barking commands. I waited for Father Lou to remember I was on the line and tell me what had happened.

When he finally did, he was obviously shaken and upset. "Oh my God! A plane has crashed right in the neighborhood! Houses are burning! This is terrible!" he said in shock. "One of the EMT workers rushing over to help said his parents were on the flight."

Belle Harbor, Queens, New York had once again been the victim of tragedy, so soon after losing thirteen members of its community in the attack on the World Trade Center.

Later that day I watched the news reports of the plane crash and read of the victims in the afternoon newspaper. In all, there had been 260 passengers and five people on the ground killed. That night Father Lou called, telling me tragic stories of the five victims he knew personally; members of his parish and of the others who had lost their homes. There was even some talk about turning the gym into a temporary morgue, he told me. The press had swarmed to the scene and the usually private priest found himself giving interviews.

Unbearably depressing as it was to hear these stories, I never anticipated that I would become part of the tragedy's aftermath. But just a few days later, on a gray fall afternoon, my colleague Joe and I were sitting in the funeral home office when a fax came through from the New York State Funeral Directors Association, requesting volunteers to handle the removals and shipment of remains from the plane crash back to the Dominican Republic, where many of the passengers were from, or to receiving funeral homes.

The directives read:

a. Business attire must be worn

b. Removal by unmarked hearse

c. Embalming or preparation of remains using the best methods available; preparing all viewable remains as if they were to be viewed and wrapping all non viewable remains in cotton.

d. Remains placed in new white zippered disaster pouch and then labeled in a dignified manner with the name of decedent and appropriate ME number.

e. Pouch then placed in the casket and labeled at the foot end with decedent name and ME number. Casket will be locked, screw "endcap" placed in the box that contains the locking tool and that box will be taped to the casket handle at the foot of the casket.

f. Minimum of coverall or plastics as necessary.

g. Appropriate preparation and filing of all required paper-work necessary to inter, cremate and/or transport human remains to include, but not limited to the Death Certificate, Burial, Cremation and/or Transit permits.

h. Preparation and sending/faxing all tracking forms.

i. Transfer by hearse to receiving funeral home or airport.

"I think we should volunteer. Do you want to help?" I asked.

"Do you?" Joe asked in surprise, knowing how badly I'd reacted to working on plane crash victims in the past.

"I think so," I said contemplating. "Yes, I feel we ought to do it. We'll need a hearse," I said rereading the fax. I turned to Joe questioningly.

"We have a hearse," he replied.

I nodded. "I'm not a member of the NYSFDA and they want the volunteers to be members." I'd long ago vowed not to join any funeral director organizations.

"I am," Joe said.

"Okay!" I took a deep breath. "We meet the requirements."

"You always choose the hard things," Joe said, agreeing to join me in volunteering, as I bit my lip, self-consciously. "Remember you and I and my brother, Ray, are in this together," he said. "It's going to be hard work. There are many victims and the bodies will be in terrible shape." He added, "I've had experience with several previous plane crashes."

"Oh Joe, I'm sure many people will want to help; they may not even call us."

I couldn't have been more wrong.

On Thanksgiving, Joe paged me to tell me we had been assigned our first case from the crash. We were to remove, prepare the remains and ship a young woman back to the Dominican Republic the next day.

For a few moments I thought of how terrible I always felt when the deceased had been young. Then I stiffened my resolve. *I have to*, I said to myself.

Early the next morning I went to the funeral home so Joe and I could take the hearse and go to the New York Medical Examiner's office to retrieve the remains. The New York Medical Examiner's building is located on First Avenue and 30th Street in New York City. It was a place I'd been to countless times before, but on this day the scene was quite different from my previous experiences. Crowded and congested, First Avenue for several blocks was lined with hearses. There was a round-the-clock police presence as well, with checkpoints for anyone entering the building and another one inside. Getting out of the hearse, I got out my driver's license and funeral director's license, both of which were required, and showed them to the policeman, while Joe waited behind the wheel.

Once inside, I was checked again. Then I waited my turn to meet with one of the "Disaster Team" volunteers, who had come to the city to help. I waited and waited. I wondered if Joe was getting worried about why I was there for so long. Finally they called me. One of the volunteers photocopied my identification, while I filled out the necessary paperwork. Then the mortuary team was alerted that Joe and I were on our way to the tent, as it was called.

"Drive around to the back of the building," a police officer instructed Joe as I got back into the hearse. As he turned the corner of the building, in front of us was the makeshift morgue, which had been constructed for the World Trade Center disaster. I saw about a dozen refrigerated tractor trailers bearing out-of-state license plates, still loaded with not yet identified body parts from the victims of the September 11 attack. Now, those from Flight 587 were among them. By each trailer I saw a flower piece adorned with a ribbon, which read *Rest in Peace*.

Among those working at the site, was the DMORT (Disaster Mortician) Team, a federal organization composed of funeral directors and emergency personnel from around the country who come to disaster sites in order to facilitate identifications and death registrations, the handling and distribution of remains, as well as manning the mortuary. Later I talked with a number of them and was impressed with their sincere dedication, especially under such trying circumstances.

Two members of the DMORT team, dressed in Army fatigues, as they all were, for the purpose of identification, came over to greet us. They were surprisingly upbeat and exceedingly polite, given the very grave circumstances. With great care, they loaded the remains onto our stretcher and wished us a good day.

Because of the holiday weekend, the streets were almost empty as we drove back to Queens. *Good thing*, I thought, knowing it was imperative that we get in touch with the Dominican Consulate. As soon as we got to the funeral home, I began calling but there was no answer. *Where could they be? Had they taken the holiday weekend off!? How could they in the midst of such disaster that had befallen so many of their countrymen?* I racked my brain trying to figure it out. After repeated unanswered calls, I had no choice but to take the subway, a mode of transportation I hadn't utilized in twenty years and one about which I didn't feel very comfortable, into Manhattan to their offices.

Once on the train, I quickly read through the paperwork and saw that the woman whose body we had picked up had been a mother. I wondered sadly whether her children were killed as well or were they now orphans? Either way, the tragedy of this crash was enormous.

The Dominican Consulate turned out to be open, just not answering the phone because of the high call volume due to the crash. I was surprised that in spite of the disaster, their attitude seemed to be very much "business as usual." Funeral directors shipping plane crash victims back to their homeland were not given any priority. I was fortunate to get some quicker-than-usual assistance from an employee who understood the time constraints we funeral directors were under. Within two hours, I was out of there and back on the subway. As the train pulled out my mind drifted back to wondering about the woman we were going to prepare for her funeral. Engrossed in my thoughts, before I realized it, I missed my stop, going several stops out of the way.

When I finally got back to the funeral home, it was time to open the wrapped remains and embalm or chemically treat the remains. On the pouch was a fuzzy Polaroid snapshot and the name of the deceased.

Joe and I unzipped the pouch, to uncover two more zipped pouches, on top of which was the clothing the woman had worn during the flight, bearing the strong, unmistakable and overpowering odor of jet fuel. We set the clothing aside, unzipping the other pouch, until we uncovered the remains. My first reaction was horror! The putrid smell was overpowering. My hand went involuntarily to my face, covering my nose and mouth. Yet, that did little to diffuse the stench. I stared at the charred remains which held no semblance of a "real body." The wrapping had made it look whole. But I now could see it was only part of an entire body, with not one identifying human feature.

Joe stared at me, as we both tried not to gag.

"Are you sure you want to do this? This is pretty horrible," he said somberly.

I nodded. "We have to do this." I gritted my teeth.

Embalming was impossible, but, with great difficulty, we chemically treated the remains. We used phenol, a caustic, toxic chemical, which always made my throat constrict and my eyes water. This time it was an almost welcome smell. After casketing the remains and placing the casket in a shipping container, we were, mercifully, done.

I was totally exhausted as the day turned into night. Worn out despite my early resolve, I hoped they didn't call us again, but I couldn't tell that to Joe. I didn't want to hear any "I told you so's."

The entire next day, a state of sadness enveloped me. I could think of nothing but the horror of plane crashes. Visions of happy vacationers, people returning to their homelands, visiting relatives, etc., all their lives cut short, passed through my mind again and again. One woman on the plane, we were told, was accompanying her mother's casket back to the Dominican Republic for burial. That was beyond eerie!

That night, Joe and I left for JFK Airport to deliver the remains of the woman for shipment. The ride, only several miles from the funeral home, seemed longer than usual, probably because we spent most of it in silence. There wasn't much to say. My thoughts ran to the irony of the bodies being shipped back on the same airline which had crashed and killed them.

The weekend brought no respite, for we received another assignment and I knew we had to return to the NYME for another victim on Monday morning. My gloomy feelings did not abate.

As I suspected, Monday turned out pretty much to be a carbon copy of that Friday, except that we delivered the second person's remains to a funeral home in the Bronx, where a closed casket visitation would take place. Tuesday no one called.

But on the evening of Wednesday, November 28, Joe and I once again returned to the NYME, for yet another body from the plane crash. After giving in our paperwork, we waited for what seemed longer than usual. "Your paperwork was mis-placed," the volunteer told us. Several hours passed, as we sat amongst colleagues, also waiting, in full view of the mortuary's reception area. The decorated Christmas tree and lit Menorah seemed glaringly out of place among all this tragedy. It seemed even more so, if that could be, given the unseasonably warm November temperatures. Police officers manned their stations outside in shirt-sleeves.

Unable to sit still any longer, I walked over to the volun-teer's desk. A poem was tacked to the wall which read in part, "If I am silent about what I've seen during my day, please under-stand. There are things I cannot share with you until I am ready. Just now, it is too difficult to voice the horrors I've seen." A long sigh escaped my lips. I walked back to my seat. The words echoed in my thoughts.

Finally, they found our paperwork and I was called. By now, Joe had gone out to sit in the hearse. I dashed out the door with the paperwork. Once again, Joe and I drove to the tent.

Wheeling the stretcher over to the trailer, I wondered how badly decomposed this victim was. By now, I knew there were no "whole" bodies.

"You won't be needing that," the DMORT volunteer offered, as he emerged from the trailer carrying a small plastic bag, not unlike what one's groceries are packed in at a supermarket.

"That's our body?" I said aghast, giving voice to the horror I felt.

Back in the hearse, I looked at Joe. "I don't know if I can't do one more of these!"

"But you will. I've learned that," he said.

And we did—three more, to be exact.

A few mornings later, I took a camera with me intending to snap a photograph of the DMORT team to accompany a future article, should I decide to do one. In an instant, the police were all over us. But, surprisingly, they allowed me to keep the camera and film. One of the DMORT team later told me another funeral director who attempted to take a photo had his camera confiscated, along with the film and, worse yet, was forbidden to return.

Ten days later, Ray and I returned from the Medical Examiner's late one afternoon, as darkness approached with the last crash victim we'd been assigned, to the awful news that Steve, one of our most well-liked colleagues, had died. I felt like I was on death overload first, with some of the worst victims of disaster I had ever seen, and now, with the loss of my friend and peer.

And as if this wasn't bad enough, early that evening my colleague and friend Vincent called me to do some work at his funeral home on a woman who had shot herself in the head. As the newspaper account told it, she had been widowed in the World Trade Center attack and was unable to come out of her deep depression. I agreed to work on her. But it was just one more dark day of a young person going far too soon, something I had been seeing far too often.

The next morning, I had to go to a family's home to arrange a Jewish funeral. It was Hanukkah and their home was decorated for the holiday and gifts were visible. The husband had died suddenly. "He'll never open his gifts," sobbed his wife. Two days later, I attended Steve's funeral.

Funeral directors, family and friends filled the room to overflowing at the Schawaroch Funeral Home. It was like a sea of black. No one said much as they waited for the funeral to begin. People always seemed to be left speechless by tragedy. Some colleagues got up to briefly say a few words about Steve. Ray was one of them, telling an anecdote about their hunting trips, hoping to infuse a lighter moment into all the tension.

The funeral Mass was held at St. Matthias, a beautiful, old church in Ridgewood, Queens, across the street from Steve's funeral home. It had been Steve's church all his life. Seven years before, his wife had died in her forties and the funeral Mass had been said there.

Embraces among colleagues were heartfelt, as we found seats in the pews. The Mass was prayerful and I reflected once again on how comforting I always found the Catholic funeral Mass. Programs of the service were distributed. A photograph of Steve, handsome in a tuxedo jacket, smiled up at the mourners from the cover of the program.

Just before the end of the Mass, Steve's twenty-one-year-old son went up to the altar to deliver a eulogy. Now, forced by the death of both his father and mother to be mature beyond his years, he spoke lovingly and eloquently about his father. Funeral directors, usually so composed, had tears in their eyes.

How patently unfair for him to lose both his parents when he is still so young and being an only child, left all alone, I thought.

I gazed over at Steve's girlfriend, who had visited him each day of his illness and thought of all the things they would never get to do together. Steve had finally found happiness again after enduring his beloved wife's death, when some people never find happiness at all. Things were going well for him; he had recently purchased another funeral home and looked forward to his son's graduation from mortuary school. Yet, inexplicably, his time had run out, reinforcing my belief that our day of death is written in a big book in the sky, the day we are born.

After the mass, colleagues talked about getting together for lunch or seeing each other more often; about how quickly time was passing...how fast life had gone. The same things all people talk about when confronted with mortality. For the moment, the fact that life is finite and often brief, is impressed upon them. But before long, most forget and get comfortable in the notion that they have endless days in which to see the people they want to see and do the things they want to do. My funeral director colleagues seemed to be no more enlightened than the mourners we saw everyday.

Their conversations made me think of a line from *Gone With The Wind.*

"Do not squander time. That is the stuff life is made of." An adage of which, in view of the sorrow I'd seen in the past month, we should all be mindful.

CHAPTER 17

The Funeral of John Gotti

Fortunately, in the business of death there are funerals akin to galas, as well as those which bring funeral directors to tears. I spent June 10, 2002, at the beach with my friend George. Passing through Howard Beach, Queens on the way to Belle Harbor Beach, we began talking about famous people whose families had prearranged their funerals, because death was said to be imminent and who, it turned out, lived longer than predicted. Our conversation turned to John Gotti, as he had outlived the dire predictions of imminent death that some people in the previous year had voiced.

"It's amazing. They said he didn't have much time and he's lived another year beyond what the doctors expected," I said.

After a relaxing day of soaking up the sun, George dropped me at my car. Less than fifteen minutes later, as I drove home to Long Island, my cell phone rang.

It was George. "John Gotti is dead," he said.

"How ironic that we were just talking about him," I mused. For a few moments I thought about reworking the *Funerals of The Infamous* article I wrote in 2000, in which I'd reported on some of the country's most notorious mobsters, a proliferation of whom were buried in St. John's Cemetery. "I'd really like to write something on his funeral," I told George.

After we hung up, I made some phone calls. One was to the Ed, the editor of *American Funeral Director* magazine. Without much coaxing on my part, Ed agreed to allow me to write about Gotti's funeral and I set to work.

I thought I knew for sure where the funeral would be held. The funeral home in Ozone Park, which had handled previous funerals for the Gotti family, seemed the natural choice and since I knew the owners, I'd be allowed easy access, as well. I called them first. They too, had heard the news, but surprisingly did not yet have the funeral assignment. By the next morning, there was still no word, so I called several more funeral homes, none of which had been contacted by the family. Later that day George telephoned, saying, "I have it on good authority that the funeral and the wake, which is to be on Thursday, is to be handled by the Papavero Funeral Home in Maspeth, Queens." It seemed a surprising choice.

Where is the connection? I asked myself.

At work on Thursday, I mulled over ways to get into the wake. If I called the Papavero Funeral Home ahead of time, they might say no. Better not to call. Just show up, I decided. So, on that rainy evening after I left work, I drove less than a mile to the site of the funeral home. As I neared the street where the funeral home was located, I could see a crowd milling around outside, the police in attendance and a multitude of news vans.

Parking my car, I approached several reporters to ask what the situation was and whether I could get in. They told me they had heard that the people in the crowd would be allowed inside.

Like so many others, I waited patiently outside the funeral home until visiting hours began again at 7:00 P.M.

While I stood there, I struck up a conversation with some *Daily News* reporters and, in the driving rain sans umbrella, huddled behind the police barricades with them. Aside from the reporters, the throng of people lining the Maspeth, Queens streets that unseasonably chilly June night included Gotti family members, blood and otherwise, friends, neighbors, law enforcement officers, curious onlookers and a few celebrities. "Grandpa Munster" actor, Al Lewis, spoke to reporters about how Gotti had liked him as a performer and come to see his shows. He said Gotti treated him better than anyone in Hollywood had.

For various reasons, they all were intent on getting into the wake, which word had it, was open to the masses by popular demand.

"He was a public person and this is a public funeral," was the position taken by his wife and children.

However, this gracious welcome was not extended to members of the press, save a select, hand-picked few. "Hanging with us may prevent you from getting in," warned one reporter.

"I'll get in," I assured him.

We occupied ourselves as we waited by trading Mob stories. One reporter had a most thought-provoking take on the spectacle. "This is the first time since September 11 that we have been able to publicize a funeral. This heralds a return to normalcy."

"Who are you writing for?" one of the *Daily News* reporters asked me.

"Well believe it or not there is a magazine called the *American Funeral Director*. We do a series called 'Funerals of The Famous'—or in this case, infamous."

"I know that magazine."

"You do!?" I was pleasantly surprised that anyone outside our insular world of funeral directing knew of it. I felt legitimized as a writer.

"Sure, one of our *Daily News* reporters, Brian Kates, his family owns part of it."

"Small world! Brian Kates, profiled me way back when I was just a fledgling funeral director, modeling on the side."

As 6:45 P.M., I looked around as visiting hour approached. Then I saw my chance to get in. Trying not to get caught on camera, several of which rolled continuously, I crossed the narrow street and waited outside the door, under a small awning, along with some neighborhood women there to pay their respects to "John."

"He was my neighbor. Always such a gentleman. I want to say goodbye," said one woman with a tear in her eye.

"I hope they let us in. Do you think they will?" asked another hopefully.

"Yes, I heard they've opened it to the public," I replied

The well-dressed, muscular "bouncer" stationed at the front door, kept glancing at his watch, waiting for the evening visitation hours to begin. Then, taking pity on us rain soaked women, he invited us in.

I made my way through the crowd to the front of the room. After a short wait on line, I stepped up to the tasteful, elegant, gold-colored, bronze casket, manufactured, I noticed, by Henry's casket company. The closed casket, flanked by a bleeding heart of roses and a blanket of Casablanca lilies, was bedecked by family photos. Daughter Victoria's wedding photo perched atop it, as well as photos of John and his cronies. Finally, a huge charcoal drawing of a very distinguished looking John Gotti hung over the casket.

After bowing my head and saying a silent prayer, I walked away, finding a seat in the back where I could survey the room inconspicuously.

Floral arrangements were everywhere, even filling the three other visiting rooms. In the room where Gotti reposed, those sent by close loved ones and the most creative were on display. Among them, flowers which formed a Cohiba cigar, the New York Yankees insignia, a martini glass, a deck of cards, the numeral 13, several racehorses, a piece spelling out 101 (for 101st Avenue—the location of Gotti's social club) and a floral piece in the shape of the state of Missouri. I couldn't help but smile.

However, the mood among the mourners, appropriately dressed in suits and ties for the men, dresses, skirts and pantsuits for the women, was as appropriately somber despite all the fanfare.

On my way out, I took a prayer card, of which there were hundreds, for myself and a couple of extras for the reporters outside. The cards were frequently replenished and bore the images of various saints on the face along with the "I did not die" verse on the back. It was said that cards with a photograph of Gotti were kept aside for special mourners.

The next morning, I dressed carefully for John Gotti's funeral. Aiming for "chic but understated mourner," I ended up looking more like "Italian widow" in my black dress, sweater and dark hose. Deciding to bypass the funeral home, where a huge crowd had gathered, some intent on being part of the funeral procession, I drove directly to St. John's Cemetery.

The first stop I had planned was the third floor of the magnificent Cloister building to see if the cover had been removed from the Gotti crypt, signifying that the entombment would take place with the family in attendance.

Afterward, as I walked away from the building I stopped by several crypts of people I have known, some of whom I have buried. Then, since I was in no hurry, I began to walk leisurely back toward the front entrance, deciding to get an idea of the size of the crowd outside the main gate held at bay by a sizable police presence. News helicopters flew overhead, recording the goings on.

On my way back to the Cloister, a kindly dark-haired woman stopped her car beside me and asked if I'd like a ride back.

"It's a long walk," she said, "especially in high heels."

I politely declined, preferring to walk, but not before she told me she had grown up with Gotti and that, "He was the handsomest guy in the neighborhood. All the girls were in love with him."

As I continued walking I met a man who told me that his brother, a doctor, had delivered Gotti's children. He also had something else to tell me.

"Miss," he said ever so politely, "the groundskeepers were talking about you on their walkie-talkies. They said you are a writer and may have a camera and that you should be watched. I didn't think that was very nice. I just wanted you to know."

I wondered why, with the hoards of reporters on and around the grounds, I was being singled out?

"Thanks for telling me."

I had reached the Cloister by then and I saw the groundskeepers giving and receiving messages on their walkie-talkies.

I walked over. "I heard you were talking about me. Why?"

"We saw you on the third floor," said one.

"So."

"Do you have a camera?"

"No, I don't have a camera. Search my bag if you like," I said as I held out my Louis Vuitton pocketbook to him.

"That's okay. We believe you. But you have written about this cemetery before and you were on the third floor."

Getting annoyed now, I responded, "For your information, I was visiting my grandparents." Then I added, "Is Gotti's crypt the only one on the third floor?"

I began perspiring. People were looking at me and I was feeling self-conscious. Moreover, I did not want to get thrown out, before I finished taking notes for my story.

As this exchange took place, out of the corner of my eye, I saw a group of "wiseguys," unmistakable by their mode of dress and stance, looking my way.

"Hey, you," the one dressed in a charcoal suit called out to the groundskeeper, "leave that girl alone. You're upsetting her. She told you—she was visiting her grandparents."

"We have to be careful with security today..." the groundskeeper said.

The mobster cut him right off. "Apologize to her! Now!"

And the groundskeeper did.

"It's alright, I understand," I said benevolently, as I involuntarily shivered from the cool, overcast weather.

"Here, take my jacket!" the Mr. Charcoal Suit quickly offered.

"Thanks, but I'm okay. I have a sweater with me."

"Put it on," directed one of his compatriots.

I did as told. The groundskeepers hurriedly left the scene and I turned to my protectors to say thanks.

"Thank you, gentlemen. Imagine, a girl can't even visit her grandparent's crypt."

"Who you kidding, honey? You ain't here visiting any grandparents. You're here for John, right?"

I couldn't help but laugh. "I didn't want them to get angry at me. I'm a funeral director and have to come here on funerals," I explained.

"You're a funeral director?" Mr. Charcoal Suit asked, surprise evident in his voice. The others eyed me skeptically.

As if on cue, two funeral directors said to have Mob connections appeared. They hugged and kissed me, then turned and embraced several members of the group of men. Suddenly, it was like old home week.

"So, you really are a funeral director!" one of the guys exclaimed.

They invited me to hang out with them as we waited for the funeral cortege to arrive. From time to time they telephoned friends who were in some of the limousines for updates. Of course, the drive to the cemetery took longer than usual as there were many places of special meaning to be acknowledged by the funeral cortege.

Meanwhile, the guys kept up a rousing conversation, talking of the "old days." Jilly Rizzo's nightclub, Sinatra concerts, Atlantic City, Vegas and the best Italian restaurants in New York City. Turned out, we knew a number of people in common and had frequented many of the same places. I felt comfortable enough to confide, that yes I was writing something. Assuring them, "it's not going to be negative."

One of the men, clutching all four major daily newspapers, complained bitterly about the press's intrusion on the Gotti family's grief. Another bemoaned the way in which, "A good man had suffered so terribly with cancer."

The praise was lavish and glowing.

"What a good man he was!"

"So generous!"

"A standup guy!"

All were united in the sentiment that John Gotti would be greatly missed.

With mixed emotions, I stood and watched with them, as the nineteen flower cars, each fully and carefully loaded, prominently displaying the most elaborate pieces, slowly rolled in, leading the massive funeral procession. I wondered aloud where all the flower cars had come from, in an era when they are seldom used.

"I wonder who sent the state of Missouri floral piece—the inmates or the governor?" I heard a woman nearby say to another.

Though this was the funeral of a notorious godfather, I felt I was not only witnessing history, but the incarnation of a fast-fading tradition. Whatever his deeds, Gotti also had been a husband, father, grandfather, brother, uncle and friend to many. And these people were all here to honor him with a most traditional funeral. The kind of funeral that I, my colleagues and those of my age group and ethnicity had grown up with, albeit on a substantially less grand scale. Looking around I saw the past duplicated here—the funeral home visitation, the well-dressed, respectful mourners, numerous flower pieces, Mass cards, religious effects, limousines, a funeral cortege, passing of the home and places which had held meaning for the departed and a priest officiating. In fact, the consensus of those attending was indignation that a Catholic had been denied a Mass of Christian Burial, no matter what sins he may have committed in life.

Between my musings about traditional funerals and the rousing conversation I was having with the guys about "times gone by" and the lack of respect for value and tradition these days, I didn't realize, nor did anyone else, that the prayer service for John Gotti was taking place.

Then one man, almost out of breath, ran over to us. "Geeze, we got the Irish priest saying the prayers! And he's almost done! C'mon, hurry!"

We dashed into the chapel just in time to lay roses on Gotti's casket. It was then I realized that his funeral was no longer just about John Gotti, alleged "mob boss," but about the time-honored tradition of commemorating the dead, no matter whom or what they may have been.

Afterward, I said goodbye to my new friends who graciously invited me to "stop by our club if you're ever in the neighborhood." Mr. Charcoal Suit pressed a business card with the address and telephone number into my palm.

Driving home that day, I thought about how meaningful and comfortingly familiar I had found the whole funeral to be, despite the reputation of the deceased. I hadn't expected that. How strange, I thought, that the atmosphere at the funeral of a godfather was in such contrast to the mood at many funerals today. So many people now feel a funeral is just something to be gotten over with, in the simplest way possible. Customs and observances, both religious and cultural, have taken a back seat to expedience and economy. Tradition, with all its ritual and pomp and circumstance, is increasingly viewed as wasteful and ostentatious. I wondered, after having watched the Gotti funeral unfold with so much symbolism, why our funeral customs have devolved to such an extent.

As I parked my car I reflected on having experienced first-hand and read in much death, dying and grief literature, that funerals, with their numerous components, serve many functions. They fulfill our need for ceremony, afford closure and mark the end of our mortal life, while comforting those left behind in tangible as well as spiritual ways, allowing them a venue in which to grieve. Sometimes, even I have lost sight of these functions, but that day, I felt renewed appreciation for them.

After the Gotti funeral, I got together with some funeral directors who talked about whether this funeral might serve as a model for others and herald a return to tradition. "I doubt the general public will opt for a casket which retails at more than twenty thousand dollars or send thousands of dollars worth of flower pieces and order numerous flower cars in which to transport them to the cemetery, but it may get them to thinking that tradition and old-fashioned rituals, are good things, not bad," I observed.

Later, when I thought more about it, I could not escape the irony. Who would have supposed that the funeral of such an infamous figure would get people thinking about a return to traditional values and how we honor our dead?

Epilogue
Winter 2003

A s the publication of this book draws close, I can't help but reflect on my life and the funeral industry which has been at its center. Perhaps it is because in this year of amazing confluence of events, all the components and areas of my interest have come together, enhancing one another. Funerals have seemed to come to me in abundance and I have continued to contribute my thoughts about death and dying in articles written for the general public and for other professionals in my field and published in *American Funeral Director, American Cemetery* and *Newsday*. In addition, my notebook is chock full of future articles and ideas for my industry, which I am eager to pursue.

I have spent much time reflecting on the state of the funeral business. In the nineties, merger-mania hit our business, just as it did nearly every other. Big corporations began to buy up smaller, family-owned funeral homes, sometimes closing them entirely. I began to collect articles from trade magazines and newspapers, the *Wall Street Journal*, in particular, which chronicled these changes. I found that predictions for the future of funeral service, now commonly called the "Death Care Industry,"

see more full service funerals ending in cremation, more cremation merchandise such as urns, crematable caskets, even cremation jewelry and a rise in the cost of cremation. Fewer open casket
visitations, less expensive caskets being selected, more graveside
and memorial services, as well as more mergers and consolidation
of cemeteries and funeral homes are foreseen as well; even better
educated funeral directors are predicted.

Today, despite our uncertain world and the tragedy of
September 11, more and more people are questioning the value
of funerals and focusing on celebrations of life, rather than just
mourning death. This seems to me a good omen for the future.

Just as my industry is changing, my personal life has also
changed for the funeral industry. To my joy, a few months ago the
director of the theatre group to which I belonged asked if I would
accept a role in the Daphne DuMaurier classic *Rebecca*. He wrote
a part for me as the spirit of Rebecca, the subject of the play. The
notation in the playbill under my name playfully reads,
"Alexandra, who is a funeral director, was a natural choice for a
'spirit' as she has had much experience with the 'spirit' world." It
goes on to mention that I am writing articles about death and
completing my book on my life and career in the funeral business.

Opening night of the play, the message our director gave
to the cast seemed to have special meaning for me:

"There are no accidents; we are meant to be here together,
doing what we are doing. We are all meant to be where we are in
life and with whom. And many of the people we meet along the
way end up playing pivotal roles in our lives."

This is a belief I have always held, as well. We are all fated
to follow a certain path. That is our destiny. And I am living the
life God meant for me.

This year has brought me back in touch with many people from my past: old friends with whom I had lost touch, acquaintances, colleagues, media associates, editors and talk show hosts as I revisited my past. Completing this book is, I feel, the culmination of long preparation and hard work. In my heart, I always felt this day would come, but there were times when doubt crept in.

An old friend expressed surprise at any uncertainty I may have had, saying "Was there ever a doubt you'd do this book? You knew you would! You've always had both incredible 'intestinal fortitude' and an even more incredible life."

His words ring true, however, I knew the story of a woman who works with the dead would not appeal to everyone. Yet, I believe my story is about much more than that. It's about what one person can accomplish with strong drive, determination and dreams, despite an emotionally and physically abusive childhood, one which lacked love, security or comfort.

As I've matured, I have come to feel sure that my strong drives and forceful ambitions stem from my difficult early family experiences. Because of them, I have had a quest for forging an identity, finding a place for myself in the world and even attaining some sort of immortality. The issues and longings of my past coupled with the knowledge of the deaths of my natural parents have caused me to gravitate toward finding an answer to the ultimate mortal question: What happens when life ends? To seek this I entered the world of death and made it my own.

As I review my journey, I realize it is my role as a funeral director that has grounded me the most. It has allowed someone who has been through much personal torment to focus on helping others going through traumatic experiences. Surely, it has made me a better, more compassionate person.

Yet, I still grapple with self-doubts: Have I done enough good? Served real needs? Actually helped those who were grieving? Fulfilled the enormous sense of mission with which I have been entrusted? There have been times when I truly believed I did. However, in the aftermath of the most difficult cases that I handled, I have asked myself, What did I do that I should not have done? What didn't I do that I should have? Perhaps these are questions we all should ask ourselves as we travel through life.

Being on such intimate terms with death has impacted all aspects of my existence and changed me forever. There are gripping images that will always haunt me. But my job has also taught me many lessons. When you constantly look at life from the perspective of death, a very different picture emerges.

Sooner or later, I believe, everyone carries a very heavy burden on this journey. I have learned that people truly show you who they are in grief and adversity. Occurrences which impact our days shape and mold us. They can make us unsteady in our efforts or they can strengthen us in our resolve. Courage, to me, is the greatest virtue to cultivate as we move forward. We all know that time for each of us is not of infinite duration and that one day we will have no more left. So we must live more intensely; do what we're going to do or let it go. At funerals I've seen people vow that in the future they will do it all differently, not waste one more moment. Yet many soon forget and return to their old ways, putting off living to the fullest once again.

Having achieved what many people said I could not and weathered much controversy, tragedy and adversity, it is little wonder that "What doesn't kill you, makes you stronger," is my favorite adage. I hope I can inspire people not to let the adverse circumstances in their lives deter them from pursuing their goals and dreams.

For me, the gift of being a funeral director has put much into perspective. And the words I wrote in my first magazine piece are as true to me today, as they were when I wrote them: "It is the greatest of ironies that the business of death has so enriched my life. I have learned valuable lessons about living that I would not have gotten elsewhere. Oddly enough, by being a funeral director, I have gained worldwide notoriety and the chance to branch out in so many directions—acting, modeling, writing and television—that I may not have otherwise. I have accomplished so much more than I set out to do and have done what people said I could not do. Now, I look ahead with much more work to do and new dreams to fulfill." Only now my dreams have changed, as have I.

My intimacy with death has given me an appreciation for living. It has taught me to chase dreams, but also to stop and savor the small moments. Revere each day and the happiness that is offered. And value life as a precious gift. Then you will not fear death when it comes.

Appendix:
Funeral Arrangement Tips

Arranging a funeral is a task that virtually all of us will have to deal with at some point in our lives, and the better prepared we are in advance, the easier it will be when the time comes.

The best way to choose a funeral director is on the recommendation of friends or relatives who recently had a death in the family. Ask the name of the firm and the funeral director who helped them. Was he or she compassionate, honest and sensitive to their needs? Were all their questions answered to their satisfaction? Did they feel pressured to spend more than they planned?

The least reliable method of choosing a funeral director is through the telephone book or other advertising. Ads are often misleading. However, a prior good experience with a funeral home is not always a guarantee of future satisfaction. Like any other business, funeral homes change hands, often keeping the original owner's name. Check to see if the establishment is under new ownership.

Prearranging a funeral is becoming a more and more common practice today. *Prearrangement* simply involves meeting with a funeral director and planning the details of a funeral in advance. You can prearrange your own funeral or that of a family member, and you have the option of prepaying. If you decide to prepay, the money will be deposited into a special, interest-bearing account by the funeral home. Many funeral homes guarantee that the future interest on the savings will offset any rise in costs; others do not guarantee this. Check with the funeral home about their policy and be sure to get it in writing. An additional benefit for prepaying is found in the case of an elderly person applying for Medicaid. The law allows the prepayment of funeral arrangements.

By prearranging your own funeral or that of a loved one's, you can rest assured knowing that last wishes and instructions will be followed. You can also decide in advance how much you plan to spend. In other words, you'll be thinking with your head and not your heart. There's no denying that a funeral can be expensive, but prices vary, as do alternatives to the "traditional" funeral, which includes embalming, open casket visitation and burial. All funeral homes are required by law to furnish their prices to you over the telephone and in person with a printed price list.

Cremation is steadily gaining in popularity as an alternative to burial. The actual cost of cremation is approximately one-third less than the cost of a grave opening. And if you don't already own cemetery property, the savings are even more substantial. However, other variables such as the casket, embalming, visitation, etc., can make a funeral which ends in cremation as costly as a funeral which ends in burial.

People are often confused by the difference between *cremation* and *direct cremation*. Cremation may be the end result of a traditional funeral, with all its frills. In direct cremation, the remains are taken directly from the place of death to the crematory, with no embalming or preparation of any kind and no services. This is the simplest and least expensive mode of disposition. *Direct burial* is another alternative. As with direct cremation, there are no services, but the body is buried. Bear in mind that if this type of funeral is selected, a religious or memorial service may be held at a later time.

Visitation at the funeral home is not mandatory. It is up to the family or whoever is planning the funeral to decide whether to have a "wake," the common term for visitation. You may decide to meet at the funeral home the morning of the funeral for a private viewing by family and friends. Or you may bypass the funeral home entirely and meet at the place of the religious service, cemetery or crematory. If you decide to have a wake, you are not bound by a particular time period. It may be for a brief hour or several days. In general, long visitation periods of two or three days are, except in certain circumstances, a thing of the past. These days, one day of visitation is common.

The statement "Embalming is not required by law" is a fact in most states, yet misleading. Embalming is certainly unnecessary and not done in cases of direct cremation or direct burial or in some cases of closed caskets. However, if you select a funeral with an open casket visitation, embalming becomes necessary. Embalming makes visitation possible by delaying inevitable post-mortem changes to the body.

Aesthetically, embalming has a lot of value. Tissues can be filled out to restore a softer, more pleasant appearance. After seeing someone through a debilitating illness, such as cancer, this last memory of him or her can be a great comfort.

A casket makes up a substantial portion of the entire funeral cost. Caskets are priced from several hundred dollars to five thousand dollars and more and can be made from wood, steel, copper or bronze. Some caskets are called "sealer caskets," which simply means that they have a sealing gasket to help retard decomposition by keeping out the elements. To some families this is important, to others it is insignificant.

Choose a casket in a price range with which you feel comfortable. Most people choose a particular casket for personal reasons, such as color or decoration.

Remember, the casket is a major purchase which will soon be either buried or cremated. There is no need to feel you must spend beyond your means. Your love for the deceased is not measured by the amount spent on the casket. One casket is as dignified as another, regardless of the price.

Burial vaults, which enclose the casket and are available in steel, concrete or wood, are generally not required by most cemeteries. They are a personal choice.

Other cost savings can include doing without "frills" such as memorial cards, preprinted acknowledgment cards, metal plates on the casket with the deceased's name and death notices. Some or all of these are often not necessary.

Family and friends may also serve as pallbearers instead of using men hired by the funeral home for this purpose. Not only will this result in a monetary savings, but it lends a touch of personalization to the funeral services as well.

Instead of costly limousines hired by the funeral home, one can drive one's own car to the religious services and cemetery, which are often nearby, thus keeping expenses down. These days, almost everyone drives and funeral attendees can car pool together. Another way to contain costs is to use a favorite outfit, perhaps one with special meaning, in which to dress the deceased rather than purchasing costly "burial" clothing from the funeral home.

Today, many cemeteries limit the amount of floral pieces they will accept. Family and friends can pool resources when it comes to flowers, rather than each one sending an individual arrangement.

Funerals are a major expenditure and can be very costly, especially if there is no life insurance to cover the costs. In addition to the service charges and merchandise contracted for with the funeral home, one must consider the outside costs which combine to produce the total price of the funeral. Outside costs include cemetery or crematory charges, the hearse and limousines, pallbearers and clergy.

For a traditional funeral with visitation, religious services and either burial or cremation, you can expect the cost to be between $5,000 and $10,000, depending upon such variables as the casket you select and whether or not you need to buy cemetery property, which in itself can exceed $3,000.

Funerals today are more focused on personalization and honoring the deceased, rather than caskets and visitations. One should strive to have the type of funeral which affords the most meaning for family and friends and which best honors the deceased's wishes and memory. Discuss your needs with your funeral director. He or she will work with you to ensure a funeral for your loved one that is uniquely personal, as well as within your financial means.